FIRST YEAR LAW SCHOOL SUCCESS

Law School Thinking, Essay Exam Writing, and Analysis

Professor Ira L. Shafiroff

Third Edition

To Cindy and Hannah

About the Author

Ira L. Shafiroff is a professor of law at Southwestern Law School where he teaches Property, Wills and Trusts, and Selected Topics in American Law, a course he designed to prepare students for the California Bar Exam. Professor Shafiroff has been teaching at Southwestern since 1982. He began lecturing for BARBRI Bar Review in 1985, when he created and began teaching BARBRI's first essay writing course for its general bar review program. He subsequently created and taught essay exam writing for first-year law school students. Professor Shafiroff has taught thousands of students essay writing for the California Bar Exam and law school. Earlier editions of Professor Shafiroff's FIRST YEAR LAW SCHOOL SUCCESS have been used in several law schools as part of their academic support programs.

borbri

Table of Contents

borbri

borbri

borbri

barbri
INTRODUCTION

You who are reading this book are undoubtedly a law school student. In fact, you are probably a first year student, a so-called "1L." If so, the chances are virtually guaranteed that you have given some thought as to how you are going to succeed in law school: What is it that you will have to do in order to pass your courses? What will you have to do to end up in the top of your class and make law review? Further, how do LSAT scores, undergraduate grade point averages (GPAs) and other factors affect the outcome? Before I discuss what you need to do in order to succeed, I first want to examine how LSAT scores, GPAs, undergraduate majors, and prior work experiences affect the outcome. What I am going to tell you may well be a surprise.

Let us first address LSAT scores. I have been a law school professor since 1982 and a dean of students from 1990-1993. I have also been involved with bar review since 1985. Consequently, I have taught, counseled, and met literally thousands of students from many law schools and a variety of educational backgrounds. Moreover, while the LSAT may be a good predictor of success in some cases, it cannot explain why a student with an average LSAT score graduates with high honors—or why a student with a top LSAT score struggles. In fact, for most students, LSAT has only a modest correlation to law school grades.

Now let us examine undergraduate GPAs. Although four or five years of an undergraduate record may be a better predicator of success in law school than a three-hour examination, a GPA (especially one that is a number of years old) may not tell the whole story. For example, an undergraduate GPA of 2.75 would not be considered outstanding by an admissions committee— unless achieved by a single parent working a forty-hour week on an assembly line.

How do undergraduate majors affect performance in law school? In short, in my experience (I was on Southwestern's admissions committee for many years) they do not. Music majors as well as political science majors become attorneys. What about prior work experience as a factor in law school success? Suffice to say that my own students have come also from a wide variety of employment backgrounds: nurses, doctors, paralegals, clergy, teachers, salespeople, accountants, construction workers, and even professional athletes. Of course, many outstanding law school students have come directly out of college.

The point is this: Once admitted to law school, it does not matter what your LSAT score was. Nor is your undergraduate major, GPA, or employment history important. Once in law school, there are only two things that you need to succeed.

The first is industry. This is something that no standardized test will ever be able to measure. Success in law school requires hard work. It is as simple as that. As you proceed through these materials (and law school), you will come to understand that the law school learning process is one that is a continuing process. You will not get an "A" on a torts exam simply by "cramming" the day before the final. Rather, you begin studying for your final exams the first day of class for each course. The outstanding students are willing to devote this amount of time to their studies. They know that if they do, they will not just pass. Rather, they will get excellent grades. They get the A grades.

Nonetheless, working hard is not enough. In addition to working hard, you must also work "smart." By this, I mean you must understand the law school learning process. Why is this so? The answer is simple. The learning process in law school is different from the learning process of any academic discipline that you have ever encountered. The "A" student understands this process intuitively. Importantly, however, this is a process any law student can learn—and do well.

In the materials that follow, I will teach you the law school learning process. I will do so in a manner that will allow you to make total sense of law school and law school exams, regardless of your undergraduate major or your LSAT score. In fact, when you finish reading these materials, you will find the law school learning process quite comfortable. Consequently, you will maximize your potential on your law school examinations.

The two critical factors for success are, therefore, (1) industry and (2) understanding the law school learning process. If you have the industry, I will teach you the law school learning process.

Let us now begin.

barbri

CHAPTER 1
RULES AND ELEMENTS

If you want to be successful in law school and on your law school exams, you must understand the law school learning process, something that your professors too often assume that you know intuitively. The first step in understanding the law school learning process is for you to grasp what constitutes "the law." Please do not fret: I am not going to give you a dissertation dealing with philosophy or economics. For that, I leave you to your law school professors—or friends at a cocktail party.

LAW IS MADE UP OF RULES AND RULES ARE MADE UP OF ELEMENTS

What constitutes "the law"? The answer really is quite simple. Indeed, the answer can be reduced to two maxims: (1) all law is made up of *rules*; (2) all rules are made up of component parts, what I call the *elements*. Rules and elements. That is what constitutes the law: rules and elements of rules.

ALL LAW IS MADE UP OF RULES

Let us now examine these simple—but crucial—maxims in some depth. First, we shall explore the first maxim: All law is made up of rules. Let us look at a basic hypothetical that will illustrate this maxim.

Hypothetical #1: A Rule Called Battery

Abel and Baker are neighbors. One day Abel and Baker have an argument. Baker hits Abel with his fist. Will Abel prevail in a lawsuit against Baker for damages?

On the facts that I have given you, Abel will successfully sue Baker. Why is this? Because of a *rule* of law that we call *battery*: an intentional and unpermitted harmful or offensive touching of the person of another. Because Baker intentionally hit Abel and Abel did not give permission to be hit, Baker will be found to have committed a battery.

You have seen one basic illustration of the first maxim: All law is made up of rules. Now let us explore yet another illustration of this truism.

Hypothetical #2: A Rule Called Transferred Intent

Abel and Baker are neighbors. One day Abel and Baker have an argument. Baker gets furious at Abel and attempts to hit Abel in the face. However, when Baker tries to hit Abel, Baker misses and accidentally hits Charlie, a bystander. Can Charlie successfully sue Baker for battery?

The answer is, yes. Why is this? Because there is a rule called *transferred intent*. This rule states that if X tries to commit an intentional tort, such as a battery, against Y but accidentally

commits it against Z, Z will be able to hold X liable. Because Baker hit Charlie while intending to hit Abel, Baker is liable to Charlie for battery.

Once again, I have given you an illustration of the maxim that all law is made up of rules. Now let us alter the facts to the Abel-Baker hypothetical one more time. In the hypothetical that follows, we shall add one set of facts to the original hypothetical, Hypothetical #1 (in law, changing the facts even slightly can often drastically change the outcome).

Hypothetical #3: A Rule Called Self-Defense

Abel and Baker are neighbors. One day they get into an argument. Abel pulls out a loaded gun and, in an wrathful voice, states that he is going to shoot Baker in the head. Baker hits Abel with his fist, but only for the purpose of disarming Abel. If Abel sues Baker for battery, will Abel prevail?

The answer is, no. Why is this? Because there is a *rule* called *self-defense*: A person is allowed to use reasonable force to prevent another from harming him. Because Baker used reasonable force to disarm Abel, there is no battery.

Recapping Hypotheticals 1-3

From the three foregoing hypotheticals, you are beginning to understand that all law (and as we shall see with Hypothetical #5, not just tort law) is truly made up of rules.

Why do we have rules of law? We have rules of law to help govern us in our lives and to have an orderly society. Thus, there is a rule that prevents one person from hitting another (battery). There is another rule that still makes it a battery even if the defendant misses his target and hits the wrong person (transferred intent). Nonetheless, there is another rule, which makes it lawful to hit another in order to prevent oneself from being shot (self-defense).

One more time: All law is made up of rules.

ALL RULES ARE MADE UP OF ELEMENTS

Now let us focus in on the second maxim: All rules are made up of elements. Let us examine a hypothetical that will illustrate this principle.

Hypothetical #4: Elements to Battery: In General

Dawn does not like Ellen. One day, Dawn tosses a bomb at Ellen. Dawn sincerely does not intend to hurt Ellen in any manner; she only wants to scare her. Nevertheless, after Dawn lights the bomb and hurls it at Ellen, it explodes at Ellen's feet and Ellen is injured. Did Dawn commit a battery against Ellen?

The answer is, yes. Now let us examine why this is so. I have previously stated that there is a rule of battery: This rule can be broken down into its component parts, into six distinct elements: [1] An intentional [2] and unpermitted [3] offensive or harmful [4] touching [5] of the person [6] of another. Reducing this rule to an equation, we have the following:

$$\text{Intentional} + \text{Unpermitted} + \text{Offensive or Harmful} + \text{Touching} + \text{Person} + \text{Of Another} = \text{BATTERY}$$

Let us stipulate for purposes of this hypothetical that there is no question that the bombing by Dawn was unpermitted, harmful, and that the bomb fragments hit (touched) Ellen's person. It looks like we are on our way to finding a battery. But wait! I stated that Dawn did not *intend* to injure Ellen--she only wanted to scare Ellen. For Ellen to prevail, she must prove that each *element* of the rule is satisfied. Can she prove the first element, the element of intent? Yes. Let us see why this element is satisfied.

Hypothetical #4: Elements to Battery: Intent

For purposes of the law of battery, what does the word "intentional" mean? For the law of battery, "intentional" (an element of battery) is defined to mean: the defendant is *substantially certain* of the consequences, that contact with the plaintiff will occur, and an unrealistic hope that the plaintiff will not be touched, however sincere, is irrelevant. When someone tosses a lighted bomb at someone's feet, he or she is deemed to know that there is a substantial certainty that contact will occur. Because all of the elements of battery—including the intentional element—are satisfied, Dawn is liable to Ellen for battery.

You are now starting to see that all rules are made up of elements. Let us now look at one more hypothetical.

Hypothetical #5: Elements of a Gift Causa Mortis: In General

Fran and George are riding together in an automobile. Fran is the driver and George is the passenger. Fran loses control and the car crashes. George is not injured but Fran is severely injured and is near death. Fran, sensing that her death is imminent, takes out her monthly savings account statement from the bank—there is a $25,000 balance in the account—and gives it to George. Fran then expires. Fran never executed a will. Is George the owner of the $25,000?

The answer is, yes. Why is this the case? To answer this question, you need to know that in the law of property, a person typically needs a will to make a testamentary gift of property (a transfer to take effect at death). However, there is a rule of law called, *gift causa mortis*. This rule states that a gift of personal property (real property is excluded) made by a donor in contemplation of imminent death is valid so long as the donor makes a *delivery* of the property to the donee and the donor dies soon after delivery is made. Again, we can break down this rule into distinct elements: [1] An intent to pass title immediately [2] of personal property [3] made by a donor [4] in contemplation of imminent death [5] with delivery of the property to the donee [6] and the donor dies soon after delivery is made. Reducing this rule to an equation, we have the following:

Intent + Personal Property + By Donor + Contemplation of Imminent Death +
Delivery + Death of Donor = GIFT CAUSA MORTIS

Did Fran make a valid gift causa mortis to George of the $25,000? Let us stipulate that Fran intended to pass title of the cash (which is personal property). Let us also stipulate that she did so in contemplation of imminent death. Moreover, Fran did die after she gave the statement to George. Still, was there *delivery* (the next to the last element) of the $25,000 to George? The answer is, yes. Let us see why this is the case.

Hypothetical #6: Elements of a Gift Causa Mortis: Delivery

For the law of gift causa mortis, delivery may be one of several types. One type of delivery is what we call a manual or actual delivery. The definition of a manual or actual delivery is this: The donor gives the donee the property. Fran did not make a manual delivery to George: She did not give him the $25,000 cash. The second type of delivery recognized in law is what we call a symbolic delivery. We define a symbolic delivery as follows: The donor gives the donee something representative of the underlying property, typically some writing or document which establishes ownership rights to the property. A monthly statement may be such a document. Because Fran gave the monthly statement to George, Fran made a valid symbolic delivery in contemplation of her imminent death. Therefore, George takes the cash in the account.

All law is made up of rules. All rules are made up of elements.

SUMMARY OF CHAPTER 1

If you have any further doubts that law is made up of rules and that rules are made up of elements, I suggest that you go to any legal encyclopedia, such as American Jurisprudence 2nd or Corpus Juris Secundum. Turn to any page of any volume in either of these works and start reading. Lo and behold, you will be reading a discussion of (1) rules of law and (2) elements of rules.

At this point, we are now ready to proceed to the next chapter of this book where we shall explore the relationship of rules and elements to case law—the heart of law school study.

CHAPTER 2
HOW TO READ CASES: THE BASICS

If you have been in law school for even one week, you know that case law is an integral part of our common law heritage (and being a lawyer). You also know that reading appellate cases and discussing them in your classes will be your day-to-day concern during your law school career, especially during your first year. Unfortunately, many first year students (and even many upper division students) do not readily understand the significance of reading and studying these cases—and their relationship to law school exams. However, by the time that you finish studying this chapter and the few that follow, you will.

RULES AND ELEMENTS—AGAIN

To understand the importance of these appellate cases, let us first go back to the two maxims that we discussed at length in chapter 1: (1) All law is made up of rules and (2) all rules are made up of elements. What is the significance of these maxims to the cases that you will be studying? In every appellate case that you will read in law school (and during your legal career), a court is attempting to resolve a dispute between two parties—and the dispute revolves around *rules or elements of rules*. Let us examine why this is necessarily so.

Rules and Elements: The Heart of a Legal Dispute

At the appellate level, in virtually all the cases you will read in law school, every time people or entities have a legal dispute, it is always because they cannot agree on (1) the rule of law that should be used to resolve the dispute, or (2) the definition of an element of a rule.[1] Consequently, when these people decide to go to court to resolve their dispute, they are each asking the court to adopt a particular (1) rule or (2) definition of an element of a rule. When the court resolves the dispute, it will do so by determining what it believes to be the correct (1) rule or (2) definition of an element of a rule.

Rules and elements are the heart of law and appellate cases. They are also the heart of law school.

Let us now look at some appellate cases, which are often found in standard casebooks. We shall examine them and see very clearly that in each one, the parties are fighting over a rule or an element of a rule. In each case, the court will resolve the dispute by stating a rule or defining an element of a rule.

---

[1] At the trial level, the underlying basis for the dispute may also be, and often is, a question of fact. For example, there may be a factual question as to whether the defendant ran a red light. One witness says yes, while another witness says no. It is up to the trier of fact (judge if a bench trial, jury if a jury trial) to decide which witness is to be believed. In law school cases, rarely will you read anything but appellate cases, which virtually never deal with questions of fact. Appellate cases typically only deal with questions of law.

Rules and Elements: *Armory v. Delamirie* (Which Rule to Use)

The first case that we will examine is *Armory v. Delamirie*, a property case. The facts in *Armory* were these: A chimney sweeper's boy found a jewel and delivered it to a goldsmith for an appraisal. The smith, however, refused to return the jewel to the sweeper's boy. The boy sued the smith. The problem was this: As between the boy and the smith, who had better rights to the jewel? Read the case. We shall then see how the court solved the problem.

ARMORY v. DELAMIRIE
King's Bench, 1722
1 Strange 505

The plaintiff being a chimney sweeper's boy found a jewel and carried it to the defendant's shop (who was a goldsmith) to know what it was, and delivered it into the hands of the apprentice, who under the pretence of weighing it, took out the stones, and calling to the master to let him know it came to three halfpence, the master offered the boy the money, who refused to take it, and insisted to have the thing again; whereupon the apprentice delivered him back the socket without the stones. And now in trover against the master these points were ruled:

1. That the finder of a jewel, through he does not by such finding acquire an absolute property or ownership, yet he has such a property as will enable him to keep it against all but the rightful owner, and consequently may maintain trover.

***

3. As to the value of the jewel several of the trade were examined to prove what a jewel of the finest water that would fit the socket would be worth; and the Chief Justice (Pratt) directed the jury, that unless the defendant did produce the jewel, and shew it not to be of the finest water, they should presume the strongest against him, and make the value of the best jewels the measure of their damages: which they accordingly did.

This dispute revolved around who had better rights to the jewel. The plaintiff (the sweeper's boy) claimed that his rights were superior to the defendant's (the goldsmith). The defendant claimed that his rights were superior to the plaintiff's rights. As between the plaintiff and the defendant, they could not agree who had a superior right to the jewel. The case does not reveal the arguments that each side made. Still, it is certain that the plaintiff sought to convince the court to adopt one rule (the finder of a jewel has rights to it that are superior to all but the true owner), while the defendant had tried to convince the court to adopt another rule (a subsequent possessor[2] of a jewel has superior rights to the finder).

If the court had adopted one rule, the boy would win. On the other hand, if the court had adopted another rule, the goldsmith would win. What did the court do? It solved the dispute by adopting the rule that the finder of a jewel has rights to it that are superior to all but the true owner. Hence, the plaintiff (sweeper's boy) won.

(The court also adopted another rule: If the smith could not present the jewel for a valuation, the smith would be liable for monetary damages equal to another jewel of the finest quality. As *Armory* illustrates, a court may sometimes have more than one problem to address. In *Armory*, there were two. In the edited cases found in your casebooks, property or otherwise, there will typically be one or two problems for the court to resolve. In the unedited cases, in the "real world," the court may have to resolve more than just a few problems or issues.)

Rules and Elements: *Li v. Yellow Cab Co. of California* (Again, Which Rule to Use)

To summarize, in *Armory*, the court stated a *rule* of law to solve a problem. Now let us look at another case, *Li v. Yellow Cab Co. of California*. These were the facts in *Li*: The defendant negligently (that is, carelessly) caused an automobile accident by driving fast, injuring the plaintiff. Importantly, the plaintiff also acted negligently by making an improper left hand turn. Thus, the plaintiff was partially to blame for her own injuries. There is a common law rule, which provides that a negligent person is liable for the damages he causes. However, there is another rule, which is an exception to the common law rule of negligence. That exception provides that if the plaintiff himself negligently contributed—however slightly—to his own injuries, the plaintiff cannot recover any damages from the defendant. This is the rule of "contributory negligence." Thus, under contributory negligence, a plaintiff who was only 1 at fault cannot recover anything from defendant who was 99 percent at fault. In *Li*, the court had a choice: It could have continued to use the common law rule of contributory negligence (the rule favored by the defendant) or it could have adopted another rule, the rule of "comparative negligence" (favored by the plaintiff). Under the doctrine of comparative negligence, a negligent plaintiff may have his damages reduced to the extent that it was caused by his own negligence, but need not necessarily lose his entire cause of action. Let us now read *Li v. Yellow Cab* and determine which rule the court decided to use to resolve the problem.

---

[2] We assume for these purposes that the goldsmith even had possession. As we explore later, it may well be that the goldsmith did not have possession, but something less than possession.

LI v. YELLOW CAB CO. OF CALIFORNIA

Supreme Court of California

13 Cal. 3d 804 (1975)

[The plaintiff, Nga Li, while driving her automobile, improperly made a left hand turn into an intersection at the same time the defendant's automobile was approaching from the opposite direction. The defendant then entered the intersection at an unsafe speed. The trial court found the defendant was negligent. However, it also found that the plaintiff was contributorily negligent. On that ground, the trial court entered judgment for the defendant. The plaintiff appealed, contending that her negligence should not have entirely barred her claim, as the common law required.]

SULLIVAN, J. delivered the opinion of the court.

In this case we address the grave and recurrent question whether we should judicially declare no longer applicable in California courts the doctrine that contributory negligence, which bars all recovery when the plaintiff's negligent conduct has contributed as a legal cause in any degree to the harm suffered by him, and hold that it must give way to a system of comparative negligence, which assesses liability in direct proportion to fault.

* * *

It is unnecessary for us to catalogue the enormous amount of critical comment that has been directed over the years against the "all or nothing" approach of the doctrine of contributory negligence. The essence of that criticism has been constant and clear: the doctrine is inequitable in its operation because it fails to distribute responsibility in proportion to fault.

[The Court then rejected various arguments to retain the doctrine of contributory negligence.]

It remains to identify the precise form of comparative negligence which we now adopt for application in this state. Although there are many variants, only the two basic forms need be considered here. The first of these, the so-called "pure" form of comparative negligence, apportions liability in direct proportion to fault in all cases. This was the form adopted by the Supreme Court of Florida in *Hoffman v. Jones*, supra, and it applies by statute in Mississippi, Rhode Island, and Washington. Moreover, it is the form favored by most scholars and commentators.

The second basic form of comparative negligence . . . applies apportionment based on fault *up to the point* at which the plaintiff's negligence is equal to or greater than that of the defendant—when that point is reached, plaintiff is barred from recovery. Nineteen states have adopted this form or one of its variants by statute. The principal argument advanced in its favor is moral in nature: that it is not morally right to permit one more at fault in an accident to recover from one less at fault. Other arguments assert the probability of increased insurance, administrative, and judicial costs if a "pure" rather than a "50 percent" system is adopted, but this has been seriously questioned . . . .

We have concluded that the "pure" form of comparative negligence is that which should be adopted in this state. In our view, the "50 percent" system simply shifts the lottery aspect of the contributory negligence rule to a different ground. As Dean Prosser has noted, under such a system "[i]t is obvious that a slight difference in the proportionate fault may permit a recovery; and there has been much justified criticism of a rule under which a plaintiff who is charged with 49 percent of a total negligence recovers 51 percent of his damages, while one who is charged with 50 percent recovers nothing at all." Prosser, Comparative Negligence, supra, 41 Cal. L. Rev. 1, 25 . . . .

We also consider significant the experience of the State of Wisconsin, which until recently was considered the leading exponent of the "50 percent" system. There that system led to numerous appeals on the narrow but crucial issue whether plaintiff's negligence was equal to defendant's.

* * *

For all of the foregoing reasons we conclude that the "all or nothing" rule of contributory negligence as presently exists in this state should be and is herewith superseded by a system of "pure comparative negligence," the fundamental purpose of which shall be to assign responsibility and liability for damage in direct proportion to the amount of negligence of each of the parties.

* * *

The judgment is reversed.

* * *

CLARK, J., dissenting. * * *[T]he Legislature is the branch able to effect transition from contributory to comparative negligence or some other doctrine of negligence.

* * *

By abolishing this century-old-doctrine today, the majority seriously erodes our constitutional function. We are again guilty of judicial chauvinism.

In *Li*, the California Supreme Court addressed the problem of whether the plaintiff should be totally barred from recovery when her own negligence contributed to her injuries. The court determined that the plaintiff should not be so barred. In lieu of the common law rule of contributory negligence, the court adopted the rule of pure comparative negligence (the Court had a choice between two types of contributory negligence doctrines). Pure comparative negligence only reduces the plaintiff's recovery in proportion to the plaintiff's responsibility for her injuries. Consequently, if a defendant is 99 percent responsible for the plaintiff's injuries and the plaintiff is 1 percent responsible for her own injuries, the plaintiff's damages are reduced by 1 percent. Again, the court solved the dispute by articulating a rule of law.

Remember: All law is made up of rules.

Rules and Elements: *Lucy v. Zehmer* (Once More, Which Rule to Use)

We shall now read one more case where the court had to determine which rule of law was going to be used to solve the problem. In *Lucy v. Zehmer*, a contracts case, the defendants claim that the plaintiffs made an offer "in jest" and that their own acceptance was in jest. The problem for the court was whether the defendants accepted this offer, even if the acceptance was in jest.

LUCY v. ZEHMER
Supreme Court of Appeals of Virginia
196 Va. 493 (1954)

BUCHANAN, JUSTICE. This suit was instituted by W.O. Lucy and J.C. Lucy, complainants, against A.H. Zehmer and Ida S. Zehmer, his wife, defendants, to have specific performance of a contract by which it was alleged the Zehmers had sold to W.O. Lucy a tract of land owned by A.H. Zehmer in Dinwiddie county containing 471.6 acres, more or less, known as the Ferguson farm, for $50,000. J.C. Lucy, the other complainant, is a brother of W.O. Lucy, to whom W.O. Lucy transferred a half interest in his alleged purchase.

The instrument sought to be enforced was written by A.H. Zehmer on December 20, 1952, in these words: "We hereby agree to sell to W.O. Lucy the Ferguson Farm complete for $50,000.00, title satisfactory to buyer," and signed by the defendants, A.H. Zehmer and Ida S. Zehmer.

The answer of A.H. Zehmer admitted that at the time mentioned W.O. Lucy offered him $50,000 cash for the farm, but that he, Zehmer, considered that the offer was made in jest; that so thinking, both he and Lucy having had several drinks, he wrote out "the memorandum" quoted above and induced his wife to sign it; that he did not deliver the memorandum to Lucy, but that Lucy picked it up, read it, put it in his pocket, attempted to offer Zehmer $5 to bind the bargain, which Zehmer refused to accept, and realizing for the first time that Lucy was serious, Zehmer assured him that he had no intention of selling the farm and that the whole matter was a joke. Lucy left the premises insisting that he had purchased the farm.

Depositions were taken and the decree appealed from was entered holding that the complainants had failed to establish their right to specific performance, and dismissing their bill. The assignment of error is to this action of the court.

* * *

The defendants insist that the evidence was ample to support their contention that the writing sought to be enforced was prepared as a bluff or dare to force Lucy to admit that he did not have $50,000; that the whole matter was a joke; . . .

* * *

In his testimony Zehmer claimed that he "was high as a Georgia pine," and that the transaction "was just a bunch of two doggoned drunks bluffing to see who could take the biggest and say the most." That claim is inconsistent. . . . The record is convincing that Zehmer was not intoxicated to the extent of being unable to comprehend the nature and consequences of the instrument he executed, and hence that instrument is not to be invalidated on that ground. C.J.S., Contracts, §133, b., p. 483; *Taliaferro v. Emery*, 124 Va. 674, 98 S.E. 627. It was in fact conceded by defendants' counsel in oral argument that under the evidence Zehmer was not too drunk to make a valid contract.

* * *

The appearance of the contract, the fact that it was under discussion for forty minutes or more before it was signed; Lucy's objection to the first draft because it was written in the singular, and he wanted Mrs. Zehmer to sign it also . . . the discussion of what was to be included in the sale, the provision for the examination of the title, the completeness of the instrument that was executed, the taking possession of it by Lucy with no request or suggestion by either of the defendants that he give it back, are facts which furnish persuasive evidence that the execution of the contract was a serious business transaction rather than a casual, jesting matter as defendants now contend.

* * *

If it be assumed, contrary to what we think the evidence shows, that Zehmer was jesting about selling his farm to Lucy and that the transaction was intended by him to be a joke, nevertheless the evidence shows that Lucy did not so understand it but considered it to be a serious business transaction and the contract to be binding on the Zehmers as well as on himself . . . .

Not only did Lucy actually believe, but the evidence shows he was warranted in believing, that the contract represented a serious business transaction and a good faith sale and purchase of the farm.

In the field of contracts, as generally elsewhere, "We must look to the outward expression of a person as manifesting his intention rather than to his secret and unexpressed intention. 'The law imputes to a person an intention corresponding to the reasonable meaning of his words and acts.'" First Nat. Exchange Bank of Roanoke v. Roanoke Oil Co., 169 Va. 99, 114, 192 S.E. 764, 770.

* * *

The mental assent of the parties is not a requisite for the formation of a contract. If the words or other acts of one of the parties have but one reasonable meaning, his undisclosed intention is immaterial except when an unreasonable meaning which he attaches to his manifestations is known to the other party. Restatement of the Law of Contracts, Vol. I, §71, p. 74.

* * *

Whether the writing signed by the defendants and now sought to be enforced by the complainants was the result of a serious offer by Lucy and a serious acceptance by the defendants, or was a serious offer by Lucy and an acceptance in secret jest by the defendants, in either event it constituted a binding contact of sale between the parties.

* * *

Reversed and Remanded.

Once again, you see that all law is made up of rules. In *Lucy*, the defendants wanted the court to articulate a rule based upon a subjective theory of contracts: When an offeror makes an offer secretly in jest, or the offeree accepts in jest, there is no offer or acceptance. The plaintiffs, however, wanted the court to adopt a rule based on an objective theory: When an offer or acceptance is made secretly in jest and the other party does not know or have reason to know that the offer or acceptance is in jest, a binding contract may nonetheless result. The court solved the problem by adopting the latter rule. The plaintiffs therefore prevailed.

All law is made up of rules.

Rules and Elements: *Fisher v. Carrousel Motor Hotel, Inc.* (Defining an Element of a Rule)

Let us now read a case where the dispute revolves not around a rule, but an element of a rule. In *Fisher v. Carrousel Motor Hotel, Inc.*, 424 S.W.2d 627 (Tex. 1967), an African-American man (the plaintiff) was standing in line in a cafeteria-style restaurant when a white bigot (the defendant) yanked a plate from the plaintiff's hand. Could the plaintiff sue the defendant for battery? Both parties agreed on the rule of law of battery: the intentional, harmful or offensive, unpermitted touching of the person of another. They also agreed that what the defendant did was an intentional, offensive, and unpermitted touching. What, then, was the controversy? It was this: For the law of battery, what constitutes a "person" when the defendant did not touch the plaintiff's body, but a plate that the plaintiff had been holding?

Let us learn how the court defined a "person."

FISHER v. CARROUSEL MOTOR HOTEL, INC.
Supreme Court of Texas
424 S.W.2d 627 (1967)

GREENHILL, JUSTICE. This is a suit for actual and exemplary damages growing out of an alleged assault and battery. The plaintiff Fisher was a mathematician with the Data Processing Division of the Manned Spacecraft Center, an agency of the National Aeronautics and Space Agency, commonly called NASA. The defendants were the Carrousel Motor Hotel, Inc. . . . and Robert W. Flynn, who as an employee of the Carrousel was the manager of the Brass Ring Club.

* * *

[A buffet style luncheon was given at the Brass Ring Club. Fisher was an invited guest and was standing in line.] As Fisher was about to be served, he was approached by Flynn, who snatched the plate from Fisher's hand and shouted that he, a Negro, could not be served in the club. Fisher testified that he was not actually touched . . . but did testify that he was highly embarrassed and hurt by Flynn's conduct in the presence of his associates. * * *

Under the facts of this case, we have no difficulty in holding that the intentional grabbing of plaintiff's plate constituted a battery. The intentional snatching of an object from one's hand is as clearly an offensive invasion of one's person as would be an actual contact with the body. "To constitute an assault and battery, it is not necessary to touch the plaintiff's body or even his clothing; knocking or snatching anything from plaintiff's hand or touching anything connected with his person, when done in an offensive manner, is sufficient." *Morgan v. Loyacomo*, 190 Miss. 656, 1 So. 2d 510 (1941).

Such holding is not unique to the jurisprudence of this State. In *S. H. Kress & Co. v. Brashier*, 50 S.W.2d 922 (Tex. Civ. App. 1932, no writ), the defendant was held to have committed "an assault or trespass upon the person" by snatching a book from the plaintiff's hand. The jury findings in that case were that the defendant "dispossessed plaintiff of the book" and caused her to suffer "humiliation and indignity."

The rationale for holding an offensive contact with such an object to be a battery is explained in 1 Restatement of Torts 2d §18 (Comment p. 31) as follows:

> Since the essence of the plaintiff's grievance consists in the offense to the dignity involved in the unpermitted and intentional invasion of the inviolability of his person and not in any physical harm done to his body, it is not necessary that the plaintiff's actual body be disturbed. Unpermitted and intentional contacts with anything so connected with the body as to be customarily regarded as part of the other's person and therefore as partaking of its inviolability is actionable as an offensive contact with his person. There are some things such as clothing or a cane or, indeed, anything directly grasped by the hand which are so intimately connected with one's body as to be universally regarded as part of the person.

We hold, therefore, that the forceful dispossession of plaintiff Fisher's plate in an offensive manner was sufficient to constitute a battery * * * *

37

By defining a "person" to be anything closely connected to the plaintiff (all the other elements of battery were clearly satisfied), the plaintiff prevailed.

All rules are made up of elements.

Rules and Elements: Summarizing What Appellate Courts Do

You should not have any doubt now what appellate courts do. Appellate courts resolve disputes by pronouncing a rule of law (such as the rule in *Armory*: a finder has better rights to property than anyone but the true owner) or defining an element of a rule of law (such as the definition in *Fisher*: for purposes of battery, a person is anything connected with the plaintiff's person). When you read your cases you, therefore, will want to attack each case from the following perspective: Why are these parties before the court? Is it because they disagree on what rule of law should be used? Alternatively, is it because they disagree on the definition of an element of a rule? Note that parties may have a dispute because they disagree on which rule should be used *and* how to define an element of a rule? Now that is a dispute!

READING FOR MORE THAN RULES AND ELEMENTS

Now you know that when you read cases, you must read from a narrow perspective. That perspective is, which rule or definition of an element of a rule will the court adopt? Still, is it enough for you just to extract a rule or a definition of a rule of law out of a case? The answer is, no. You should be getting still more out of each case that you read. Let us now examine what additional information it is that you should come away with from each case.

Understanding the Court's Reasoning: In General

In addition to learning a new rule of law or definition of an element of a rule, you should also grasp the underlying reasoning of the court: *Why* did the court use the rule that it did? *Why* did the court define the element in the manner that it did? Although sometimes a court (such as in *Armory*) will not articulate its reasoning, that is rare. A court will typically state its reasoning. Let us now explore the typical reasons that a court will give to support its adoption of a rule or definition of an element of a rule.

Understanding the Court's Reasoning: Policy Considerations in *Li* and *Fisher*

In *Li v. Yellow Cab*, the reason given by the court for its having adopted the rule of comparative negligence was fairness. In *Fisher v. Carrousel Motor Hotel*, the court defined "person" as anything connected to the plaintiff's body because of "the offense to the dignity involved in the unpermitted and intentional invasion of the inviolability of his person." Both *Li* and *Fisher*, therefore, involved public policy. However, let us examine the rationale in *Lucy v. Zehmer* and see how the rationale in *Lucy* was different from the rationale in *Li* and *Fisher*.

Understanding the Court's Reasoning: Legal Precedent in *Lucy v. Zehmer*

In *Lucy*, the court ruled that an offer or acceptance made secretly in jest might nevertheless result in a binding contract. The reasoning, however, was not based expressly on public policy. Rather, it was based on two other well-established rules of law. In a word, it was based on *precedent*. One of these precedent-setting rules was articulated by the Virginia Supreme Court (recall that the *Lucy* case took place in Virginia): In contract law, we look to the outward expression of a person as manifesting his intention rather than to his secret and unexpressed intention. The second rule was based on the persuasive (not binding) authority of the Restatement: The mental assent of the parties is not a requisite for the formation of a contract. With these two rules as the foundation, the court declared that an acceptance made secretly in jest could nevertheless be a valid acceptance. The decision in *Lucy* therefore is an *extension* of preexisting legal principles (whether found in other cases or treatises, such as the Restatement), what I call "collateral rules" (because it is not the "main" rule or definition of the case).

The reasoning of a case may, therefore, be based on (1) policy, such as in *Li* or *Fisher*, or (2) legal precedent (the "collateral rules"), such as in *Lucy*.

SUMMARY OF CHAPTER 2

Let us now summarize the main points that we have covered in this chapter. When you read a case, you should ask yourself the following: What are the parties in this dispute fighting about? Is it about which rule of law (all law is made up of rules) should be used, or is it about the definition of an element (all rules are made up of elements) of a rule? Once you make this initial determination, ascertain the rule or definition the court articulates in order to solve the parties' dispute. Remember that you will also want to be able to understand the reasoning of the court. Sometimes the reasoning will be based on nothing more than public policy (fairness, politics, economics, sociology, etc.). Other times the reasoning will be based upon previously stated rules or precedent, what I have referred to as "collateral rules." (Sometimes it will be based on grounds of both policy and precedent.) You will especially want to pay attention to the reasoning when these collateral rules are the foundation for the court's decision. Why is this so? Because when you take your final examination, your professor may test you, not just on the "main" case rules and definitions, but also on the "collateral" rules and definitions.

barbri®

CHAPTER 3
MORE ON CASES: THE IMPORTANCE OF FACTS (AND HOW THEY TRIGGER THE LEGAL ISSUES)

"Just the facts, ma'am." These are the famous words of fast-talking, deadpan, Sgt. Joe Friday (played by the late Jack Webb) from the old, long-running Dragnet series (a wonderful police drama with no "action" whatsoever).[1] In this chapter, we are going to spend some time on "just the facts."

AN INTRODUCTION TO FACTS

Facts are critical to lawyers. When a wronged party enters your office to tell you about his or her problem, you will find that the typical client will spend much more time than is necessary to tell you what the problem is. Why is this? The reason is that clients do not understand the significance of "just the facts." To put it another way, clients cannot distinguish between facts that are important to their case from facts that are not important. Lawyers do. That is one reason why we are paid: to separate the relevant from the irrelevant. Moreover, that is what law school is about (at least in part): facts—and getting the student to separate the relevant from the irrelevant. Further, to do well on your exams, you are going to have to be able to separate the relevant facts from the irrelevant facts—as you will soon see.

THE THREE CATEGORIES OF FACTS

If you are going to understand the art of reading cases (and doing well on law school exams—but that will be just a little later in these materials) you must learn to separate the facts out. What I do is consider three categories of facts when I read cases or teach my students to read cases: (1) "key" facts, (2) "background" facts and (3) "colorable" facts. Let us now discuss each type of fact.

CATEGORY #1: KEY FACTS

Key facts are those facts that create the dispute between the parties. Key facts, therefore, are those facts, which, if they were changed or eliminated, would change the outcome of the case. The following hypothetical will illustrate what a key fact is.

> *Xavier is riding his bicycle when he sees Yetta walking down a residential street at 11:30 AM. Xavier thereupon dismounts from his bicycle, goes over to Yetta, and intentionally punches Yetta. Xavier then remounts his bicycle and peddles away.*

Xavier clearly committed a battery. Still, what are the *facts* that created the battery? Let us break out each set of facts and see. The first set of facts is "Xavier is riding his bicycle." Is this a

---

[1] If you are interested (when you take a break from your studies) and want to learn about this icon in American television, you can start here, http://en.wikipedia.org/wiki/Dragnet_(series).

key fact? No. That is because we can change this fact (and make Xavier be driving a car) or even eliminate this fact and, assuming that all other facts remained the same, we would not change the outcome of the hypothetical. Xavier would still have committed a battery. What do we make of the fact, "he sees Yetta walking down a residential street"? Are there any key facts in this clause? Again, the answer is, no. Xavier could have seen Yetta walking in a business section of town, but if all the other facts were the same, we would still have the same outcome: a battery. Is it a key fact that all of this happened at about 11:30 AM? No. If we changed the time to 10:30 AM or 7:00 PM, and all of the other facts were the same, we would not have changed the outcome of the hypothetical. Therefore, the time is not a key fact. Is it critical that "Xavier thereupon dismounts from his bicycle"? Of course not: if Xavier had punched Yetta intentionally while riding by, we would still have a battery. Hence, Xavier dismounting is not a key fact.

What do we make of the fact about Xavier "intentionally punches Yetta"? Is this a key fact? Remember what a key fact is: it is a fact, which, if we changed it or eliminated it, we would change the outcome of the hypothetical. If we eliminate "intentionally punches Yetta" from the hypothetical, we would no longer have a battery. Indeed, we would have nothing. We will have changed the outcome of the hypothetical. Consequently, "intentionally punches Yetta" is indeed a key fact. Finally, of course, it is not a key fact that the actors were Xavier and Yetta. The actors could have been Abel and Baker. Thus, the ultimate key facts are, "A intentionally punches B."

The balance of the facts—"Xavier then remounts his bicycle and peddles away"—are not key facts. Xavier could have left his bicycle there and run away. If he had done this, we would still have a battery.

The Importance of Key Facts and the Legal Problem

It is imperative that you determine what the key facts are in every case you read. Why is it crucial? The reason is simple: the key facts trigger the legal dispute or problem between the parties. As we have already discussed, in every case that you read, there is a legal dispute between the parties. The key facts create the legal dispute or problem. In the hypo we have been working with, the key facts are Xavier (or some actor) intentionally punched Yetta (or some other actor). These facts triggered the legal problem of battery. As you will see, you have to determine what the legal problem is when you read cases; you also have to determine what the legal problem is on your final exams. We will spend more time on framing the legal problems in chapters 5 and 14-17.

Factual and Legal: The Two-Part Composition of Every Issue Statement

As stated in the preceding paragraph, when you read cases and, eventually, when you write your final exams, you will have to write an issue statement. What is the issue statement of a case or on a law school exam? In every issue statement that you frame (whether in your reading of cases or on law school exams), there will always be two parts: the factual part and the legal part. The factual part is the key facts. The legal part is the legal problem: the rule or element in dispute (all law is made up of rules; all rules are made up of elements) that the parties are fighting over. Going back to the Xavier-Yetta hypothetical, the factual part is Xavier intentionally punched

Yetta;[2] the legal part is battery. Again, we cover this in much greater depth in chapters 5 and 14-17. Suffice to say for now, the "formula" for every issue statement is this: *(Key Facts) + (Legal Problem) = Issue Statement.* Thus, *(Xavier intentionally punched Yetta) + (Battery) = Issue Statement.*

Framing the Issue Statement as a Question

Now that you know that an issue statement is comprised of the key facts and the legal dispute between the parties, we are ready to discuss how to frame the issue. When you frame the issue in your mind (we will discuss writing the legal issue in chapter 5), frame it in the form of a question. Thus, again using our Xavier-Yetta hypothetical, the proper way to frame the issue is: *When Xavier intentionally punched Yetta, did he commit a battery?* Note that the first clause is the key facts; the second clause is the legal problem.

Why is it important to frame the issue as a question? Because this is exactly what you will be doing when you write your case briefs (chapter 5) and when you write your law school exams (chapters 14-17). Get into the habit now!

CATEGORY #2: BACKGROUND FACTS

What, then, are the facts that we did not classify as key facts? The facts that we did not classify as key facts (such as, "Xavier is riding his bicycle when he sees Yetta walking down a residential street at 11:30 AM") are what I call (my own terminology) "background facts." These facts just round out the story, whether the story is a hypothetical or a case (or, as you will learn, an essay question on an examination). Courts will always give you background facts to round out your knowledge of the case. Typically included in this background is a summary of what transpired in the trial court or intermediate appellate court below.

It is important for you to realize that it may not be easy for two reasonable people always to agree as to what the key facts are in a certain case. In the hypo that we have just gone over, it is very clear what the key facts are. Some hypos—or cases—may not be that clear. Nevertheless, that is okay. The study and practice of law is in part a science, in that we must work with great precision. Simultaneously, however, law also is an art, in that people can look at matters differently and reasonably disagree. Sometimes we can disagree as to what rule should be applied to resolve a dispute (see chapter 2). Sometimes we can even disagree as to what the key facts are in a case. (A dear colleague of mine, John Gallagher, Professor of Law Emeritus, Southwestern Law School, in describing my art-science dichotomy, coined the expressive term that I now often use, "ambiguity with precision.") All that is required of you when you read a case is to recognize that there are indeed key facts—the source of the parties' dispute. In most cases, the facts that are the key facts will be reasonably clear.

CATEGORY #3: "COLORABLE FACTS" (THE WAR HERO CASE)

---

[2] As stated earlier in this chapter, the key facts are not that the actors are "Xavier" and "Yetta." I use Xavier and Yetta (X and Y) to indicate two individuals. I could just as easily have used descriptive terms "Defendant" (for Xavier" and "Plaintiff" (for "Yetta").

The last type of facts that you should be familiar with are what I call (again, my own terminology) "colorable facts." What are colorable facts? These are emotionally charged facts which should have no impact at all on the case (they are not key facts)—but they do, even though the court will not acknowledge that they have impact. One of the best examples of colorable facts is *State v. Peery*, 224 Minn. 346 (1947), a criminal law case, which I read when I was a law school student. Here are the "facts" of the case. The defendant, in 1946 (World War II ended in 1945), had been convicted of exposing himself in public. After stating the procedural history of the case, the court summarized the evidence presented at trial. The first sentence of this part of the opinion states: "The evidence presented at the trial indicates that defendant, 23 years of age, a veteran of four major campaigns of the United States army in the South Pacific. . . ." I remember my professor asking someone to read these opening lines. After the student read, "United States army in the South Pacific," the professor said, "Stop!" He then asked, "Does anyone have any doubt how this case is going to turn out?" Of course, the court reversed the conviction.

Is it a key fact that the defendant was a veteran of four major campaigns? Of course, it is not. Elsewhere in the opinion, the court wrote, "He is a combat veteran of four major campaigns of the South Pacific, honorably discharged as a staff sergeant, seeking a college education, and working part time to help defray his expenses." It is not a key fact the first time the court stated the defendant's military background; it is not a key fact when the court states it a second time. It also is irrelevant to his arrest and the subsequent litigation that the army honorably discharged him as a staff sergeant. Nor is it a key fact that the defendant is working his way through college. It would appear that the key facts are whether he exposed himself and whether he had the requisite intent. So why did the court focus in on his status—a veteran of four major South Pacific campaigns? The answer is, it was a "colorable fact," meaning, an emotionally charged fact that indirectly and silently affected the outcome. Even though these facts do not go to the issue of whether the defendant committed the crime in question (as the dissent points out), the court reversed the conviction. Put simply, the court was not going to send a veteran of four major campaigns to jail for the crime of indecent exposure. You may agree or disagree with the outcome. It is, however, reality. Look at it this way: Who is the more "likeable" defendant? Is it a veteran charged with indecent exposure, or a hardcore gang member charged with murder? The answer is obvious. Colorable facts ultimately drove the *Peery* case.

Colorable facts should have no impact on the outcome and should only round out your understanding of the case (like a background fact). However, colorable facts are so emotionally charged that they can actually affect the outcome. Indeed, sometimes you cannot explain the outcome of a case any other way.

CATEGORY #3: "COLORABLE FACTS" (THE STOCKBROKER CASE)

Here is another example of colorable facts, the case of *Chapter House Circle of King's Daughters v. Hartford Nat. Bank and Trust Co.*, 121 Conn. 558 (1936). During the Great Depression that started in 1929 with the stock market crashing, a major stockbrokerage firm failed to register securities in the names of its clients. Rather, it registered the securities in its own name. There was no fraud involved by the firm. It engaged in this practice because it was customary and made record keeping easier. Still, the law was that if a broker did not "earmark" (register the securities in the name of the clients) stock shares correctly, the broker was liable for any loss, even if the failure to earmark did not cause the loss. As stated earlier, the stock market crashed in 1929. Nonetheless, the court refused to apply the common law rule of liability for failure to earmark. What was the reason for this? At that time, all brokerage firms registered securities in their own name. Further, and importantly, the stock market would have crashed even if the broker had registered the securities correctly. If the court had applied the common law rule, every major stockbrokerage firm on Wall Street would have gone into bankruptcy because all stocks had crashed: the Great Depression had begun. To apply the common law rule of earmarking would have made a terrible economic situation even worse. Therefore, the court refused to apply the common law rule. Was the Great Depression a colorable fact or a key fact? I think it was significant that the court's opinion for refusing to apply the common law rule did not even mention the fact that the stock market had collapsed and the country had entered the worst depression in its history. Nonetheless, I believe that the Depression was a colorable fact in this case: The economic collapse of the nation was a highly charged emotional (as well as an economic) fact, which had a silent but obvious impact on the outcome of the case.

That stated, do not go looking for a colorable fact in each opinion. They are not that common. They do come up from time to time, however. Be aware that they exist.

SUMMARY OF CHAPTER 3

To summarize, when you read your cases, be sensitive to key facts on the one hand and mere background facts on the other. Remember, not all facts are critical to your understanding the case. You have to get into the habit of knowing what is relevant and what is not. Key facts trigger the legal dispute between the parties. The key facts plus the legal dispute equal the issue before the court. Frame your issue statement in the form of a question. Be aware, too, that some facts may not be part of the court's legal reasoning—but these colorable facts (like a war hero and the Great Depression) may nevertheless affect the outcome of the case.

CHAPTER 4
MORE ON CASES: THE RULE IN LIGHT OF THE FACTS (ALSO KNOWN AS THE HOLDING)

You will recall that in chapter 1, we learned that all law is made up of rules and all rules are made up of elements. In chapter 2, we began to see that cases involve disputes between parties and that the court resolves the dispute by articulating a rule or a definition of an element of a rule. In chapter 3, we saw the need to distinguish key facts from non-key facts: the key facts create the legal controversy or issue that the court must address. In this chapter, we shall explore the relationship between the key facts and the rule or definition of an element that a court pronounces in a case.

THE INTERRELATIONSHIP BETWEEN THE RULE AND THE FACTS

The key facts of a case and the rule (either the rule of law, as per *Amory* or *Li* cases, or the definition of an element, as per the *Fisher* case)[1] stated by the court to solve the legal dispute between the parties are not separate and distinct features of a case. Rather, the key facts and the rule are interrelated. Indeed, only when you understand this relationship between the key facts and the rule will you be able truly to comprehend what the case means—and understand what a holding is.

The Interrelationship between the Key Facts and the Legal Problem

In the last chapter, we learned that you frame each issue statement in the form of a question. We also learned that each issue statement is comprised of two parts: the factual and the legal. The factual aspect is the key facts and the legal aspect is the legal problem that is the center of the parties' dispute (e.g., the meaning of "person" for purposes of the law of battery).

The Holding of a Case Answers the Legal Question Presented

The holding of a case is simply the answer to the legal issue presented. Moreover, just as an issue statement is comprised of two parts (factual and legal), so, too, is the holding. Each holding has a factual and legal part. What, then, is the difference between an issue statement and a holding? Simply put, while we always frame the issue statement of a case (key facts and legal issue) in the form of a question, we always frame the holding of a case (key facts and legal issue) in the form of an affirmative statement. Thus, for example, in the hypo that we covered in chapter 3 dealing with Xavier and Yetta, the issue statement is, *When Xavier intentionally punched Yetta, did he commit a battery?* The holding, which answers the issue statement, is, *When Xavier intentionally punched Yetta, Xavier committed a battery.*[2] Better yet, my holding is, *When X intentionally punches Y, X has committed a battery.*[3]

---

[1] See chapter 2.

[2] Recall from chapter 3 that it is not a key fact that "Xavier" did the act. I use the name "Xavier" simply to designate an actor. I could just as easily have used "Defendant."

[3] See preceding footnote.

What is the purpose of doing essentially one exercise twice? You will see shortly in chapter 5 that you ultimately do not have to do this twice. For now, however, we walk before we run. Thus, for now (and only for now), we do it twice.

THE HOLDING IN *ARMORY*

To illustrate this further, and to make this just a little more challenging, let us now look at the *Armory* case (discussed in depth in chapter 2). Recall that in *Armory*, a chimney sweeper's boy found a jewel. The boy brought the jewel to a goldsmith in order to have it weighed or appraised. The smith took the jewel to weigh it but refused to give the jewel back to the boy.

The Key Facts in *Armory*

What were the key facts in *Armory*? Was it significant that the plaintiff was a chimney sweeper's boy? No. If the plaintiff had been a carpenter's assistant, the outcome of the case would have been the same. Would the outcome have changed if the defendant had not been a goldsmith but a silversmith? Of course, the answer is, no. Would the result have been different if the boy gave the jewel to the smith, not for the limited purpose of weighing the jewel, but merely to admire it for a few minutes? Again, this would not have changed the outcome in any way. What would have happened if the smith had been just an acquaintance of the plaintiff? Yet once more, there would not have been any difference. Finally, would the outcome have been any different if the object of the dispute happened to be an antique watch instead of a jewel? No.

What, then, were the key facts? They were these: the plaintiff found a chattel, gave the chattel to another for a limited purpose, with the intent that the defendant would not secure possession.[4] These then are the key facts in *Armory*.

The Legal Dispute in *Armory*

What was the legal problem or dispute in *Armory*? It was this: as between the plaintiff (the chimney sweeper's boy) and the defendant (the goldsmith), who owned the chattel? Ownership was the legal issue that was in dispute.

The Issue Statement in *Armory*

You will recall from chapter 3, we always frame the legal issue in the form of a question. This question includes two parts: (1) the key facts that are triggering the legal dispute between the parties and (2) the nature of the legal dispute. Thus, the issue statement in *Armory* is, *When A finds a chattel and gives it to B for a limited purpose, with the intent that B would not secure possession, as between A and B, does A own the chattel?*[5] Put another way, saying essentially the

---

[4] It was clear from the facts that there was no question as to the plaintiff's intent. The plaintiff gave the chattel to the defendant for an appraisal—and not for making a gift of the chattel to the defendant.

[5] Possession, you will learn in your property course, is an important concept. With respect to personal property or chattels, possession might give the possessor ownership of the chattel. Although this can get somewhat complicated, more than that is not necessary for you; the purpose of these materials is to teach you to understand the

same thing (yes, there may be several ways of framing a correct issue statement, as we have seen with the "ambiguity with precision" calculus we discussed earlier), we might succinctly state, *Does a finder of a chattel have better rights to it than anyone except the true owner?*

The Holding in *Armory*

What then is the holding in *Armory*? It is this: *A finder of a chattel has better rights to it than anyone except the true owner.* Yes, you will note that the holding essentially is simply the issue stated as a question put into an affirmative statement.

What Is Not the Holding in *Armory*

We should carefully note what the holding is not: The finder of a *jewel* has better rights to it than anyone except the true owner. Why is the holding not limited to jewels? Perhaps I can answer this question (in the true tradition of law school) with a question: If you think that the decision is limited to jewels, what happens in the next case when the plaintiff finds a watch or a rare coin? Are we going to have to have one legal principle for jewels, another one for watches, and still another for rare coins? The answer is obvious: of course not. You, therefore, will want to be able to recognize that the holding in *Armory* deals with any *chattel*. In this way, you can readily apply the holding in *Armory* to a situation where the plaintiff finds any chattel. You can now see why it is important to make certain that the key facts in your issue statement and, ultimately, in your holding are not too narrow. If they are too narrow, they lose their utility in resolving subsequent problems—and in answering your law school essay exams.

Holdings and Law School Exams

Why is it important not to make the holding too narrow for your law school exams? As you will soon learn, on your exams, you will not get a fact pattern where the plaintiff finds a jewel. You may get one where the plaintiff finds a rare stamp, however. Of course, the rule in *Armory* works just as well for rare stamps as it does for jewels.

THE HOLDING IN *LI*

Now let us look at *Li* (discussed in chapter 2). The facts, we will recall, were that the defendant was driving at an unsafe speed and consequently injured the plaintiff, who had made an unsafe left hand turn, which contributed to her injuries.

The Key Facts in *Li*

Was it a key fact that the plaintiff made an unsafe left hand turn? Of course not: If the plaintiff had made an unsafe right hand turn, all other facts being the same, the outcome would have still been the same. Was it a key fact that the injury was due to an auto accident? No. If instead of driving autos, the plaintiff and defendant had been driving speedboats, the outcome would still have been the same. The key facts in *Li* were therefore these: The defendant

---

law school learning process and write exceptional law school exams—not teach substantive law per se.

negligently injured plaintiff; however, the plaintiff's injuries were also caused by her own negligent conduct.

The Legal Dispute in *Li*

What was the legal dispute of *Li*? The defendant wanted the court to retain the rule of contributory negligence; the plaintiff wanted the court to adopt the rule of comparative negligence. (Remember, all law is made up of rules and all rules. . . .)

The Issue Statement in *Li*

The issue statement may be stated as follows: *When the plaintiff's own negligence was a legal cause of her injury, should the doctrine of contributory negligence, which bars all recovery, be replaced by comparative negligence, which assesses liability in proportion to the defendant's fault?* Remember to always frame the issues statement in the form of a question. Remember also that each issue statement has two parts: one part factual (key facts) and one part legal (the rule or element in dispute).

The Holding in Li

What, then, was the holding in *Li*? Once again, you must appreciate that the court's decision, to adopt the rule of comparative negligence, was not limited to a situation where there was an automobile accident. Rather, the holding applies whenever the plaintiff's own negligence was a contributing cause of her injuries. Hence, the holding is simply the issue statement that was in the form of a question transformed into an affirmative statement: *When the plaintiff's own negligence was a legal cause of her injury, the doctrine of contributory negligence, which bars all recovery, is replaced by comparative negligence, which assesses liability in proportion to the defendant's fault.*

Holdings and Law School Exams—Again

Remember, on your law school exam, you will not get a hypo dealing with an automobile accident—but you will get a hypo dealing with a hunting accident. *Li* works just as nicely for hunters as it does for drivers.

THE HOLDING IN *FISHER*

Now let us explore the *Fisher* case (discussed in chapter 2). In *Fisher*, an African-American man was in line in a cafeteria-style restaurant and holding a plate. A white man yanked the plate away in a rude manner.

The Key Facts in *Fisher*

What were the key facts in the case? Was it significant that the plaintiff was in line in a cafeteria? What if the plaintiff had been standing in line in a grocery store and the bigot yanked a bag of groceries from the plaintiff's hands? Would we still have a battery? Of course, we would. Therefore, it does not matter that the plaintiff was in line in a cafeteria-style restaurant; he could have been seated at a very elegant dining establishment. Nor does it matter that he was holding a plate, a tray, a fork—or a bag of groceries. The key facts are therefore these: The defendant intentionally and offensively pulled an object that was held by the hands of the plaintiff. Alternatively, better yet (this is the art aspect of law school), we can say that the defendant intentionally and offensively pulled an object closely connected with the person of the plaintiff.

I make one final point now: Does it matter that the defendant in *Fisher* was a bigot? It does, but only for the purpose of showing that the touching was offensive and unpermitted (which was not disputed by the defendant). Appreciate the following differences: (1) The white bigot yanked the plate yelling, "You have no right to be here" (the actual facts in *Fisher*). The touching was clearly offensive and unpermitted. (2) A waiter in the restaurant had believed that the plaintiff was finished eating and took the plate, politely stating, "Sir, please allow me to take that plate from you." The touching of the plate was not offensive and permission would be implied by the circumstances in the second scenario.

The Legal Dispute in *Fisher*

The dispute centered on how we define an element of a rule: How does one define "person" for purposes of battery?

The Issue Statement in *Fisher*

Putting the key facts together with the legal dispute, the legal issue is, *For purposes of battery, is the offensive touching of anything closely connected with the plaintiff's person deemed to be the plaintiff's person?*

The Holding in *Fisher*

What was the holding in *Fisher*? Was it limited to holding a plate? Certainly not. The holding was this: *Anything closely connected with the person of the plaintiff can be deemed the plaintiff's person for purposes of battery.* Again, note how we simply take the issue statement and turn it around from a question into an affirmative statement. Further, note, too, how on the exam, you will not get a bigot yanking a plate from the plaintiff, but you will get a bully yanking a briefcase from the plaintiff.

THE RELATIONSHIP BETWEEN KEY FACTS AND THE HOLDING

You now see how important it is to determine what the key facts are in any given case: The more broadly we can describe the key facts, the more broad the holding. Further, if we can state the holding broadly, we can apply it more generally to other disputes that arise in the future. Thus, in *Armory*, the holding deals with the finder of a chattel, not only the finder of a jewel.

A Court May Want a Narrow Holding

Nonetheless, you must also be aware that in some cases the court purposefully wants to state a very narrow holding. For example, in the *Lucy* case (discussed in chapter 2), these were the key facts: The defendant made an acceptance in jest and the plaintiff (offeree) did not know and had no reason to know that the acceptance was in jest. The holding stated by the court was that an acceptance made secretly in jest is a valid acceptance. Here, the facts—and the holding—dealt with acceptances made secretly in jest.[6] This is a somewhat narrow rule of law in that it has absolutely no application except in the limited and unusual circumstance of an acceptance made in jest. (Note, however, that it was not a key fact that the subject matter of the offer was the sale of the defendant's *farm*. Consequently, the holding is not limited to offers to sell farms.)

Key Facts, Holdings, and *Stare Decisis*

You now see the relationship between key facts and holdings. There also is a related point that you should know: the policy of *stare decisis*. This means that a decision by one court is binding on courts of equal or lower rank in subsequent cases where the law and facts are the same. (See *Black's Law Dictionary*, "Stare Decisis," fifth ed. at 1261.) With this doctrine in mind, it is not uncommon for litigation in a lower court to revolve around whether a decision of a higher court (such as a state supreme court) is binding on the parties to the present controversy. Thus, if the plaintiff in a lawsuit wants a rule stated in a published opinion (traditionally, only published opinions can be cited as authority) by a higher court to apply to the present litigation, she will try to convince the court of one of two matters. She will assert that either (1) the key facts in both cases are identical or, (2) even if the key facts are not identical, the holding stated by the higher court should be broadly interpreted and the holding extended so that it encompasses the facts of the present case and therefore is applicable to the present litigation. On the other hand, if the defendant does not want the holding stated by that higher court to apply, he will try to convince the court that (1) the key facts in both cases are different and, (2) the holding in the higher court case should be given a narrow reading and the holding should not be extended to the present controversy.

SUMMARY OF CHAPTER 4

Let us now summarize the highlights of this chapter: When you read a case, to the extent that you can make the key facts very narrow, you will have a very narrow holding. The consequence of this will be the holding will have limited application in future controversies (or examination hypotheticals). For example, if *Armory* had dealt only with found jewels, it would have very little application in future disputes. However, to the extent that you can broaden the key facts, you will have a broad holding with greater application. Thus, a rule dealing with found chattels has greater application than a holding dealing with found jewels. It is not uncommon for a dispute to arise because one party to the controversy believes that a holding in a prior opinion is

---

[6] Of course, the holding might well also include *offers* made secretly in jest. Again, this is the art aspect of "ambiguity with precision," something we have discussed earlier. Eventually, you will get used to working with uncertainty and ambiguity.

applicable because the court that wrote the opinion had intended a broad-based holding, while the other party believes that same opinion is inapplicable because that court had intended a very narrow-based holding.

CHAPTER 5
CASE BRIEFING: WHAT TO DO—AND WHAT NOT TO DO

To brief a case is simply to write a summary of the case. In this chapter, we will discuss what a good brief should have. We also will discuss what a good brief should not have. First, however, we will discuss why you should brief.

REASONS TO BRIEF

There are four good reasons why you, a law school student, especially a 1L, should brief your cases. Let us go over them now.

Reason #1: Briefing Helps You Learn, Understand, and Memorize the Law

The first reason is to enable you to learn the holdings and collateral rules of the case. There is nothing like writing something out to see if you really do understand it and to hardwire it in to your mind. In the process, you will end up memorizing without trying to memorize the cases. Yes, you will have to memorize, but when you memorize by understanding and not by rote, you are on your way to an "A" grade. If you start to write out a brief but you bog down, it is because you really do not fully understand the case. Of course, there is nothing wrong in such a situation. That happens to everyone at some time (and to 1Ls a lot). It is just part of the learning process. When you are stuck, all that you need to do is go back, re-read the case, and try to determine where you are having a problem.

Reason #2: Briefing Allows You to Participate in Class

The second reason for briefing is to give you a short summary of the case so that you can readily follow or participate in the class discussion. Without a short summary of the highlights of a particular case in front of you, it is possible, if not likely, that you will forget the facts or issue of a case, or confuse the facts of one case with those of another.

Reason #3: Briefing Will Help You Construct Your Course Outline

The third reason for briefing is that your case briefs will become one of the tools that you will use when you begin constructing your course outline (more on that later in the next chapter of these materials). As you will see, your course outline will be your most significant tool in learning the material on a week-to-week basis, but briefing your cases day-to-day will be a major prerequisite for your outline.

Reason #4: Briefing Gives You Practice Writing Law School Essay Exams

The fourth reason that you will want to brief is so that you can get immediate practice in writing law school exams. Every time you write out a case brief, you are isolating the relevant facts from irrelevant facts and framing an issue statement—something that you will have to do on your essay examinations. As you will see when we cover essay examination writing, practice really does make perfect (or at least an "A" for a final grade).

Why "Book-Briefing" Is Not Good Enough

Now I know that some of you are saying to yourselves. "I can get just as much out of a case by *book briefing*." What is "book briefing"? Book briefing is a term that means the student annotates and underlines the major principles in his or her casebook—as is also done by students who do case briefing—but without doing the final step of writing out a brief. With all due respect to those who just book brief, I do not think that most first year law school students can understand what they need to understand without writing out a brief. Moreover, when you are just starting out (I won't object if you want to book brief Estate and Gift Tax in your last semester), it will be difficult for you to understand *and remember* the materials that you previously read without taking notes in some organized manner. Book briefing will not hardwire the material into your mind; writing a case brief will. Further, except for not being prepared at all, few things are more embarrassing in law school than to be called on in class and to stumble around on the facts and issue of a case, while your professor and one hundred of your colleagues are watching you and listening to every word that you are saying. If you do not write out a case brief, you will almost certainly stumble.

One Final Point on Briefing

I have one final point to make regarding why you should brief. I have authored these materials to make the law school learning experience understandable and to help you write excellent law school exams. Consistent with these goals, I have absolutely no desire to make you do anything that you will not find to be beneficial. In short, everything that I am teaching you has one objective: to help you succeed. Briefing your cases really will help you.

CONTENTS OF A CASE BRIEF

Now that you understand why you should brief, what should your case brief—the summary of the case—contain? Let us now see.

Law as Science and Art

Preliminarily, it is important to point out that neither the law nor the study of law is pure science. There is a science-like aspect to the law, to be sure. That is the precision that we need when we deal with the law. Yet, law also has an art-like aspect to it. We discussed this "ambiguity with precision" earlier. As such, there may well be not just *one* right answer. There may be a number of right answers. You have already seen this to some extent in Chapter 3, "More on Cases: The Importance of Facts." It was there that we learned that reasonable people might sometimes disagree on what the key facts are in a given case. Briefing illustrates the point that law is a science because it needs to be precise. Nonetheless, briefing also is an art—two students can each attack a case differently and both can be correct. It, therefore, does not matter if you use some variation of what I am going to suggest; I assume that you will. What matters is that you know what you are doing so that your brief gives *you* a proper understanding of the case.

The "3-Point" Brief

Nevertheless, all "correct" briefs will have the following components: (1) There will be an issue statement, which includes the key facts.[1] (2) There will also be a holding. (3) In all probability, there will be the rationale or reasoning of the court. That is it. I know that some professors and writing instructors will want you to use a 7-point or (even) an 9-point brief. I disagree, however, as I next explain.

Brevity as Key

By using this 3-point brief system, your case briefs will necessarily be brief. It is important to remember that your *case briefs should be brief.* That is why we call it a "brief" and not a "long." That briefs should be brief is, of course, necessary if the purpose of the brief is to give you a short summary of the major points of the case.

Yet, if all "good" briefs have the foregoing characteristics, "bad" briefs also have certain common characteristics. We shall see this in some of the sample briefs that follow.

SAMPLE CASE BRIEFS: *ARMORY V. DELAMIRIE*

Now let us take a detailed look at a sample brief of *Armory v. Delamirie*, a case that we have been referring to regularly since we first read it in Chapter 2, "How to Read Cases: The Basics." Perhaps this is a good time to go back and refresh your memory of *Armory*. After you do, let us analyze Sample Brief #1A to see what is good about it and what needs improvement.

Sample Case Brief#1A: A Good Brief

This is a good brief, especially for a 1L, who has never done any significant briefing before. Still, as you will see, we can certainly improve it.

---

[1] See Chapter 3, "More on Cases: The Importance of Facts," for definition and significance of "key facts."

Sample Brief #1A: A Good Brief

ARMORY v. DELAMIRIE
King's Bench, 1722

Issue #1: Does the finder of a jewel, though he does not by such finding acquire an absolute right to the jewel, have rights superior to all but the rightful owner?

Holding #1: Yes. The finder of a jewel, though he does not by such finding acquire an absolute right to the jewel, has rights superior to all but the true owner.

Reasoning for Holding #1: None given.

Issue #2: Is the measure of damages for the conversion of the finder's jewel by the smith the full value of the jewel?

Holding #2: Yes. The measure of damages for the conversion of the finder's jewel by the smith is the full value of the jewel.

Reasoning for Holding #2: None given.

Sample Case Brief #1A: A Good Brief: General Observations

There are a number of good things about this brief. To begin with, the brief is indeed brief. Many first-year law school students have a habit of writing briefs that are so lengthy that they are several pages long. When that happens, the brief is no longer brief and it loses its effectiveness; it no longer is a summary of the major points of the case. Second, the brief has all of the critical components of the "3-point brief." Importantly, the brief has the legal issue and the holding.

Sample Case Brief #1A: A Good Brief: Specific Observations

Now let us turn to the specifics of the brief.

1. *Issue statement.* First, let us tackle the issue statement. You may be thinking, "What exactly is an *issue*?" It is really quite simple. Indeed, we have already covered it earlier in Chapter 2, "How to Read Cases: The Basics," and Chapter 4, "More on Cases: the Rule in Light of the Facts (Also Known as the Holding)." You may remember that we learned that courts solve disputes between parties. Consequently, the issue statement tells us exactly what the dispute between the parties is. Alternatively, to put it in terms that a layperson could understand, why are the parties fighting? In *Armory*, there are two issues because the parties were fighting about two matters: (1) Who has better rights to the jewel[2] and, (2) assuming that the plaintiff prevails on the first matter, what will be the extent of the defendant's liability? Let us now focus our attention on Issue #1, which addresses the question of who has better rights to the jewel.

2. *Two parts to the issue statement: factual and legal.* If you examine Issue #1 of Sample Case Brief #1A carefully, you will note that it contains two parts: (1) a factual part and (2) a legal part. In the factual part, we are told what happened: Someone found a jewel ("Does the finder of a jewel"). In the legal part, we are told what the legal question is ("though he does not by such finding acquire an absolute right to the jewel, have rights superior to all but the rightful owner?"). As we have already seen, every issue statement will include two parts—factual and legal. Indeed, in Issue #2, we likewise have a factual part ("the conversion of the finder's jewel by the smith") and a legal part ("Is the measure of damages . . . the full value of the jewel?"). Now that you know that each issue statement has two parts to it (factual and legal), let us explore the factual aspect in a little more depth.

3. *Factual part: key facts.* What kind of facts are to be found in the factual part of an issue statement? The answer is this: key facts. Recall that the statement of facts should be limited to the key facts. The issue statement should likewise include only key facts. If you examine Issue #1 carefully, you will determine that it contains *mainly* key facts. But why does it not have *only* the key facts? It should, and we shall see how Sample Brief #1B, infra, is an improvement in this regard.

4. *Phrasing the issue affirmatively or negatively.* One final point on the issue statement is

---

[2] Give yourself a well-deserved pat on the back if you are presently saying to yourself, "The dispute really involves who has better rights to the *chattel.*" If you do not understand the significance of this statement, do not worry. Just keep reading along in these materials until we get to Sample Brief #1B and the explanatory text. At that point, you will see very clearly the significance of the italicized statement.

appropriate. You will note that the issue statement is phrased in such a manner that it can be answered in the affirmative or the negative—it can be answered in a simple "yes" or "no." You should always phrase an issue statement in a manner so that it can be answered, "yes" or "no."

5. *The holding.* Now let us proceed to the next part of the brief, the holding. The holding also consists of two parts. The first part is the answer to the issue statement ("yes" or "no"). The second part of the holding is merely the issue statement—a question—turned around and put into a positive statement. Thus, the second part of the first holding is, "The finder of a jewel, though he does not by such finding acquire an absolute right to the jewel, has rights superior to all but the true owner." The second part of the second holding is, "The measure of damages for the conversion of the finder's jewel by the smith is the full value of the jewel." Both of these positive statements are of course rules of law (remember: all law is made up of rules) and may be used by courts in subsequent cases to resolve controversies that arise between parties. These rules will also be used by you, in addressing the issues raised on your final examination.

6. *Reasoning.* *Armory* is unusual in that it does not have any reasoning.[3] We shall soon come to briefs of other cases where the court's reasoning is stated.

Summary of Sample Case Brief #1A

To summarize, this first sample brief was a fairly good brief. The brief, however, did have its drawbacks: Because the statement of facts in the issue statement was drawn so narrowly, the issue statement was likewise narrowly stated ("Does the finder of a jewel . . . ."). When the issue is narrowly drawn, the holding must likewise be narrowly drawn ("The finder of a jewel . . . ."). The point is simply this: The principles in *Armory* are not limited to finders of jewels. Let us now look at another brief and see how it is superior to Sample Brief #1A.

Sample Case Brief #1B: A Better Brief

The case brief that follows is superior to the case brief that we just examined. Why this is superior will become clear as we dissect it.

---

[3] It would have been very appropriate for the student to take a stab at the reasoning, even though the court itself did not provide it. You should always try to push yourself intellectually as far and as hard as possible. The more you do, the better you will be as a student and, ultimately, as a lawyer. See Sample Case Brief #1C.

Sample Brief #1B: A Better Brief

ARMORY v. DELAMIRIE
King's Bench, 1722

Issue #1: Does the finder of a chattel, though he does not by such finding acquire an absolute right to the chattel, have rights superior to all but the rightful owner?

Holding #1: Yes. The finder of a chattel, though he does not by such finding acquire an absolute right to the chattel, has rights superior to all but the true owner.

Reasoning for Holding #1: None given.

Issue #2: Is the measure of damages for the conversion of the finder's chattel by the defendant the full value of the chattel?

Holding #2: Yes. The measure of damages for the conversion of the finder's chattel by the defendant is the full value of the chattel.

Reasoning for Holding #2: None given.

Sample Case Brief #1B: A Better Brief: Specific Observations

Sample Brief #1B is superior to sample Brief #1A because the former recognizes that the problem between the parties does not exist because the property in question is a jewel. For this reason, the statement of facts contains only key facts: "the finder of a *chattel*."[4] Because the key facts of the issue statement are narrowly drawn, so, too, is the holding. Still, as good as Sample Brief #1B is, it can be better. Sample Brief #1C illustrates how to make it better.

Sample Case Brief #1C: A Great Brief

Sample Case Brief #1C is a great brief because it is specific where it should be and, importantly, the student goes further by trying to understand the court's reasoning—even when the court does not state it.

---

[4] Is it a key fact that the plaintiff took the chattel to the defendant "for an appraisal"? No, because the plaintiff could have taken the chattel to the defendant for the purpose of giving the defendant the pleasure of admiring it. Nevertheless, it is important to recognize that when the plaintiff gave the chattel to the defendant, he did so for a limited purpose only and not with the intent that the defendant could keep the jewel. In this regard—and only in this regard—it is important to recognize that the plaintiff took the chattel to the defendant "for an appraisal."

Sample Case Brief #1C: A Great Brief

ARMORY v. DELAMIRIE
King's Bench, 1722

Issue #1: Does the finder of a chattel, though he does not by such finding acquire an absolute right to the chattel, have rights superior to all but the rightful owner?

Holding #1: Yes.

Reasoning for Holding #1: None given. (Perhaps the holding is based on the need to maintain an honest social order.)

Issue #2: Is the measure of damages for the conversion of the finder's chattel by the defendant the full value of the chattel?

Holding #2: Yes.

Reasoning for Holding #2: None given. (Justice, seemingly, requires that the burden be on the defendant to prove that the chattel was not of the highest quality.)

Sample Case Brief #1C: A Great Brief: Specific Observations

This brief is excellent for several reasons: First, the issue statements contain the key facts only (as was done in Sample Brief #1B). Second, the holdings are simply a "yes"—there is no second part to the holding ("The finder of a chattel . . ."). The reason for this omission is simple: The fictitious student who wrote this brief *knows* that the holding is merely an affirmative statement of the question asked in the issue statement. Why, then, state the same thing twice? In all frankness, there is no need to write out a complete issue statement *and* a complete holding. If you have the former, you do not also need the latter. Remember, briefs should be brief. Finally, the student thought what the reasoning of the court was—even though the court itself did not state the reasoning. Wow! For these reasons, Sample Brief #1C is outstanding.

To summarize, Sample Brief #1C is truly an outstanding brief. It contains only the key facts in issue statement. Moreover, it does not have duplication: Although it has a complete issue statement, it does not *also* have a complete holding. Rather, the holding is simply the "yes" or "no" answer to the issue. Finally, the student pushed to excel by stating the reasoning.

Sample Case Brief #1D: A Poor Brief

Now let us examine one other sample brief and see what problems exist with it— problems that are especially common among first year law school students.

Sample Case Brief #1D: A Poor Brief

ARMORY v. DELAMIRIE
King's Bench, 1722

Facts: The plaintiff is a chimney sweeper's boy. He found a jewel and carried it to the defendant's shop. The defendant was a goldsmith. The plaintiff took the jewel to the goldsmith to "know what it was." The sweeper's boy delivered it to the goldsmith's apprentice. The latter, under pretense of weighing it, took out the stones, and called to the goldsmith. The goldsmith offered the plaintiff three halfpence. The plaintiff refused to take the money and insisted on having the "thing" again. The goldsmith refused to deliver the jewel to the plaintiff, who commences an action in trover against the goldsmith.

Issue #1: Who owns the jewel?

Holding #1: The plaintiff. The finder of a jewel, though he does not by such finding acquire an absolute property or ownership, yet he has such a property right as will enable him to keep the property against all but the rightful owner, and consequently may maintain trover.

Court's Reasoning for Holding #1: None Given.

Issue #2: Damages?

Holding for Issue #2: As to the value of the jewel, several of the trade were examined to prove what a jewel of the finest water that would fit the socket would be worth; and the Chief Justice (Pratt) directed the jury, that unless the defendant did produce the jewel, and shew it not to be of the finest water, they should presume the strongest against him, and make the value of the best jewels the measure of their damages: which they accordingly did.

Sample Case Brief #1D: A Poor Brief: Specific Observations

1. *Statement of facts is superfluous and not limited to the key facts.* The first problem is the statement of facts: This student includes a statement of "Facts." First, it is not necessary. One simply has to put the key facts into the issue statement. A separate statement of "Facts" is superfluous. Second, this statement of "Facts" is not limited to key facts. Indeed, it has far too many non-key facts. As we have previously discussed in Chapter 3, "More on Cases: The Importance of Facts," key facts are those facts which, if changed or eliminated, would change the outcome of the case. Key facts, therefore, trigger the dispute before the court. As we previously covered, would it make a difference if the plaintiff were a carpenter's helper instead of a chimney sweeper's boy? Did the chattel have to be a jewel? Would there have been a different outcome if the defendant had been a silversmith? Did it matter that the plaintiff took the jewel to the defendant "to know what it was"? It is it critical that the defendant's apprentice took the jewel from the plaintiff and gave it to the defendant? Is it at all important that the defendant offered the plaintiff only three halfpence and not four? We must answer all of these questions in the negative. Quite simply, we do not need them in the statement of facts. When students include all of these facts in their statement of facts, their briefs are no longer brief and, more importantly, the student fails to comprehend the importance of the case.

2. *The first legal issue is too broad.* Now let us look at Issue #1 in Sample Case Brief #1D. We shall recall that the issue statement is composed of two parts: (1) a factual part—key facts and (2) a legal part (the rule of law or element of the rule that is in dispute). This issue statement of this brief does not contain a factual part ("Does the finder of a chattel. . . ."). Moreover, the legal part that is stated in the brief ("Who owns the jewel?") is far too broad. While ownership is involved in *Armory,* the point of the case is that ownership is relative. The issue statement here does not even address that relative nature of ownership (that is, who has better rights to the chattel).

3. *A lesson in precision.* There is an important lesson (one that we will visit again in great depth in the context of identifying the issues on your examinations) that we can learn from Issue #1 in Sample Brief #1D: If we are not clear as to what the key facts are, we will have a difficult time in identifying the issue before the court. Why is this? Recall that an issue statement is composed of the (1) factual (key fact) part and (2) the legal part. The factual part is the foundation of the legal part. Consequently, if we do not do a good job with the first part, the chances are excellent (as this sample brief illustrates) that the second part will not be accurate.

4. *The second legal issue is again too broad.* Now let us examine Issue #2, "Damages?" What damages are we discussing? From whom? How? Why? This issue statement is not going to be much help to a student who is trying to understand the case for the purpose of participating in class discussion or preparing a course outline (see Chapter 6, "Preparing a Course Outline").

5. *The holdings are not just "yes" or "no."* The two holdings are legally correct but there are still two problems. First, the holdings are not just "yes" or "no" answers to the issues. As we have seen with Sample Brief #1C, we do not need full-blown holdings if we frame the issue statement correctly. Where we frame the issue statement correctly, the second part of the holding (where we take the issue statement and put it into an affirmative statement so that it becomes a

rule of law that we can use in subsequent controversies) becomes superfluous for purposes of our understanding the case. Nevertheless, because Sample Brief #1D does not have a correct issue statement, it would be impossible for the holding to be in abbreviated form.

6. *The holdings are copied from the case.* Second, there is a problem with the holdings as they are written. The holdings are verbatim and not in the student's own words. Is it important that you state the holding in your own words? Yes. If you write the brief in your own words, you will be assured that you understand it (if you do not, you will not be able to write it out in your own words) and, consequently, it will be easier for you to remember for purposes of class discussion and your final examination. Let us be frank. Which of the following two holdings do you think will be easier to remember? (1) "The finder of a chattel, though he does not by such finding acquire an absolute right to the chattel, has rights superior to all but the true owner." (2) "The finder of a jewel, though he does not by such finding acquire an absolute property or ownership, yet he has such a property as will enable him to keep it against all but the rightful owner, and consequently may maintain trover." I think that the answer is obvious. The second is verbose (courts often are!) and does not add anything to what is in the first. The moral: Use your own words—you will understand the legal principles in the case better and memorize[5] it much more easily.

SAMPLE CASE BRIEFS: *LI V. YELLOW CAB*

Let us now examine other sample briefs, for the case of *Li v. Yellow Cab.* You may wish to refer back to Chapter 2, "How to Read Cases: The Basics," where the case is reproduced.

Sample Case Brief #2A: A Great Brief

This brief is a great brief because, as we shall see, the student does everything correct, from keeping it short to putting the brief in his or her own words.

---

[5] Yes, you must memorize to do well in law school. Anyone who tells you differently is not being straightforward with you. I have stated this earlier. More on this later in Chapter 6, "Preparing a Course Outline."

barbri®

Sample Case Brief #2A: A Great Brief

LI v. YELLOW CAB CO. OF CALIFORNIA
Supreme Court of California, 1975

Issue #1: When the plaintiff's own negligence was a legal cause of her injury, should the doctrine of contributory negligence, which bars all recovery, be replaced by comparative negligence, which assesses liability in proportion to the defendant's fault?

Holding #1: Yes.

Reasoning for Holding #1: Contributory negligence is not equitable with its "all or nothing" approach; fault is not distributed in proportion to responsibility.

Issue #2: When the plaintiff's own negligence was a legal cause of her injury and the doctrine of comparative negligence is adopted, should "pure" comparative negligence be adopted, which apportions liability in direct proportion to fault, in lieu of the "50 percent" system, which bars a plaintiff from recovery if the plaintiff's negligence is equal to or greater than the defendant's negligence?

Holding #2: Yes.

Reasoning for Holding #2: The "50 percent" system is a de facto contributory negligence system when plaintiff's liability is 50 percent. This is inequitable when just 49 percent liability on the part of the plaintiff would allow plaintiff to recover 51 percent of damages. Further, it may be too difficult to distinguish between 49 percent fault on the part of the plaintiff (recovery allowed) and 51 percent fault on the part of the plaintiff (recovery not allowed).

Dissent: It is up to the legislature to make such a change in law.

Sample Case Brief #2A: A Great Brief: Specific Observations

1. *The issue statement for the first issue properly makes use of key facts and the legal issue triggered by those facts.* This brief is indeed quite good. The first issue statement, Issue #1, is clearly articulated. The first part of the issue statement contains the key facts, the factual part: "When the plaintiff's own negligence was a legal cause of her injury. . ." The second part of the issue statement contains the legal part: "should the doctrine of contributory negligence, which bars all recovery, be replaced by comparative negligence, which assesses liability in proportion to the defendant's fault?"

2. *The holding for the first issue is simple.* The holding is a simple, "Yes." We will recall that there is no need to restate the issue into an affirmative rule of law; to do so would duplicate work. If the student is called on in class, he or she will be able to state what the issue is. If necessary, the student also will be able to take the question and easily reformulate it into an affirmative statement—a full-blown holding: "When the plaintiff's own negligence was a legal cause of her injury, the doctrine of contributory negligence, which bars all recovery, should be replaced by comparative negligence, which assesses liability in proportion to the defendant's fault."

3. *The reasoning of the court for the first issue is clear.* The reasoning of the court is based on fairness and is clearly stated in the section of the brief titled, "Reasoning for Holding #1."

4. *The issue, holding, and reasoning of the second issue also are addressed competently.* For similar reasons, Sample Brief #2A does a good job of summarizing the critical points of the second issue. The issue statement is composed of a factual part consisting of the key facts: "When the plaintiff's own negligence was a legal cause of her injury and the doctrine of comparative negligence is adopted. . . ." The issue statement also contains the legal part, consisting of the legal problem: "should 'pure' comparative negligence be adopted, which apportions liability in direct proportion to fault, in lieu of the '50 percent' system, which bars a plaintiff from recovery if the plaintiff's negligence is equal to or greater than the defendant's negligence?" The holding is, "Yes," and the reasoning is clearly stated.

5. *The dissent.* We should note that the brief contains a summary of the dissenting opinion. Some students believe that it is not important to read dissents. This is fallacious thinking. First, casebooks do not necessarily present the majority position for a given principle of law. Consequently, a dissent for one jurisdiction may well be the majority rule in another jurisdiction. Second, what is the dissent today may well be the majority tomorrow. Third, the dissent may further explain the majority opinion. Fourth, law school study is not just for the purpose of getting out and getting a license. The skills that you will learn in law school will be critical to you in practice. Reading a dissent will help sharpen your reasoning skills.

Sample Case Brief #2B: A Poor Brief

Now let us look at Sample Brief #2B. This brief illustrates how a student can get too wrapped up in the facts. When that happens (as we saw in Sample Brief #1D of the *Armory* case), the issue statement and the resulting holding (remember that the holding is just an affirmative statement of the question presented in the issue statement) may be incorrect.

Sample Case Brief #2B: A Poor Brief

LI v. YELLOW CAB CO. OF CALIFORNIA
Supreme Court of California, 1975

Facts: Plaintiff, Nga Li, was driving her automobile, a 1967 Oldsmobile, when she improperly made a left hand turn into an intersection at the same time that defendant's automobile was approaching from the opposite direction. The defendant's automobile entered the intersection at an unsafe speed after the traffic light had turned yellow. Plaintiff was injured in the ensuing crash. However, plaintiff was denied recovery in the trial court because plaintiff was herself contributorily negligent. Plaintiff appeals on the ground that her negligence should not totally bar her claim, which is mandated under the doctrine of contributory negligence.

Issue #1:When a plaintiff drives an automobile by negligently making a left hand turn into an intersection at the same time that a defendant's auto entered the intersection at an unsafe speed, negligently injuring the plaintiff, should the doctrine of contributory negligence, which bars all recovery, be replaced by comparative negligence, which assesses liability in proportion to the defendant's fault?

Holding #1: Yes.

* * *

Sample Case Brief #2B: A Poor Brief: Specific Observations

There are a number of problems with this brief. First, Sample Brief #2B contains a section or statement of "Facts." Remember that such a section is not necessary. Second, in any event, this section has far too many non-key facts. It is quite irrelevant to the outcome of the case that the plaintiff's name was Li, that she was driving a 1967 model year auto, and that the auto she was driving was an Oldsmobile. What do we make of the fact that she made an improper left hand turn? Would the outcome of the case have been the same if instead of having made an improper left hand turn, she made an improper right hand turn? Of course, it would have. What is important in *Li* is that the negligence of the plaintiff will not be a bar to her stating a cause of action against the defendant for negligence.

Sample Brief #2B loses sight of this, however. Look at the issue statement. Observe how it is far too narrowly drawn. Certainly, the principle in *Li* is not applicable only to cases of automobile accidents.

SAMPLE CASE BRIEF: *FISHER V. CARROUSEL MOTOR HOTEL*

Let us now examine a brief of *Fisher v. Carrousel Motor Hotel*, a case that was reproduced in Chapter 2, "How to Read Cases: The Basics."

Sample Case Brief #3A: A Good Brief

This is a good brief, even though the facts are not limited to the key facts. Nevertheless, as will be seen, it accomplishes its job: a summary of the critical points of the case.

Sample Case Brief #3A: A Good Brief

FISHER v. CARROUSEL MOTOR HOTEL, INC.
Supreme Court of Texas, 1967

Issue: Is the offensive touching (by a white bigot) of anything closely connected with the plaintiff's person (an African-American) deemed to be an offensive touching of the plaintiff's person so as to constitute a battery?

Holding: Yes.

Reasoning: The key to battery is the offense to the plaintiff's personal dignity, which is no less violated when something closely connected to the plaintiff is offensively touched than when plaintiff's body is so touched.

Sample Case Brief #3A: A Good Brief: Specific Observations

Sample Brief #3A is a good brief. The issue statement (excluding the facts in parentheses) is broad enough to encompass any situation where the plaintiff is holding something that the defendant touches offensively: a briefcase or cane, for example. Nonetheless, what should we say of the facts within the parentheses? Certainly, the plaintiff did not have to be African-American. Certainly, the plaintiff did not have to be a white bigot. Why then does this brief still qualify as a good brief?

Sometimes, the non-facts in a case may be so unusual that stating them in your issue statement (albeit in parentheses, to make it clear that they are not key facts) will enable you to remember them and the holding more easily.

SAMPLE CASE BRIEF: *LUCY V. ZEHMER*

Let us now peruse one final brief. Sample Brief #4A is a good brief of the *Lucy* case, also reproduced and discussed in Chapter 2, "How to Read Cases: The Basics."

Sample Case Brief #4A: A Good Brief

This is a good brief. It is important for us to study it because it is different from the other briefs that we have previously covered.

Sample Case Brief #4A: A Good Brief

LUCY v. ZEHMER
Supreme Court of Appeals of Virginia, 1954

Issue: Is a writing which otherwise appears to be a valid contract enforceable (for the purchase of a farm) when one of the parties was merely joking and the other party did not in fact know or have reason to know that the other party was joking because the negotiations went on for forty minutes?

Holding: Yes.

Reasoning: (1) In contract law, the law looks to the outward expression of a person as manifesting his intention rather than his secret intention. (2) If the words or acts of one party have only one reasonable meaning, his undisclosed intention is immaterial.

Sample Case Brief #4A: A Good Brief: Specific Observations

1. *Reasoning based on collateral rules.* This brief is different from the others that we have examined. First, let us look at the section labeled, "Reasoning." We should take note that the prior cases (*Li* and *Fisher*) involved reasoning based on fairness. Not so with the *Lucy* case. The foundation for the court's holding is based on what I have referred to in Chapter 2, "How to Read Cases: The Basics," as *collateral rules*: holdings in other cases or statements previously articulated in other sources (e.g., Restatement) which now serve as the building blocks for the present holding.

2. *Issue statement contains non-key facts but. . . .*We should also take a close look at the issue statement in *Lucy*. Note that the facts state that one party owned "a farm" (in parentheses). In the study of Sample Brief #3A (*Fisher v. Carrousel Motor Hotel*), we learned that the plaintiff did not have to be an African-American. Similarly, in *Lucy,* the subject matter of dispute did not have to involve a farm. Nevertheless, if stating that the property was a farm (again, in parentheses, to make it clear that this is not a key fact) helps you to remember the case, there is nothing "wrong" and nothing has to be corrected—so long as the student understands that the case does not revolve around farms. In Sample Brief #4A, the issue statement (excluding the material in parentheses) is drafted broadly. That is good: On the final examination, the student will not be surprised when the subject matter of an offer or acceptance that is made secretly in jest does not deal with a farm—but deals with an antique automobile, for example.[6]

3. *Forty minutes as a key fact?* One final point about Sample Brief #4A: Note that the statement of facts indicates that the negotiations went on for "forty minutes." Recall that in your issue statement, you want to limit the facts to the key facts (unless you quite purposefully want a background fact or two to jog your memory). Is the fact that the negotiations went on for forty minutes a key fact? Keep in mind that what we are dealing with is a situation where the defendant had accepted the plaintiff's offer, secretly in jest. If the negotiations had gone on for ten hours, that would be very relevant in establishing that the plaintiff did not know or have reason to know that the acceptance was in jest. Likewise, if the negotiations had gone on for a mere fifteen seconds, that fact could very possibly have caused a court to find that no reasonable person would believe that a farm could seriously be sold with so little negotiation. In this regard, the fact that the negotiation went on for forty minutes is a key fact: If we were to change the forty minutes to fifteen seconds, we may very well have a change in the outcome of the case.

Still, what would have been the outcome if the timeframe for the negotiations had been thirty-nine minutes? Would this have changed the outcome? What would the result be if the timeframe had been thirty-eight minutes? What would have happened if it had been thirty-seven minutes? Would the answer have changed if the time had been thirty minutes? The point here is this: As we discussed in Chapter 3, "More on Cases: The Importance of Facts," in any given case

---

[6] It might also be that on the examination the hypo will not deal with an acceptance or offer secretly made in "jest" (the most narrow key facts in *Lucy*), but where there is no jesting and the other party still had no reason to doubt that the other party made a sincere offer or acceptance. For example, it might be that the "offeror" made the "offer" only to practice a sales technique. The "offeree" then accepted. Of course, does this now mean that the "jesting" was itself not a key fact? Is the brief too narrow? Hmm. Welcome, yet again, to the "ambiguity with precision" problem of law school!

we may disagree as to what the key facts are. That being so, Sample Brief #4A states that the negotiations lasted forty minutes, a fact relevant to show that the plaintiff had reason to believe that the defendant was serious and not jesting. Still, at what point would the timeframe for the negotiations change the outcome? That is not clear and it is something about which reasonable people can reasonably disagree.

FINAL POINTS ABOUT CASE BRIEFING

Before we end this chapter, we should address some other points that may be of concern to students.

Procedural History of a Case

Should you include the case's procedural history (what happened at the trial or intermediate appellate court level) somewhere in your brief (perhaps in a short section of the brief titled, "Procedural History")? As we alluded to in Chapter 3, "More on Cases: The Importance of Facts," that is going to be determined by the course and the professor. For example, in Civil Procedure, it may well be that you will include the procedural history of the case—but typically only if that procedural history was a key fact (and then you will include it in the issue statement). However, in any subject you will include the procedural history, even if the history is not a key fact, if it is something that your professor covers in every case. If you do include the procedural history, however, make it brief.[7] Remember, briefs are brief, not long!

Minutia and the Obsessive Professor

Should you include minute details that are not key facts in your issue statement because you have a professor who always discusses (or obsesses over) the insignificant facts of the case? My opinion is that I do not think so. If you have a professor who is going to ask you questions on the year of the car, its make and model, and how many miles per hour the defendant was driving, *when these are not key facts*, your briefs will get hopelessly long and confusing, and you will go astray. In such a scenario, accept the wrath of the professor. Frankly, that is better than writing terribly lengthy briefs that lose their purpose.[8]

SUMMARY OF CHAPTER 5

To summarize the main points in this chapter: A brief is merely a summary of the main points of the case. A case brief should include an issue statement, which has two components: (1) the key facts and (2) the legal problem. Remember to draft the issue statement in such a manner that it has usefulness in other situations, i.e., in any situation where the *key* facts are the same. Recall that the holding is merely the answer to the issue. Importantly, if you draft the issue statement properly, the holding can be as simple as either "yes" or "no." Of course, if you want to, immediately after the "yes" or "no," you can reformulate the issue into an affirmative statement of

---

[7] If your case brief does have a section titled, "Procedural History," your brief will not be a "3-point" brief, as we earlier discussed. Rather, you will have a "4-point" brief.

[8] See also Chapter 7, "I Don't Understand What's Going on in Class."

law. Remember also not to ignore the rationale, especially when it includes "collateral rules." On your examination (as you will learn very soon) you may be tested on these rules as well as on the holdings—the "main rules." You should also not ignore a dissenting opinion;[9] it may explain the holding of the majority. It may also be the rule in most jurisdictions. If you must include a procedural history of the case, keep it brief.

Remember, too, that there are definitely wrong ways to brief. This we have seen in Sample Brief #1D. There are, however, many right ways, too. You may want to include something in a brief that I would not want to include. I may want to include something in a brief that you may not want to include. Can we both be right? Absolutely! All that a brief does is give a short summary of the major principles of the case. It is nothing more and nothing less. Reasonable people can reasonably disagree on certain aspects of a case. Do not be concerned if you disagree with a colleague—or even a professor.

---

[9] If you include a dissent, you will end up with a "4-point" brief, not a "3-point" brief, which is fine.

CHAPTER 6
PREPARING A COURSE OUTLINE

Preparing a course outline is an iconic part of law school. In that great movie, *The Paper Chase*, the 1973 classic about 1Ls at Harvard Law School, one scene deals with the study group preparing course outlines. Why you should prepare course outlines and how you prepare them is the subject of this chapter.

THE BANE OF MEMORIZATION

If you are going to do well on your exams, you will have to memorize many rules and definitions of elements of rules. Even if you have an open-book exam, you will still have to memorize rules and definitions of elements because you will not have the time to flip through materials to retrieve the definition of every element that is on the exam. Moreover, in addition to memorizing all of these rules, you will also have to *understand* how these rules fit together into an organized body. How can you memorize the rules and put these rules into an order? There are two ways. Let us now explore these two ways.

Memorization by Rote

The first way to memorize is simply to do it by rote. You sit down with a commercial outline or pre-packaged flash cards and you memorize every rule and every definition without doing any thinking.[1] When I was in seventh grade, I had to memorize the Preamble to the Constitution. It took a lot of time and effort to memorize it. Still, I did it—by rote. To this day, I can recite the Preamble to the Constitution. Is there a reason why you cannot memorize your rules in the same manner? The answer is that there are too many rules to memorize by rote. How many rules are there in contracts, property, torts, and criminal law? There are not just dozens, but hundreds of rules and definitions of elements. Further, assuming that you memorize all of these rules, you still have to understand the flow—the organization—and put all the pieces of the puzzle together. Moreover, just reading a commercial outline or pre-packaged set of flashcards is what I refer to as "passive learning." In passive learning, the student merely reads something that someone else has prepared. Without more, passive learning is in fact a very ineffective method to learn and retain information. Indeed, studies have shown that a person will forget 90 percent of what he or she reads within a matter of hours. The point is that you cannot memorize and synthesize this massive body of law by rote. How then do you do it?

Memorization by Understanding

The second way you memorize is by *understanding* the material. Allow me to give you an illustration of what I mean. If you were to ask an author of any book (this or another) to discuss any aspect of his or her work, the author could go on for hours telling you everything that you ever wanted to know—and many things that you never even thought of asking—about the contents of

---

[1] You may be surprised to know that commercial outlines can be used in a proper manner and be very beneficial. We shall discuss this matter in Chapter 7, "I Don't Understand What's Going on in Class" and Chapter 8, "Law School Traps."

such book. Indeed, I think that it is obvious that the author of a book knows more about the book's contents than anyone else in the world knows. In this regard, do you think that any critic or professor knows more about *The Old Man and the Sea* than Ernest Hemingway did? The very thought is ridiculous. Consequently, if you were to *write* a book on the law of torts—or a slightly less ambitious goal, such as a course outline for torts—you would know the material better than anyone who just read about the law of torts. In short, there is one way that will enable you to master the many rules in your courses: create a miniature treatise for each of your courses—a course outline.

GETTING STARTED PREPARING YOUR COURSE OUTLINE

In a course outline, you are going to organize an amorphous and massive body of law into something that is meaningful and understandable. You are going to synthesize the rules (holdings and collateral rules)[2] from the cases, your class notes, the professor's hypotheticals, and any other material that the professor has alluded to in the lecture, such as a note following a case in your casebook. This process—outlining—also happens to be the antithesis of passive learning: When you start from scratch and create this miniature treatise, you are engaged in what I call "active learning." In active learning, you learn by doing. *You* must know exactly what to do each step of the way. If *you* do not know something or *you* become stuck, *you* will come to a grinding halt—until *you* solve the problem. Now that is learning! Let us now examine how you actually prepare a course outline.

SAMPLE COURSE OUTLINE #1: A GOOD OUTLINE FOR BATTERY

Sample Course Outline #1 is a sample torts outline for the law of battery. As you will see, it is a very good outline. After you take a few minutes to study it, we shall examine how the student constructed it and why it is indeed a very good outline. We will also understand why, after creating this part of the outline, the student will have total mastery of the subject matter.

---

[2] See Chapter 5, "Case Briefing: What to Do—And What Not to Do" for an explanation of holdings and "collateral rules."

barbri

SAMPLE COURSE OUTLINE #1

CHAPTER 2: INTENTIONAL INTERFERENCE WITH PERSONS

I. Battery

    A. The intent to cause a harmful or offensive contact with the person of another and a harmful or offensive contact with the person of another directly or indirectly results.

        1. Intent

            a. Hostility toward plaintiff not required

                (1) Giving plaintiff a friendly unsolicited hug

                (2) Playing a good-natured practical joke on plaintiff

            b. Extends to those consequences which the actor, or a reasonable person in the actor's position, believes are substantially certain to follow from what he does

                (1) Pulling chair away just as plaintiff was about to sit down

                (2) Firing a bullet into a crowd sincerely hoping that no one will get hit

        2. Harmful or offensive contact

            a. Actual physical harm to plaintiff is not required; any contact brought about in a rude manner qualifies

                (1) Spitting in plaintiff's face

                (2) Barefooted defendant kicking police officer protected by motorcycle boots

                (3) Cutting plaintiff's hair while plaintiff is asleep

            b. But where reasonable under the circumstances, consent is assumed, and thus touching not offensive

                (1) Defendant grabs plaintiff to save plaintiff from drowning

                (2) Defendant lightly taps plaintiff on the shoulder to attract plaintiff's attention in order to obtain directions

        3. Person

        a.   Anything closely connected with the plaintiff's person

             (1)   White racist yanking plate from African-American man's hands

             (2)   Defendant ramming a car in which plaintiff is riding

    4.   Directly or indirectly

        a.   It is sufficient that defendant sets in motion a force, which ultimately produces the result

             (1)   Poisoning the food which plaintiff eats

             (2)   Digging a pit in the path on which plaintiff walks and into which plaintiff falls

II.   Assault

    A.   An intentional, unlawful, offer to touch the person of another in a manner under such circumstances as to create in the mind of the plaintiff a well-founded fear of an imminent battery, coupled with the apparent present ability to effectuate the attempt, if not prevented.

* * *

Sample Course Outline #1: A Good Outline for Battery: General Observations

Let us preliminarily make some general observations about this outline. It takes the rule of battery (all law is made up of rules) and breaks it down into its component parts (all rules are made up of elements). Moreover, each component part is defined and each definition is illustrated with a very brief set of facts, key facts. You will notice that by taking the rule of battery and breaking it down in this manner, we have organized this material carefully and thoughtfully: We go from a big concept (battery) and work our way down to the smaller concepts (intent, harmful, person, etc.). As a result, we can see the "forest" (the big concept of battery) and the "trees" (the smaller concepts, which together make up the rule of battery). In fact, this outline is so well-organized that, if you were merely to scan it, the material would virtually jump out at you. More importantly, we are able to see where each piece of the "puzzle" fits together. Now let us go over this outline in some detail.

Sample Course Outline #1: A Good Outline for Battery: Specific Observations

1. *Starting the outline.* How was the student able to start this outline? This is often a problem for students. Indeed, a common question for first year students is, "How do I begin?" The answer is very simple: use the table of contents in your casebook as the foundation of your outline. This is exactly what was done in Sample Course Outline #1. The (hypothetical) second chapter of the casebook deals with intentional torts and the first section of that chapter deals with the law of battery. The second section of the chapter deals with assault. Assuming that your professor follows the order of the casebook, the first tort that you would cover would be battery. The second would be assault. And so on.[3]

2. *Arriving at the rule of battery.* How did the student arrive at the rule of battery ("the intent to cause a harmful or offensive contact with the person of another and a harmful or offensive contact with the person of another directly or indirectly results")? There are a number of possibilities. One is that the student gleaned the rule from the first case of the section in the casebook. Another is that the student got the rule from a hornbook. Still another possibility is that the student was "led" to this definition though the professor's use of a Socratic dialogue. Perhaps the professor may have just initially "laid it out" for the student. How the student came to the rule is not important. What is important is that the student knows that all law is made up of rules—and there is a rule for battery.

3. *Breaking the rule down into component parts.* After the rule of battery is stated, the rule itself is broken down into its component parts (all rules are made up of elements) and each element is defined. For example, a "person" is defined as "anything closely connected with the plaintiff's person." How did the student arrive at this definition for this—or any other—particular element? Again, there are a number of possibilities: It may have come from a case or a note following a case. It may have come from a hypothetical of the professor. It may have come from a hornbook or another supplemental source. Once again, how the student arrived at the definition is not important. What is important is that the student *got* the definition.

---

[3] If your professor does not follow the order of your casebook, do not be concerned. All that you need do is follow the order of your professor. Remember, Professor Prosser (the late preeminent torts professor and casebook author of his time) is not going to grade your torts exam; your professor is.

4. Why define each element? Why did the student define each element? To put it in very practical terms, how does this help a student on his or her final examination? When we come to the materials dealing with essay exam writing, you will see very clearly that the chances are very good that on your final exam, you will not be tested on "battery" per se. Rather, you will be tested on an element (or elements) of battery: *person* or *touching*. If you do not know the definitions of these terms quite well, you will not be able to get outstanding grades. Conversely, if you know the definitions of these terms very well, you will be on your way to getting outstanding grades.

5. Determining the order of the elements. Another common question that first year students ask is, "In what order do I tackle each element in my outline"? Indeed, when you look at your class notes, it may seem at first that you have an amorphous "thing" on your hands. Nevertheless, the order of tackling the elements in your outline is simple: follow the order that you cover the material in the casebook. As we have just discussed, use your casebook as the foundation for your outline. If your professor and the authors of your casebook covered the subject of *intent* before the subject of *person*, how wrong can you go if your outline follows that same order? When in doubt, follow the order of your professor and casebook—and you cannot go wrong.[4]

6. Illustrating the definitions. You will note that following each definition are two or three very short fact patterns that illustrate the definition. Why does the student illustrate each definition? Because you will find it is easier to understand rules—and memorize them—if you can illustrate how the rule (the definition of the element) works. Additionally, on your final examination, you will have to grapple with unusual fact patters and determine which rule should be used to solve the problem created by those facts (just as courts must do). Consequently, the more fact patterns that you can expose yourself to, the easier it will be for you to know which rule is called into use on the final exam.

7. Illustrating the definitions with key facts. Note, importantly, that the fact patterns that are used for illustrations in Sample Outline #1 are typically key facts.[5] Where do these key facts come from? From the same place that the definitions of the elements come from: cases, a professor's hypotheticals, or supplemental reading material.

8. Continuing to the next issue. After having broken down and organized the law of battery in the manner reproduced in Sample Course Outline #1, the student will next proceed to the second intentional tort—assault. After having defined what an assault is, the student will break out the elements, define each of the elements, and give two or three illustrations for each definition.

---

[4] As stated earlier, if your professor does not go in a linear fashion (start at page 1 and end at page 1000), follow the order of your professor.

[5] Some of the illustrative facts are arguably not truly key facts. For example, look at the facts, which illustrate the definition of a "person": White racist yanking plate from African-American man's hands. As we have already discussed in Chapter 5, "Case Briefing: What to Do—And What Not to Do," the defendant did not have to be a racist for there to be a touching of the person of the plaintiff. Nor did the plaintiff have to be an African-American man holding a plate; a Caucasian woman who was holding a briefcase would have done just as nicely (if the touching were otherwise offensive and unpermitted). However, sometimes the facts in a case are so unusual (and consequently, a good learning tool) that the student will want to use these facts in the course of putting together an outline, even though they are not solely key facts. As we have previously discussed in Chapter 5, that is all right—so long as the student knows that the principle of the *Fisher* case (for the law of battery, a "person" is anything closely connected with the plaintiff's person) is not limited to bigots and plates.

SAMPLE COURSE OUTLINE #2: A POOR OUTLINE FOR BATTERY

Now let us examine Sample Course Outline #2, a brief, which is not as good as Sample Course Outline #1.

CHAPTER 2: INTENTIONAL INTERFERENCE WITH PERSONS

I.   Battery

    A.   The intent to cause a harmful or offensive contact with the person of another and a harmful or offensive contact with the person of another directly or indirectly results.

* * *

        3.   Person

            a.   Anything closely connected with the plaintiff's person

                (1)   FISHER v. CARROUSEL MOTOR HOTEL, INC.

                    (a)   The plaintiff was an African-American man on line in a cafeteria-style restaurant. As he was waiting to be served, a white racist yanked the plate from the plaintiff's hands. The trial court found that there was no battery but the Supreme Court of Texas reversed. The court held that the forceful dispossession of the plaintiff's plate in an offensive manner was a battery. This was because anything closely connected with the plaintiff's person is deemed to be the person of the plaintiff.

* * *

Sample Course Outline #2: A Poor Outline for Battery: General Observations

This outline reveals several errors that first-year students often make. First, the student has case names. Second, the fact patterns are too long. Third, the student includes law in the fact pattern. Now let us take a more detailed look at these problems.

Sample Course Outline#2: A Poor Outline for Battery: Specific Observations

1. *Use of case names.* First, the student states the case name, *Fisher v. Carrousel Motor Hotel, Inc.* Seldom is there a need to state a case name in your course outline. The name will typically not add anything to your understanding of the material. There are only two limited circumstances when you will want to know a case name: (1) when the case stands not just for a rule of law but, rather, an entire doctrine. An example of this is *Palsgraf* or *Erie*; or (2) when a teacher expressly tells you to know the names of cases (some or all) for your final examination.[6]

2. *Long fact patterns.* The second error in this outline is the fact pattern for the *Fisher* case: it is too long. The facts include not just key facts; background facts (procedural history) are also included. These facts in no way allow a student to understand how the definition works in a factual context.

3. *Law in the fact pattern.* The third error is the inclusion of law in the fact pattern. We should note that the student defined what a person is ("anything closely connected with the plaintiff's person") and restated this definition again ("the court held that the forceful dispossession of the plaintiff's plate in an offensive matter was a battery. This was because anything closely connected with the plaintiff's person is deemed to be the person of the plaintiff") in what should have been nothing more than a short clause of key facts to illustrate the definition of "person."

SAMPLE COURSE OUTLINE #3: ANOTHER POOR OUTLINE FOR BATTERY

Now let us look at Sample Course Outline #3, which illustrates still another common error by first year students.

---

[6] In my own property class, I tell my students that they do not have to know the names of cases, except for United States Supreme Court cases, when we cover zoning and takings. My reason for this is that when I cover Supreme Court cases, we are learning not just cases, but doctrines. Hence, for example, it is not the *Penn Central* case, but the *Penn Central* ad hoc analysis for regulatory takings.

SAMPLE COURSE OUTLINE #3

CHAPTER 2: INTENTIONAL INTERFERENCE WITH PERSONS

I. Battery

    A.   The intent to cause a harmful or offensive contact with the person of another and a harmful or offensive contact with the person of another directly or indirectly results.

II. Assault

    A.   An intentional, unlawful, offer to touch the person of another in a manner under such circumstances as to create in the mind of the plaintiff a well-founded fear of an imminent battery, coupled with the apparent present ability to effectuate the attempt, if not prevented.

* * *

Sample Course Outline #3: Another Poor Outline for Battery: Specific Observations

The problem with this outline is that although it has rules (battery and assault), it does not break down the rules into component parts. Remember, on your final examination, it will not be sufficient for you to know the rules; you must also know the definitions of the elements of the rules.

SAMPLE COURSE OUTLINE #4: ANOTHER GOOD OUTLINE (PROPERTY)

Sample Course Outline #4 is a segment of a Property outline. More specifically, it deals with future interests. I have included this particular outline—a good one at that—so that you can see that you can and must outline *any* course. There are some subjects or topics within a subject that students often have a difficult time outlining. I am not certain why this is so. So long as you remember that all law is made up of rules and all rules are made up of elements, you should be able to outline any course—including Property and future interests.

CHAPTER 3: FUTURE INTERESTS

I.   Future Interests in Transferors

    A.   Right of Entry

        1.   A future interest left in the transferor or his successor in interest on the transfer of an estate subject to a condition subsequent.

            a.   Left in the transferor

                (1)   Does not have to be expressly created

                    (a)   O conveys, "To A, on the condition that liquor will not be sold." O retains a right of entry.

            b.   Or his successor in interest

                (1)   Heirs at law

        2.   Alienability inter vivos

            a.   Common law

                (1)   In some jurisdictions, the transfer is held void

                    (a)   O conveys to A, "but if liquor is ever sold, O shall have the right to retake possession." Thereafter O attempts to convey his right of entry to B. Subsequently, A sells liquor. O has the right to re-enter.

                (2)   In other jurisdictions, the transfer destroys the right of entry, giving the owner in possession a fee simple absolute

                    (a)   O conveys to A, "but if liquor is ever sold, O shall have the right to retake possession." Thereafter O attempts to convey his right of entry to B. A now owns a fee simple absolute.

MISCELLANEOUS POINTS ON OUTLINING

I give you now some final thoughts on outlining. First, if you are going to use the outline of a friend or classmate, you will not be creating it yourself. You will just be reading it. You will not be engaging in active learning, but passive learning, which is an ineffective means of learning. In such case, you might as well read a good commercial outline, written by a professor.

Second, if a case contains an element of a rule that your professor does not cover in class and you are not sure if you are responsible for it, ask your professor. If the answer is that you are not, there is no reason to include it in your outline. The purpose of your outline is to enable you to understand and memorize a body of *law that you are responsible for on your final examination.* If you will not be responsible for it, do not put it into your outline.[7]

Third, you will have noticed that the good sample outlines, Sample Course Outline #1 and Sample Course Outline #4, include rules and definitions of elements of rules (whether main or collateral). There are no statements of public policy, however. Why is that? Because public policy may help explain *why* a particular court adopted the rule that it did (as we saw in *Li v. Yellow Cab,* discussed in Chapter 5, "Case Briefing: What to Do—and What Not to Do"). Once you understand why a court adopted the rule, there is no longer any need to include it in your outline. Remember that your outline focuses on rules and elements. Nonetheless, having stated that, do not think that policy has no place on final exams. It does, as you will learn.

SUMMARY OF CHAPTER 6

Let us now summarize the major points in this chapter: If you are going to master the many rules and elements for all of your subjects, you will want to create your own work of art—a course outline. When you do this, use the table of contents in your casebook as your foundation. Proceed to organize the rules and elements of the rules in a manner that makes sense to you. Regardless of how you organize your outline, however, you will start with a major concept (such as battery) and proceed to break it down into its elements (intentional, touching, person, etc.). You will define each element and illustrate each definition. You will get your rules, definitions, and illustrations from your cases, professors' hypotheticals, and, if necessary, supplemental reading materials.

---

[7] This is not to mean that you should not delve into an area of interest just because you are not going to be tested on it. To the contrary, you should. Indeed, when something in class or in your readings sparks an interest, you should plunge into that area, irrespective of coverage on your final examination. Law school is more than just a means to getting your license. Nonetheless, the sole purpose of outlining is to master a subject for an examination. If a particular subject is not going to be included on the final examination, there is no reason to put it into your outline.

CHAPTER 7
I DON'T UNDERSTAND WHAT'S GOING ON IN CLASS

The points that we shall discuss in this chapter and the next are very important. Indeed, a failure to understand this segment of the materials could undermine a student's success.

RULES AND ELEMENTS YET AGAIN

From the chapters that we have covered so far, you should now have no doubt in your mind that all law is made up of rules and all rules are made up of elements. You also now know that when you are reading your cases, you need to extract the rules and definitions of the elements of the rules. Additionally, you know that you will also want to understand the court's reasoning because (1) the reasoning, whether based on logic or policy, will often enable you to better understand the holdings (rules and definitions of elements) and (2) sometimes the reasoning is based on precedent—what I call "collateral rules."[1]

UNDERSTANDING YOUR PROFESSOR IN THE CLASSROOM

Notwithstanding what I have just stated above, if you are going to do well in law school, should you not also know what your professor is doing in the classroom? Indeed, if you do not know what your professor is doing in class, you will have a more difficult time in understanding the legal process (which includes taking essay exams) and law school will not be as enjoyable or educational as it can be.

WHAT ONE PROFESSOR DOES IN THE CLASSROOM: THREE OBJECTIVES

For illustrative purposes, let me tell you what I do in my classes. You will see that I have "three objectives" in mind.

Objective #1: Rules and Elements

First, I conduct class sessions (sometimes by pure lecture[2], sometimes by the Socratic method, and sometimes by discussion) in a manner so that when the student walks out of the classroom, he or she understands the holding (rule or definition of an element) covered in the case, as well as any "collateral rules" that were discussed in the case. Nevertheless, I also expect my students to get more out of the class than just a rule or element.

Objective #2: Reasoning Skills

Second, I also want to sharpen my students' reasoning skills; I do this by discussing whether the court's decision was "correct." By "correct," I may mean any of a number of things. For example, a case that states a well-established legal principle and purports to follow it but does

---

[1] See Chapter 2, "How to Read Cases: The Basics," for a discussion of "collateral rules."

[2] In recent years, I have begun using PowerPoint; I distribute the hard copy of the slides to minimize the note taking of my students.

not may not be *internally* correct. Alternatively, or additionally, a case may not be morally, socially, economically, or politically correct or incorrect. For example, a case which allows a landlord to discriminate on the basis of a potential tenant's occupation may involve moral, social, economic, and even political implications. Hence, I suspect that for a law school professor, "correct" here means whatever the professor says it means.

Objective #3: Advanced Reasoning Skills

Finally, after I believe that the students have mastered the material covered in the casebook, I may explore hypotheticals (sometimes my own; sometimes from another source such as a treatise or a case that I read) with my students. My purpose in going over these hypotheticals—slight variations of the key facts from the principal case—is not just to have the students learn another rule or definition. I do it primarily to further hone their analytical skills. In this regard, I also try to get the students to see patterns of consistency and distinctions between cases. In this way, students learn not only "law"—they learn to stretch further their reasoning skills.

To summarize, what I (and many of your professors) cover in our classes are, (1) the holdings (rules and definitions of elements), along with any collateral rules; (2) discussions of whether a case is correct (however broad that term is); and (3) hypotheticals.

THREE DIFFERENT PROFESSORS COVER *ARMORY V. DELAMIRIE*

Many students, however, do not understand what is going on in class. Why is this? There are two reasons. The first is that the professor may not cover the three objectives in an *overt* manner. For example, if a professor says, "What is the holding in *Armory*?" the students can easily follow the discussion that follows. They know that the discussion will seek to establish the rule (that is, the holding) in *Armory*. Yet, if the professor is not that conspicuous in what he or she does, students may not readily follow along.

The second reason is that not all professors have "three objectives" in mind. Some teachers may have only one or two.[3]

In the fictitious transcripts that follow, we illustrate all of these points. In Sample Class Session #1, the professor will examine the *Armory* case in a very overt manner. As a result, you will probably feel quite comfortable in reading the transcript (and would probably feel comfortable if you were in such a class). In Sample Class Session #2, however, you will probably feel a little less comfortable with what the professor does: the professor discusses "law" but does not cover the holding of *Armory* at all. Finally, in Sample Class Session #3, you may feel downright uncomfortable: the professor does not discuss any "law" at all. If you were a student in this professor's class, you may not understand what is "going on."

---

[3] In any given class, I may attempt to accomplish only one or two of the three objectives; I may not do all three in each class.

barbri

Before we read and analyze the transcripts of these sample class sessions, it may be helpful for you to reread and for us to summarize *Armory*.[4]

You will recall that in *Armory*, the question that the court had to address was who had better rights to certain property: the finder, a chimney sweeper's boy, or the goldsmith (to whom the finder had given the property for the purpose of weighing and appraising it). The court held that the finder of the property has better rights to it than anyone, except for the true owner.

Sample Class Session #1: The Overt Professor

Now let us read Sample Class Session #1. When you read it, you will probably feel very comfortable because the professor is quite overt in what he or she is doing and trying to accomplish.

---

[4] If you wish to reread *Armory v. Delamirie*, see Chapter 2.

SAMPLE CLASS SESSION #1

PROFESSOR: Mr. Brown, please tell us what the issue is, including the key facts,[5] in *Armory*.

MR. BROWN: Well, when X finds a jewel and—

PROFESSOR, INTERRUPTING MR. BROWN: Would the outcome of the case have been different if the plaintiff had found a watch instead of a jewel?

MR. BROWN: No. May I change my answer? (Class laughs).

PROFESSOR: Please do.

MR. BROWN: When X finds a chattel and gives it to Y to examine only, as between X and Y, does X have better rights to the chattel?

PROFESSOR: And what did the court hold?

MR. BROWN: When X finds a chattel and gives it to Y to examine only, X has better rights to the chattel; X owns the chattel.

PROFESSOR: Why do you think that the court awarded the property to X, the finder, and not to Y?

* * *

---

[5] See Chapter 3, "More on Cases: The Importance of Facts" for a discussion of the term "key facts."

Sample Class Session #1: The Overt Professor: A Study

I think that you will agree that the foregoing dialogue was clear and straightforward. The professor went over the issue, including the key facts, the holding, and initiated a discussion on the social ramifications of the court's decision. Not all professors are alike, however. Different people do things differently.

Sample Class Session #2: The Less-Overt Professor

Consequently, another professor may simply assume that the students fully understand the holding of the case and begin the class discussion with that premise. In Sample Class Session #2, this is exactly what happens: the professor never discusses the "rule" (that is, the holding) of *Armory*. Let us read this transcript and learn what the professor does—and why.

SAMPLE CLASS SESSION #2

PROFESSOR: Let us now turn our attention to *Armory*. Ms. Smith, let us suppose that Ann and Baker are walking in a public park and they each see a fifty-dollar bill on the ground. Ann declares, "I found it!" A split second later, Baker declares, "I found it!" As between Ann and Baker, who has better rights to the fifty-dollar bill?

MS. SMITH: Ann does.

PROFESSOR: Why?

MS. SMITH: Because she saw it and, thus, found the property.

PROFESSOR: Why do you equate seeing with finding?

MS. SMITH: How else could one determine ownership rights between Ann and Baker?

PROFESSOR: Is it okay with you if *I* ask the questions, Ms. Smith? (Class laughs.) If it is as you say, Ms. Smith, that ownership rights are determined by who happens to see the fifty-dollar bill first, what happens if someone, let's call her Charlene, has a telescope and, from a distance of five miles, sees the fifty-dollar bill a moment before Ann sees it. Does Charlene own the fifty-dollar bill?

MS. SMITH: I don't think so.

PROFESSOR: Why not? You just stated that as between Ann and Baker, Ann owns the fifty-dollar bill because she saw it first. If seeing property is finding it, why doesn't Charlene prevail?

MS. SMITH: Well, it just doesn't seem fair that Charlene should get the fifty-dollar bill.

PROFESSOR: But does the law revolve solely on grounds of fairness? If that is the only criterion, what guidelines will people have in conducting their lives and business affairs? Do we abolish all rules of property law, criminal law, tort law, and contract law and have one rule for all bodies of law and all circumstances: do whatever is "fair"? What is fair to you may not be fair to me. Put another way, Ms. Smith, as between Ann and Baker, is it "fair" to allow Ann to keep the fifty-dollar bill?

MS. SMITH: If fairness is not the sole criterion, and if we want something more definite, perhaps none of the actors in your hypothetical has rights to the fifty-dollar bill. I guess seeing property does not amount to finding it.

PROFESSOR: Why not?

MS. SMITH: Because there is no way a court could determine with any degree of certainty who saw the chattel first.

PROFESSOR: Can you come up with some guideline then that would enable society or a court to know when someone does find property?

MS. SMITH: Perhaps when someone actually grabs the property.

PROFESSOR: Do you mean when someone takes *possession* (placing emphasis on the word) of the property?

* * *

Sample Class Session #2: The Less-Overt Professor: A Study

Let us examine what has happened. The professor stated that he was going to discuss the *Armory* case—but proceeded to discuss a hypothetical, which, at first blush, seems to have nothing to do with *Armory*. Recall that in *Armory* the court stated that the finder of property has better rights to it than anyone except the true owner. So what did the professor do in his or her lecture (which employed a Socratic method)?

The professor started the class with the *assumption* that everyone in the class understood the holding in *Armory* (the finder of a chattel has better rights to it than anyone else, except for true owner). The professor then sought to expand the students' understanding of the rule in *Armory*—and work on their legal reasoning skills—by focusing in on an element of the rule in *Armory*: finder. What the professor did was examine what constitutes "finding." (Remember, all law is made up of rules and all rules are made up of elements.) In this regard, through questioning, the professor helped the student to reason that seeing an object, without more, cannot result in one being a "finder." Rather, "finding" requires something more. The student was eventually able to arrive at what that something is: "grabbing" the object—taking possession.

We should note that the professor never referred to any of the facts in *Armory*. Nor did the professor state the holding in *Armory*. Still, without the student understanding the facts and holding in *Armory*, the student would have had a much more difficult—if not impossible—time in understanding the professor's hypothetical. Moreover, for the final examination, the student will be responsible for the holding of *Armory* and the rule that *possession*, and not *seeing*, confers rights.

This kind of learning makes students uncomfortable because students feel insecure in this environment. They are never really quite certain that they know the holding of the principal case (because the professor never states the holding). Contrast this with Sample Class Session #1, where the professor makes certain that the students know the principle of *Armory*.

Sample Class Session #2: The Less-Overt Professor: You Must Help Yourself

How, then, does a student get used to a professor who assumes that each student knows the underlying holding of the case? Initially, if a student gets the holding by reading and briefing the case, without turning to any outside sources, that is wonderful. On the other hand, if a student needs help in understanding the holding, there are a number of outside sources. One time-tested source is the so-called "hornbook." A hornbook is a one-volume treatise that states the legal principles of a body of law by extracting the holdings from the premiere cases in the field. When you are in doubt about the principles of a case, go to a hornbook, find the case in the table of cases, and read the relevant section. Not only will you be able to get a better idea of what a given case stands for, but you will also be able to see the flow of the cases, which will assist you when you are preparing your course outline.[6]

---

[6] See Chapter 6, "Preparing a Course Outline."

You also can go into a computer database, such as Westlaw® or Lexis®, and read the head notes to get the holding of the case. Some of your professors might object to this, but the reality is that lawyers read head notes. If lawyers did not read them, Westlaw® and Lexis® would not bother to create them. If it is helpful for lawyers, it can be helpful for you, too.

There is yet another source to use if your understanding of a case is weak. You can go to a commercial outline. I must caution you, however: Many of your professors will not want you to use commercial outlines.[7] Whether you use commercial outlines (or any other outside source) or not, it is a foolish student who does not read cases and relies solely on an outside source. Reading cases is an art and that is what lawyers do. We read cases. Hone your skills now when you have the time. You will not have the time when you are a new associate.

Sample Class Session #3: The Mysterious Professor

Now let us examine another classroom scenario, one that gives students the most difficult time. In Sample Class Session #3, the professor will also discuss the *Armory* case; however, the professor will discuss only the social considerations of the case. Let us read the transcript and then explore what happened.

---

[7] There are two reasons professors typically will give for not wanting students to use commercial outlines. The first reason is that they are not accurate. Such a reason may have been valid many years ago, when the authors typically were not professors (sometimes they were students). Today, however, professors usually write the outlines. While no work is totally error-free, the outlines available today are well edited and are, indeed, quite accurate. The second reason is that students will understand the material much better if they create their own outlines. I totally agree with this second reason. In fact, we discussed this point in Chapter 6, "Preparing a Course Outline." Nevertheless, there is nothing wrong with going to a commercial outline if you need to confirm the principle (holding or collateral rule) of a case or see how that principle fits into the entire picture. When used for this limited purpose, there is nothing wrong with reading a commercial outline, any more than there is reading a hornbook.

PROFESSOR: Now let us examine the *Armory* case. Mr. Jones, why should the plaintiff win? Why shouldn't society require all finders to give the property over to the state for the public benefit?

MR JONES: That sounds like socialism.

PROFESSOR: So what if it does?

MR. JONES: Well, it just wouldn't be right to force someone who finds property to give it up. After all, it is the finder who went out of his way to take possession of the property. If he doesn't have any rights to it, it will end up in the state's treasury.

PROFESSOR: So what? That is my point. Why shouldn't the public get the benefit of the found property?

MR. JONES: If it goes to the state, then there is no incentive for this finder to pick it up. He will probably just leave it on the street and not bother.

PROFESSOR: But if Finder #1 does not bother to pick it up, perhaps Finder #2, or Finder #3 will. Someone—"a good-deed-doer"—eventually will pick it up and deliver it to the proper authorities.

MR. JONES: With all due respect, I'm not convinced someone eventually will do that. If the property belongs to the state, there is no reason for anyone to go out of his or her way to pick it up.

PROFESSOR: Mr. Jones, do you think that the jewel in *Armory* will continue for all eternity to remain in the public street, or wherever the sweep found it?

MR. JONES: Well, forever is a long time. (Class laughs.) I guess not. What I suspect could happen though is that someone may find the jewel and keep it—and never give it over to the state.

PROFESSOR: But that would be a crime—theft—since the jewel belongs to the state. Isn't that true, Mr. Jones?

MR. JONES: Yes.

PROFESSOR: So how does that relate to *Armory*?

MR. JONES: Maybe that is why finders have rights to lost property. In this way, the state does not put people to the test: if you do not hand over the jewel, the state will label you a thief.[8]

---

[8] In some classes, where a pure Socratic method is used, the professor will never acknowledge that an answer

I think that you can see what the professor was driving at: social policy and only social policy using a Socratic dialogue. The underlying (although unstated) reason for the holding in *Armory* is that we want to reward finders so that they do not become thieves, which would be the inevitable result if finders were not given rights to property. Note carefully, however, that just as we saw in Sample Class Session #2, the professor assumed in Sample Class Session #3 that the student read and understood the holding in *Armory*. Just as we saw in Sample Class Session #2, the professor did not expressly refer to the holding, which the student will be responsible for on the final examination. Here, too, the student will have to get the holding, if not from the case, then from outside sources.

SUMMARY OF CHAPTER 7

Let us now summarize the main points in this chapter. You may have a professor who examines the holding quite overtly (Sample Class Session #1). If so, your job is relatively easy. At the least, you will understand what is going on in class. You will not feel insecure. You will walk out of the classroom knowing what the holdings and collateral rules are. On the other hand, you may also have a professor who assumes that you know the basic legal principles of the cases and uses class time to emphasize reasoning and expand your knowledge of the law (Sample Class Session #2). Alternatively, you may have a professor who uses class time to discuss social policy (Sample Class Session #3). Of course, you may have a professor who one day will mirror Sample Class Session #1 and the next day Sample Class Session #3. In any case, however, you will have to know the rules and elements. If you do not, you will fall into a trap, which we shall discuss in the next chapter.

---

is correct. For example, after Mr. Jones's last comment, the professor may well come back with a question, "But doesn't the state put people to the test all the time? When you fill out your income tax return, you must determine your income and expenses. If the state can put you to the test for taxes, why can it not put you to the test for lost property?" Students either hate or love such a class.

barbri

CHAPTER 8
LAW SCHOOL TRAPS

There are traps in law school. If you fall into any one of these traps, you will not do well. What are these traps? Very simply, they all revolve around not knowing rules and definitions of elements for your final examination. Let us now explore the various ways that a student unintentionally and naively can fall into these traps.

ALLOWING CLASS DISCUSSION TO PULL YOU OFF THE TARGET

In the previous chapter, "I Don't Understand What's Going on in Class," we discussed the various ways in which a professor may conduct his or her class. One way is for the professor to make the holding (the rule or definition of an element) the focus of class discussion. Another way is for the professor to discuss nothing but policy, leaving it to the student to learn the holding. If you were in such a class—a "policy class"—it would be a grave error for you to think that you are not responsible for rules and elements on the exam. You are. Expect your professor to test on the rules and elements—even if your professor does not go over the rules and elements in class. To repeat: Make sure that you know your "black letter law," even if your professor limits class discussion to policy considerations.

OUTLINING LATE IN THE SEMESTER

As we previously discussed in Chapter 6, "Preparing a Course Outline," outlining is important. The outlining process will allow you to master and memorize the material *through understanding* the material. Moreover, as we also discussed in that chapter, preparing a course outline from scratch is "active learning," where you learn by doing and creating. This is the most effective type of learning. Nevertheless, if you start your outlining two days before your final exam, you might as well not do it at all. This is because there is no way you can take a full semester of Property or Torts, and break it down and organize it into something meaningful in a matter of hours. No one can write a book in a matter of hours. No one can write an effective and detailed outline in a matter of hours.

The moral of all this is simple: Do your outlining regularly. Doing it weekly or every other week is the ideal.[1] In this way, you will have the luxury of thinking about the material, seeing why each piece belongs where it does and, if you are unsure of something, you have plenty of time to resolve the problem—which you won't have the day before the final examination.[2]

---

[1] If you have four substantive courses, I suggest you do two one week, and then do the other two the next week. This way, you will never be more than one week down in outlining any particular course.

[2] What should you do if circumstances have in fact prevented you from outlining on a regular basis? You should read and study from a good commercial outline to help you understand and organize the rules and elements. As we discussed in Chapter 6, "Preparing a Course Outline," there is nothing wrong per se with using a commercial outline to clarify a particular point. Still, the best learning is undoubtedly "active learning," learning by doing. Although reading a commercial outline is not active learning (it is passive learning), it is, most obviously, far superior to not studying at all.

ENGAGING IN OVERKILL IN YOUR OUTLINES

You will recall from Chapter 6, "Preparing a Course Outline," that course outlines are not three pages long. Indeed, they will typically be quite substantial. That does not mean, however, that you should engage in overkill. How do you engage in overkill? There are a number of ways. One way is to define elements of a rule that are not terms of art. Not every word of a rule is a "term of art," i.e., a technical term. If the element is not a technical term, do not bother to define it in your outline (unless your professor spends time on it).

Another way to engage in overkill is to define elements of a rule when your professor expressly tells you that you are not responsible for knowing such material. Similarly, another way to engage in overkill is to include a rule when your professor states that you are not responsible for that rule.

A final way that you can engage in overkill is if there is an entire section of the casebook that your professor skips (and you confirm that you are not responsible for this material), and you include this entire section in your outline. Including this material in your outline would not be a good use of your time.

The point that you must understand is simple: Your outline should include only those rules and elements which your professor covers in class and/or for which you are responsible. Do not include material that will not show up on the exam.

ENGAGING IN OVERKILL IN READING AND BRIEFING YOUR CASES

As I mentioned above, you need to do your outlining on some regular basis. On the other hand, however, you have to read and brief your cases on a more current basis. Still, some students engage in overkill in the reading and briefing of their cases. What is overkill on cases? Spending countless hours reading and briefing a three-page case is overkill.

Now I am not telling you that reading your cases is unimportant. Indeed, we have established in the preceding chapters how important it is. Nonetheless, that does not mean that you should use your time unwisely. If there is something that you do not understand in a case and you have reading[3] for two other subjects (and are already behind in your outlining), use your time wisely and go on to the other matters (like the readings for the other two subjects or catching up on your outlining).

Remember this: As we discussed in Chapter 6, "Preparing a Course Outline," except for a case which stands for an entire doctrine (such as the *Erie* case in Civil Procedure), a case holding simply shows you the rule or element that a court applied in a given fact pattern. That you must know the rule of the case is clear, but you cannot ignore time constraints. If you do, you will not have the time to master all of the rules and elements that will be necessary for you to know for your final exam.

---

[3] In law school, students have readings or assignments; they do not have "homework." Homework is something that middle school students receive, not law school students. Never use the term "homework."

borbri

NOT DOING PRACTICE EXAMS

If you have been doing your outlines during the semester, during the study period before the final exams ("dead week"), you will only have to re-read your outlines once briefly to refresh your memory. What then do you do with the rest of your time? You do practice exams.

As you shall learn in the subsequent chapters, law school exams are quite different from other exams that you have taken. One difference is this: On the law school exams, you must deal with new and unusual fact patterns. Hence, the more practice exams that you do, the more experience you will get in dealing with unusual fact patterns. Consequently, the better you will do. Why is this? Because by having to grapple with unusual fact patterns, you are again learning the law by doing: you are again engaged in "active learning."

How many practice exams should you do? Do not do just one or two per course—as the average student does. Rather, you should do *dozens* for each course. When I was a student, I always finished my outlining by the last day of class. During the study period before exams, I did nothing but practice exams. Sometimes I wrote out the entire exam. Other times I just outlined the answer. Whether I wrote out full answers or just outlined the answers, however, I grappled with new fact patterns. Consequently, I was seldom surprised on the final exam. I may have missed a proximate cause issue once doing a practice exam, or maybe even twice. By the third time, however, it was virtually impossible for me to miss it. The professor may change the names and the places on the exam, but proximate cause is still proximate cause. Instead of a doctor botching an appendectomy operation, I dealt with a plumber botching a pipe repair.[4] Do enough hypos and you will probably never miss an issue on the examination.[5]

Where do you get practice exams? You get them from commercial publishers, your professor, and your school library.[6] That is fine, but how exactly do you go about writing a law school essay exam? It is now time for us to learn that. We are now ready to discuss law school essay examinations.

---

[4] The "key facts" (see Chapter 3, "More on Cases: The Importance of Facts") remained the same or were very similar. We will discuss key facts in the context of examinations in greater depth in coming chapters.

[5] As you will learn in the subsequent chapters, an integral part of the examination process is to identify the issue that is in dispute.

[6] If your professor does not have past exams on file, past bar exam questions are an excellent source for practice exams. They are typically sold by commercial publishers or your state bar office. The State Bar of California, for example, sells books of past bar exam questions with selected (not model) answers. The price is very reasonable. Starting with 2002, the State Bar of California puts their essay exams with selected answers on the internet, free of charge (at least at the time of the writing of this book; I fear that this policy may change). You can access this at www.calbar.org and follow the link to Bar Exam/Examinations and Statistics. The direct URL is http://www.calbar.ca.gov/state/calbar/calbar_generic.jsp?cid=10115&id=1010. Be warned, however, that bar exams are much easier than law school exams. Bar exams test minimal competency; that is not the standard for law school exams.

CHAPTER 9
LAW SCHOOL ESSAY EXAMS: AN OVERVIEW

To introduce you to law school essay exams, I think it would be helpful to first tell you of a wonderful "Peanuts" (Charlie Brown and Snoopy) cartoon that I read years ago. In the first of two frames, one of the Peanuts characters is preparing to take a history exam. The exam question was, "Discuss the causes of World War II." I remember that when I read this first frame, I chuckled to myself. Discuss the causes of World War II! Indeed! A ten-year old (how old is Charlie Brown anyway) is expected to do this in an hour or less? Public libraries contain shelf after shelf of books that discuss the causes of World War II! Yet, these young students were to answer this question in an hour. When I read the second frame of the cartoon, however, I actually laughed aloud. In the second frame, the Peanuts character continues reading the question: "Use both sides of the paper if necessary." The Peanuts cartoon was very funny. In college, I took a course in Japanese history. On the final examination, one of the two essay questions actually was, "Discuss the causes of World War II." I find this all very amusing.

UNDERGRADUATE NON-SCIENCE EXAMS

The fact of the matter is that most (if not all) undergraduate (and many graduate) final examinations are relatively quite easy. The night before the final, you cram everything possible into your head, confident that the examination will be a "tell-me-everything-you-know-about-the-course-examination," whether the exam is the causes of World War II; the philosophy of Spinoza; the meaning of the Book of Genesis; or the economic consequences of teen pregnancy. The common thread is that a student does not have to engage in any critical "thinking" to get a good grade. All that the student has to do is just tell the teacher everything you know about the causes of World War II; the philosophy of Spinoza; the meaning of the Book of Genesis; or the economic consequences of teen pregnancy. Do that and you will get your A in the course. Why is this so? Because the professor spent much class-time discussing the causes of World War II; the philosophy of Spinoza; the meaning of the Book of Genesis; and the economic consequences of teen pregnancy. All that the student has to do is restate on the exam paper what the professor stated in class. As you will see, law school exams are not like that. They are not like that at all.

UNDERGRADUATE SCIENCE EXAMS

Now some of you may have been science or accounting majors. In such case, you will object to my statements in the preceding paragraph. Science majors, you may contend, have to solve problems—and surely, "thinking" must be required to solve those problems! True. Nonetheless, in science, two plus two *must* equal four, each time. We have no exceptions to this rule. We have no "maybe" to this rule. On your law school exams, however, your answers will seldom be that absolute and concrete.

LAW SCHOOL ESSAY EXAMS ARE DIFFERENT

In short, your law school exams will be quite different from exams that you have previously taken, whether on the undergraduate or graduate level. Let us now explore some of these differences.

Identifying the Key Facts and the Legal Issue

First, for each essay question, you will have to determine which facts are "key facts." Then you will have to determine the legal issues triggered by each set of "key facts."[1]

Stating the Applicable Law

Second, once you decide what the issues are, you will have to state the law that is applicable to those issues—and those issues only. You will note that you will *not* tell the professor everything that you know about the law of Property. Thus, although you may have memorized five hundred rules for your Property course, on the final exam you may have need to use only fifty to solve the problems presented. The "trick" is to know which fifty.

Applying the Law to the Facts or Analyzing the Law in Light of the Facts

Third, after you determine which rules you need to solve the legal problems (issues) presented, you will have to apply the applicable rule to the facts or analyze the rule in light of the facts. This is what we refer to as "application" or "analysis."[2]

Concluding

Finally, you will have to state a conclusion. Then you will move on to the next issue and do the same all over again.

LAW SCHOOL EXAMS REQUIRE CRITICAL THINKING

I think that you can see that law school exams require critical thinking—and that is an understatement! To be frank, law school examinations are as demanding a test as you will ever come across. Note that I use the term, "demanding," not, "impossible."

---

[1] If you do not have a firm grasp of what "key facts" are, you will want to reread Chapter 3, "More on Cases: The Importance of Facts."

[2] Many of your professors will use the terms "analysis" and "application" interchangeably. As you will learn from the chapters that follow (and especially Chapter 11, "How to Categorize the Issues"), I use the term "analysis" to mean one thing and the term "application" to mean another. At this point, however, you do not need to know the differences that I ascribe to "analysis" and "application." Indeed, at this point, I do not think that it is even fruitful to discuss what these terms mean. Consequently, at this point, it is sufficient that you know that on your exams, you will have to perform either an "analysis" or "application" for each issue.

A LOOK AHEAD

In the chapters that follow, we will not discuss how to pass a law school essay exam. Rather, we will discuss how you can do exceedingly well on your law school exams. Up to this point, I have been setting the foundation for your success. This has been a critical part of the equation, but there is much more to learn. In the chapters that follow, we go into this in essay writing in depth. In these chapters, you will learn:

- How to read a law school essay question
- How to identify the issues
- How (and why) to categorize the issues
- How to prepare a "scratch" outline[3] of the issues
- What "analysis" is[4]
- How to do an analysis on an exam
- What an "application" is[5]
- How to do an application on an exam
- How to write your answer using my "HIRRAC"™ method

An introductory explanation about HIRRAC™ is appropriate here.

AN INTRODUCTION TO IRAC AND HIRRAC™

HIRRAC™ is my own variation of the traditional (and, as you will see, unsatisfactory) IRAC method. IRAC is an acronym for *issue, rule, analysis* or *application*[6] and *conclusion*. HIRRAC™, on the other hand, is an acronym for *heading, issue, rule(1), rule(2), analysis* or *application*, and *conclusion*. As you will see, HIRRAC™ is more precise and, thus, far superior to IRAC. Nonetheless, HIRRAC™ is merely an organizational tool for answering your law school essay exams in a lawyer-like manner. At this point, I shall give you a synopsis of how the HIRRAC™ method works, what it does—and what it will *not* do.[7]

AN INTRODUCTION TO HIRRAC™ AND LAW SCHOOL ESSAY EXAMS

In a typical three-hour exam, if your professor gives only essay questions,[8] you can reasonably expect three essay questions, each to take approximately one hour. In each question,

---

[3] A "scratch outline" for an examination, which we shall discuss in Chapter 12, "Preparing a Scratch Outline," is different from a "course outline," which we discussed in Chapter 6, "Preparing a Course Outline."

[4] See footnote 2, supra.

[5] See footnote 2, supra.

[6] See footnote 2, supra.

[7] In Chapters 13 through 18, we shall spend much time on HIRRAC™.

[8] There was a time when all professors gave only essay questions—no multiple-choice questions. Professors started using multiple-choice questions only when preparing students for the bar exam became more prominent in the curriculum than it was years ago and professors wanted to prepare their students for the multiple-choice portion of the bar exam, called the MBE (Multistate Bar Exam). Nonetheless, some professors, still give only essay examinations. For my own property and wills and trusts classes, I give only essay questions: four questions in a four-hour exam.

you will probably come across six to eight legal issues.[9] The HIRRAC™ method is nothing more than a common sense approach to tackle the issues: For the first issue, you would introduce the issue with a heading. Then you would identify the issue in a lawyer-like manner. You would then proceed to state the rules (there are typically two rules in HIRRAC™) applicable to that issue. Next, you would analyze the rule in light of the facts or apply the rule to the facts.[10] Last, you would state your conclusion. Heading, issue, rule(1), rule(2), analysis or application, and conclusion. After you finished doing a HIRRAC™ for the first issue, you would go on to HIRRAC™ the second issue.

WHAT HIRRAC™ IS NOT

HIRRAC™ is not a substitute for thinking. You must think through the problem to know what the issues are. You must understand what the relevant rules are—you do not throw in everything you know. You must also think through the analysis or application.[11] HIRRAC™ merely assists you in organizing your thoughts. We shall spend much time on HIRRAC™,[12] again, my variation of IRAC.

One final point is in order. As we proceed, you will see very clearly that if you have read and briefed your cases and prepared your own course outline, you are well on your way to doing well.

Now let us begin discussing all the preceding points in great depth.

---

[9] If you have a three-hour exam and only one essay question, you need only extrapolate: you can reasonably expect to deal with approximately twenty issues. What do you do if you get a teacher who gives you a so-called "race-horse" examination (scores of issues in three hours)? We shall discuss this matter in Chapter 15, "Using HIRRAC™ to Answer a Rule/Counter-Rule Issue."

[10] See footnote 2, supra.

[11] See footnote 2, supra.

[12] As I stated earlier, in HIRRAC™, you not only have a heading, but also two rules of law (hence, not one "R," but two "R's." I do not discuss HIRRAC™ in depth now. We shall do so in the coming chapters.

CHAPTER 10
READING A LAW SCHOOL ESSAY EXAMINATION QUESTION

At this point, you are probably saying to yourself, "I think I will skip reading this chapter. I know how to read!" I can certainly understand a student wanting to move ahead quickly. Nevertheless, I implore you not to skip this chapter. Please read it carefully. While I know you know how to read, reading a law school essay examination question is like reading a case: It is a skill that must be learned.

TWO PRELIMINARY MAXIMS

Before we get into the actual mechanics of reading an essay question, we must recognize two maxims: (1) every word on your exam is there for a reason and (2) there are only two possible reasons: the words are either (a) key facts or (b) non-key facts.

Maxim #1: Every Word on the Exam Is There for a Reason

Let us discuss the first maxim: Every word on your exam is there for a reason. Your professors create your examinations with great care. They do not create exams in ten minutes with a stroke of inspiration. Rather, your professors thoughtfully and deliberately construct their examinations. I cannot emphasize this too much. Why do I want you to recognize that each word was carefully thought through? Because it is only when you come to that realization that you will be able to appreciate the second maxim: Every word (or set of words) is either (a) a key fact, or (b) a non-key fact.

Maxim #2: Every Word is Either a Key Fact, or a Non-Key Fact

We have already discussed key facts in much depth in Chapter 3, "More on Cases: The Importance of Facts." At this point, let us merely summarize the highlights from that chapter.

BACK TO CASES: CHAPTER 3 SUMMARIZED

When you read a case, the court will state the facts of that case. These facts will include the key facts and non-key facts.

Cases and the Definition of Key Facts

You will recall that key facts are those facts which, if changed or eliminated, would change the outcome of the case. Consequently, key facts create the legal dispute between the parties.

Cases and Non-Key Facts: Background Facts and Colorable Facts

Additionally, a court will also state the non-key facts. There are several types of non-key facts. One type of non-key fact is the background fact. Background facts are pieces of information the court gives us to more fully round out our understanding of the case. Another type of non-key

fact is what I call the "colorable fact." Colorable facts are emotionally charged facts which, critically speaking, should not have any impact on the case. Colorable facts do have an impact on the case, however, albeit in a stealth-like manner. Recall the war hero case that we covered in Chapter 3.

To repeat: In every case we read, we have key facts on the one hand and non-key facts (background and colorable) on the other.[1]

Relationship between Cases and Exams

Why have I put so much emphasis on reading (and briefing) cases? When you read (and brief) cases, you distinguish and separate the key facts from the non-key facts. Of course, that is good practice because that is what you will have to do on your examinations. On your exams, you will get a fact pattern, a story, and what you will have to do is isolate the key facts from the non-key facts.

EXAMS AND THE DEFINITION OF KEY FACTS (REDUX)

On your examination, each set of facts will be either (a) key facts, or (b) non-key facts. What are key facts on the examination? Key facts are facts, which, if changed or eliminated, would change the outcome of the hypothetical. The definition of key facts for exam purposes is the same definition of the term for case briefing purposes.

IMPORTANCE OF KEY FACTS ON EXAMS

Why is it important—indeed, critical—for you to isolate the key facts from the non-key facts on your exam? You will recall that the key facts in cases trigger the legal dispute between the parties. Similarly, key facts on the exam also trigger the issues—the legal dispute between the fictional parties. Consequently, if you cannot recognize a set of facts as key facts, you will miss writing on an issue.

GUIDELINES FOR RECOGNIZING KEY FACTS ON EXAMS

Now that you understand just why key facts are critical, how do you recognize key facts on the exam? I wish I could give you a rule guaranteed to enable you to pick out the key facts easily every time, in every subject. Unfortunately, I cannot. What I can give you, however, are three guidelines to assist you. Further, if you take practice exams using these guidelines (practice makes perfect), I am confident that you will readily be able to isolate the key facts on your final exams— and identify the legal issues that the key facts trigger. Now let us discuss these guidelines.

---

[1] If you do not find this summary of Chapter 3 adequate, please go back and reread the material in that chapter before proceeding any further.

Pay Attention to Adjectives

When you read your fact pattern, pay careful attention to adjectives, words that modify a noun. Never forget that every word on your exam is there for a reason. Consequently, you must always ask yourself *why* the fact pattern states, for example, "The defendant was tall." Why is it that the defendant was tall? Why could he not have been short? Why did we have to know his height at all? It is true that not every adjective is a key fact. Still, at a minimum, you must be aware there is a good chance that it could be a key fact. If it is, it is triggering a legal issue. Remember: Every word is there for a reason.

Pay Attention to Adverbs

You will also want to pay careful attention to adverbs, words that modify a verb. For example, if the fact pattern states that the plaintiff "ran fast," we must ask, why is the plaintiff running "fast"? Why is she not running "slowly"? Why do we even have to know her speed? Not every adjective is a key fact. Likewise, not every adverb is a key fact. Nevertheless, because every word is there for a reason, there is a good chance that the adverb ("fast," for example) is a key fact. At a minimum, you must consciously ask yourself if changing the adverb or eliminating it would change the outcome of the hypothetical. If the answer is yes, you have found a key fact.

Pay Attention to Action Verbs

You must also pay close attention to action verbs. For example, you must pay attention to words such as, "signed," "telephoned," or "punched." Again, there is no guarantee that every action verb will be a key fact. Yet, because every word is there for a purpose, you must ask yourself *why* is it significant that this plaintiff "signed" the document, "telephoned" his order, or "punched" his neighbor. The chances are good that the action verb is a key fact.

IMPORTANCE OF NON-KEY FACTS ON EXAMS

Obviously, not every word on your exam is going to be a key fact. Indeed, we have already noted that not every adjective, adverb, or action verb will be a key fact. Consequently, because every word on your exam is there for a reason, the second reason for words is that they are non-key facts. Let us now explain what non-key facts are.

TYPES OF NON-KEY FACTS ON EXAMS

For exam purposes, there are three types of non-key facts: (1) background facts; (2) "red herring" facts; and (3) preclusion facts.

Background Facts

We have previously learned[2] that courts provide background facts in their opinions to round out the reader's knowledge of the case. It is for this same reason that law professors include background facts on final examinations.

---

[2] See Chapter 3, "More on Cases: The Importance of Facts."

Personally speaking, when I develop an exam—a story—I want the students to get a full feel for the problem. That is one reason why I include background facts. There is another reason, too. Simply put, I want my students to be able to distinguish the relevant (key facts) from the irrelevant (non-key facts). After all, will they not have to do this when they become lawyers and a client comes to their office? Clients do not come in and say, "My landlord has breached the implied warranty of habitability by not eradicating the rodents and by failing to provide heat in the winter." Rather, clients come in and say, "Do I have to pay rent? I moved in four years ago. I have a one-bedroom apartment. My landlord doesn't do anything about the rodents and he doesn't provide heat." As a lawyer, you would have to know that rodents and lack of heat are key facts and these facts will trigger a breach of the implied warranty of habitability. You would also know that it is irrelevant that the apartment is a "one-bedroom" apartment (it could have been a two-bedroom apartment and we would not change the outcome of the case or hypothetical). You would also deem it irrelevant that the tenant moved in "four years ago" (it could have been three years ago and we would not change the outcome of the case or hypothetical). For these reasons, professors include background facts on the exam: to round out the story and test the student's ability to isolate the relevant from the irrelevant.

Once you make the determination that a set of facts are background facts only, you will be able to discard those facts and not have any further use for them.

Red Herrings

Now let us discuss the second type of non-key facts: the "red herring." A red herring is a fact that looks like a key fact, smells like a key fact, and even walks like a key fact. Thus, a red herring is typically an adjective, adverb, or action verb. It is not a key fact, however. It is nothing. It is just smoke. It is a trick. The purpose is to get you to write on an issue which does not exist.[3]

Red herrings are somewhat similar to so-called "colorable facts," which we discussed in Chapter 3. You will recall that "colorable facts" are emotionally charged facts. Colorable facts should not have any impact on the outcome of a case, but they do, albeit silently. Although red herrings are also "sexy" or emotionally charged facts (like colorable facts), they have absolutely no impact at all on the outcome of a hypothetical (unlike colorable facts). An example of a red herring is this: "Oscar conveys Blackacre to Abel as a gift. Ten years ago, Abel was released from prison after having served five years for robbery." Now some students might be tempted to discuss the conveyance in light of Abel's criminal record and question whether the conveyance is valid. In effect, some students may write on whether someone with a felony record can take title to property. However, a convicted felon who has served his or her time is entitled to hold title to property, whether by gift or otherwise. Consequently, although Abel's criminal history looks "sexy" and seems to be a key fact, it is actually irrelevant. It is smoke. It is a red herring.

Handling Red Herrings on Your Exams

On your exams, if you spot a red herring, there are two ways to address it: (1) Ignore it and do not even mention it or (2) tell the professor why it is not an issue. Whether you will ignore it or

---

[3] Personally speaking, I rarely give red herrings.

tell the professor why it is not an issue will depend upon your professor. Some professors want to know *why* a fact is a red herring. Others do not. Handle the problem as your professor asks you to handle it. When in doubt, tell the professor the fact is irrelevant: state that such-and-such fact, although striking, is not relevant to the outcome of the hypothetical and why.[4]

Preclusion Facts

The third and last type of non-key fact is what I call a "preclusion fact." In a preclusion fact, the professor gives you a set of facts that precludes you or prevents you from writing on a particular issue. For example, consider a fact pattern that states, "Xavier negligently injured Yetta." Because the facts tell you that Xavier negligently injured Yetta, you cannot (and should not) discuss *whether* Xavier negligently injured Yetta. Why is this? It is because the facts *state* that Xavier negligently injured Yetta. Why would the professor give these facts? Perhaps because there will be an issue of proximate cause: "Yetta thereafter went to the emergency room of her local hospital. The emergency room was very busy and a doctor could not see Yetta for three hours. During that time, an infection set in that caused Yetta additional pain and suffering." The professor stated that Xavier negligently injured Yetta to prevent you from going through a discussion of whether Xavier was negligent for the initial injury. Nonetheless, you would then be required to address whether Xavier could be held liable for the *aggravated* injury due to the delay in receiving treatment: Will Xavier be liable in negligence for the added injury Yetta suffered due to the delay in the emergency room?

Here is another example of a preclusion fact: "Landlord and tenant entered into a valid lease for two years." Because the facts state that the lease is "valid," you would be precluded from discussing whether the lease satisfied the Statute of Frauds requirement. The professor simply does not want a discussion of the Statute of Frauds.

SUMMARIZING THE MAJOR POINTS COVERED THUS FAR

Let us now summarize the major points covered thus far in this chapter. Every word (or set of words) on your exam is there for a reason. There are only two possible reasons: The words are either key facts or non-key facts. Key facts are those facts, which, if changed or eliminated, would change the outcome of the hypothetical. Key facts trigger the legal issues that you will discuss. To help you to isolate the key facts, pay careful attention to adjectives, adverbs, and action verbs. Non-key facts are either background facts, red herrings, or preclusion facts. If it is a background fact, you will never have to refer to that fact again. If it is a red herring, it looks like a key fact, but it is really nothing. Depending upon your professor's requirements, you will either ignore red herrings or briefly tell your professor why the fact is not relevant. Finally, a preclusion fact is one that prevents you from writing on a particular issue.

---

[4] If you state why the fact in question is not relevant, i.e., is a red herring, you will do so in a brief manner. For example: "Although Abel is a convicted felon, Abel can still hold title to Blackacre because a convicted felon is not deprived of the right to hold title to property given to him as a gift." You will not need to HIRRAC™ your answer. We discuss HIRRAC™ in Chapters 13 through 18.

MECHANICS OF READING A LAW SCHOOL ESSAY EXAM

Now let us discuss the actual mechanics of reading a law school essay exam question. Let us assume for these purposes that the student has one hour to answer the question. (I am assuming that the exam is comprised of three essay questions, to be answered in three hours. Of course, if you have one three-hour question, you would have to extrapolate accordingly).

First Reading: Read the Fact Pattern Quickly

The first thing that you want to do is to read the fact pattern quickly. In your first reading, your objective should be very basic: to get a very broad feel for the subject matter of the test. For example, in a Torts exam, you would want to know whether you are being tested on intentional torts or negligence. For Property, you would want to know whether you are being tested on landlord-tenant law or future interests. To assist you in this limited task, the call of the question may help you. (Some students like to read the call of the question first, before reading the fact pattern.) The call of the question may consist of one, two, or three specific interrogatories. If these interrogatories are narrowly drafted, they may clue you in to the subject matter of the exam. By way of illustration, let us assume that the interrogatory after the fact pattern states, "What affirmative defenses can the tenant raise in the landlord's suit for unpaid back rent?" You would then have no doubt that the general subject matter deals with landlord-tenant law. On the other hand, the call of the question (that is, the interrogatory) may simply be "Discuss" or "Discuss the rights and liabilities of all the parties." In such case, obviously, you will not get any benefit from the call.

Second Reading: Read the Fact Pattern Carefully and Annotate

After you read the fact pattern through quickly, you will then have a "feel" for the question. You will then read the fact pattern through a second time. In this second reading, you will consciously be isolating out the key facts from the non-key facts. When you see a key fact, you will annotate in the margin the legal issue that the key fact is triggering. For example, on your Torts exam, if you see a set of facts, which read, "John punched Ken," you will write the word "battery" in the margin. On a Property exam, if the facts state that the tenant's apartment was "rat-infested and had no heat," you would write "implied warranty of habitability" in the margin.

Third Reading: Read the Fact Pattern Carefully (Again) and Annotate (More)

After you read the exam's fact pattern a second time, annotating as you go, you will do the same thing one more time. This will be your third and final reading. In this third reading, you will try to pick up any additional key facts (and legal issues) that you did not get on your second reading.

You, therefore, will do three readings. Some of you are probably saying, "If reading the fact pattern three times is good, isn't four times even better?" Of course, it would be, and five times would be even better. Nonetheless, you have a very limited amount of time within which to read, annotate, categorize,[5] outline, and write your answer. The more time you allocate for writing, the better your grade will be. You cannot leave just fifteen minutes to write your exam. What you need to do is strike a proper balance. Assuming you have a three-hour exam with three essay questions (one question per hour), you should allocate approximately ten minutes to read and annotate a question. You will also need time to categorize (if you have not been categorizing while annotating[6]) and outline, which will require another five to ten minutes, leaving you a minimum time of forty minutes to write your answer for one essay.[7]

A Recap of Reading and Annotating

To recap, you will read your question (the fact pattern) three times. The first time you will get a basic feel for the subject matter. The second and third times you will read the question very carefully, isolating the key facts and determining which issues the key facts are triggering. Once you determine what issue is triggered by each set of key facts, you will write out the legal issue (e.g., "battery") in the margin of the question sheet.

After you have fully annotated the first question *and categorized* the issues, you are ready to write out a "scratch outline" for the question. This outline will greatly assist you in writing out your answer. In the next chapter, "Categorizing the Issues," we discuss *why* you first need to categorize each issue that you have identified. We also discuss *how* to categorize each issue. After we discuss categorizing, we go on to Chapter 12, "Preparing a Scratch Outline."

---

[5] Categorization is critical. We discuss this in the next chapter.

[6] We tackle the details of categorizing in the next chapter.

[7] The overwhelming majority of students type their exams on computer using ExamSoft. Very few students handwrite anymore.

barbri

barbri
CHAPTER 11
CATEGORIZING THE ISSUES

In the preceding chapter, we learned to isolate the key facts from the non-key facts. We also learned that the key facts trigger the legal issues that we will have to discuss for the exam. Yet, it is not enough for you to identify the issues on the exam. Indeed, if you want to get an "A" on the final, you will have to do more. You will have to *categorize* each issue. In this chapter, we present a brief overview of the five different categories of issues, discuss *how* to categorize the issues, discuss the five categories of issues in depth, how to implement the categorization of issues, and, finally, spend time on *why* you must categorize the issues.

THE CATEGORIES OF ISSUES: AN OVERVIEW

In the material that follows, we shall see that irrespective of the subject matter (Torts, Property, Contracts, etc.) there are only five categories or types of issues that you can come across on your final examination. These categories are: (1) a "simple analysis" issue; (2) a "complex analysis" issue; (3) a "rule/counter-rule" issue (also known as an "application" issue); (4) a "combination" issue; and (5) a "non-issue" issue.[1] We will define and discuss all of these issues at length later on in this chapter.[2]

Before we can intelligently define and discuss the differences between the five types of issues, however, it first will be necessary for you to learn *how* to categorize the issues.[3] Let us turn to this topic now.

HOW TO CATEGORIZE THE ISSUES

To categorize the issues (and note that you may be dealing with all five types of issues on any given exam question), you must have a plan, which is actually not difficult at all

Ask Yourself One Critically Important Question

You will recall from the previous chapter that in your second and third reading of the question, you are searching for key facts that trigger the legal issues. In categorization, once you identify an issue (e.g., battery), you state the rule of battery to yourself, and then you ask this critically important question:

Are all elements of that rule of law absolutely and clearly satisfied on the facts given?

---

[1] The categories of issues presented (e.g., "simple analysis" issue) are the author's own unique terminology. I have created this terminology because it is very descriptive and allows the student to conceptualize this difficult material more easily.

[2] In fact, by the time we finish, you will see there really are only three types of issues: analysis issues, application issues, and non-issue issues.

[3] One might wonder why we do not define the categories of issues now. The author hopes that the reader will simply accept it on blind faith that the material will make more sense if we define the categories of issues at a later stage.

Why is this question so important? The reason is this: You will recall that all law is made up of rules, and all rules are made up of elements.[4] You will soon see that by asking yourself this question, you will be able to determine whether your professor is testing you on a rule of law or an element of a rule. Moreover, by the time that you finish this chapter, you will see why it is so critical for you to know whether the professor is testing you on a rule of law or an element of a rule.

Three Alternative Possible Answers to that Critical Question

Now let us go back to the critical question that you have asked yourself: *Are all elements of that rule of law absolutely and clearly satisfied on the facts given?* After you have asked yourself this question, you will be able to come up with one (and only one) of three different answers:

1. *Alternative Number 1: The answer to the question is, no.* You will say to yourself, "All of the elements of that rule of law are not absolutely and clearly satisfied because one or more elements can go either way on the facts given." To say that, "one or more elements can go either way," means that on the facts given, one or more elements of the rule are in dispute.[5] In such case, what you will do is write down that element(s) next to the issue (that you previously identified) in the margin of the question sheet. Such an element(s) is in dispute.

Let us now illustrate the preceding paragraph. Let us suppose that one of the issues that you had identified and jotted down on the question sheet of the exam was "battery." What you would then do is state to yourself the rule of battery (an intentional and harmful or offensive unpermitted touching of the person of another). You would then ask yourself, "Are all of the elements of this rule absolutely and clearly satisfied on the facts given?" After posing this question to yourself, let us stipulate that you determined that the answer to the question was "no," because on the facts given, one element of the rule—"INTENTIONAL"—was in dispute; on the facts given, this element, which has one definition, could go either way. It is possible that the plaintiff could prevail on this element, but it is also possible that the defendant could prevail on this element.

Consequently, on the question sheet, you would write "INTENTIONAL" next to the issue, "battery."

2. *Alternative Number 2: The answer to the question is, yes.* You would say to yourself, "All of the elements of that rule of law are absolutely and clearly satisfied on the facts given." If this is your answer to the question, you will write "ALL ELEMENTS OK," or "OK," or just place a check mark (✓) next to the issue that you previously identified. Let us now illustrate this point.

---

[4] See Chapter 1, "Rules and Elements."

[5] Recall our discussion in Chapter 2, "How to Read Cases: The Basics." In that chapter we learned that the parties are either fighting over a rule of law or an element of a rule. Are you now beginning to see the relationship between cases and essay exams?

Let us assume that one of the issues on the examination that you identified and jotted down on the question sheet was "negligence." You would then state the rule of negligence to yourself: duty, breach of duty, cause in fact, proximate cause, and damages. You would then ask yourself the critical question: "Are all of the elements of the rule of negligence absolutely and clearly satisfied on the facts given?" Let us stipulate that the answer is, "yes." It is so clear that all of these elements are satisfied that one cannot reasonably dispute that the defendant was negligent.

Consequently, you would write on the question sheet, "ALL ELEMENTS OK," or "OK," or place a check mark (✓) next to the issue "negligence."

3. *Alternative Number 3: The answer to the question is, no.* You would say to yourself, "All of the elements of that rule of law are not absolutely and clearly satisfied because on the facts given, one or more of the elements can never be satisfied." This answer differs from the first possible alternative in that in the first possible alternative, the element in dispute could go either way. Maybe plaintiff would win; maybe defendant would win. Here, however, one or more elements *cannot* go either way: one or more of the elements simply does not exist on the facts given. Put another way, one or more of the elements are not even *arguably* satisfied. If this is the answer to the posed question, you will write in the margin next to the identified issue the element(s) that cannot be satisfied: "NO [STATE ELEMENT]." Let us now illustrate the principles in this paragraph.

Let us assume that the issue you identified was common law burglary. You would then state to yourself the rule of common law burglary: The breaking and entering of the dwelling house of another in the nighttime with the intent to commit a theft or felony therein. You would then ask yourself, "Are all of the elements of this rule absolutely and clearly satisfied on the facts given?" Let us stipulate that all of the elements are absolutely and clearly satisfied except one: NIGHTTIME. This element does not exist in the facts by any stretch of the imagination (the action took place in the afternoon).

Consequently, you would write on the fact pattern of the question sheet, next to the issue of burglary that you previously wrote, "NO NIGHTTIME."[6] Of course, you ask this question for each issue that you identify on the exam.

Now that you have a basic feel for categorizing the issues, we shall next discuss the five categories of issues that you can run across on your exams. We will also take this time to show how you categorize. Later in this chapter, you will see the importance of categorizing and how, with categorizing, you can be on the road to your "A" grade.

FIVE CATEGORIES OF ISSUES AND IMPLEMENTING CATEGORIZATION

You now have a broad idea of how categorization works. For you to master the categorization, we shall illustrate its use for each of the various categories of issues that you can

---

[6] When you cannot satisfy one element of a rule as a matter of law, there is technically no issue. Thus, if the facts state that the breaking and entering took place in the afternoon with the sun shining brightly, you cannot have a common law burglary. Nevertheless, some professors will include these "non-issue" issues (which we discuss later) on the final exam. The reason for this is that they want to know *why* there cannot be a burglary on the facts given.

come across on your exams. We shall also take this opportunity to explain the five categories of issues: (1) the "simple analysis" issue; (2) the "complex analysis" issue; (3) the "rule/counter-rule" issue (also known as an "application" issue); (4) the "combination" issue; and (5) the "non-issue" issue.[7]

SIMPLE ANALYSIS ISSUE

The first type of issue that we will address is the simple analysis issue. Although I call this "simple," that does not mean that it is easy, as we shall see.

Simple Analysis Issue: Overview

As I just stated, by using the term "simple," you should not think that the term means "easy." Rather, a "simple analysis" issue means this: only *one* element of the applicable rule of law is in dispute. In a simple analysis issue, all but *one* of the elements of the rule applicable to the issue will be absolutely and clearly satisfied. However, with respect to one element of the rule, there will be one definition for that element,[8] and you will be saying to yourself, "Based on that definition, it could go either way; it's not clear on the facts given." The plaintiff could win on this issue, or the defendant could win on this element. In such a situation, you have a simple analysis issue. To repeat: one element of the rule is not clearly satisfied.[9] The following diagram will illustrate a simple analysis issue.

---

[7] Again, this is the author's own terminology. Note, also, as I stated earlier in this chapter: when you finish this material, you ultimately will conclude that there are only three types of issues: analysis issues, rule/counter-rule (also known as application) issues, and non-issue issues.

[8] What if there is more than one definition for an element? What if there is a split of authority? We address this matter later in this chapter when we discuss "Combination Issues."

[9] Remember, all law is made up of rules, and all rules are made up of elements.

Simple Analysis Issue: Diagram

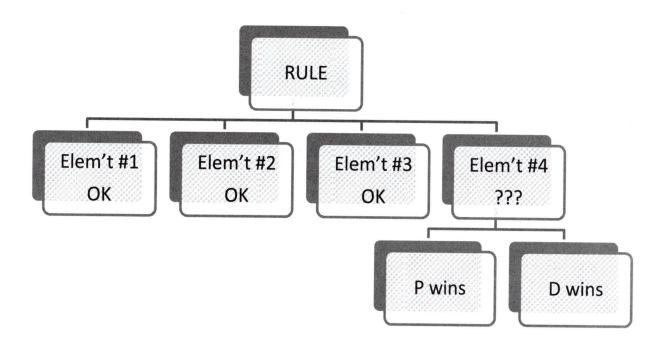

This diagram shows that Elements 1-3 of the "Rule" (e.g., battery, negligence, etc.) are absolutely and clearly satisfied on the facts given. Element 4, however, is not clearly satisfied. It can go either way. On the facts given, plaintiff may win or defendant may win.

Let us now examine a hypothetical that will illustrate a simple analysis issue.[10]

Simple Analysis Issue: Hypothetical #1

In this hypothetical, a common law burglary problem, all of the elements of common law burglary will be absolutely and clearly satisfied on the facts given, except for "dwelling house." That element will not be clear; that element may go either way.

---

[10] It is important that you note that each hypothetical that we cover in this chapter does not represent an entire essay question. Rather, each hypo illustrates only *one* category of issue that you can get on your examination. In Chapter 19, "Sample Exams," we cover entire essay questions. In Chapter 19, you will see how the professor can combine the various categories of issues into one essay question.

Hypothetical #1

[Simple Analysis Issue]

In June 2010, Charles graduated from college with a B.S. degree in accounting. Prior to beginning work in September for an accounting firm, Charles decided to travel across the United States in his 2005 Dodge minivan, seeing small towns and just enjoying himself. Not being financially well off, however, Charles felt he could economize by sleeping in the back of his minivan. In this way, he would not have to pay for a motel room nightly.

While traveling through State X, Charles pulled over from the public highway to catch a few hours of sleep. It was a cool night so Charles rolled up all of the windows of his car. For safety reasons, he also locked all of the doors of his car. By 10:30 PM, with the nighttime stars shining brightly, Charles fell asleep.

An hour later, Dan walked by. Dan saw Charles' wallet lying next to Charles. Being low on funds, Dan decided that it would be easy to take Charles' wallet. Dan then broke the glass nearest Charles with the intent of snatching Charles' wallet; Dan put his hand into the car and succeeded in taking the wallet. Charles' person, however, was not harmed in any way.

Assuming that State X's Penal Code codifies the common law, what crimes, if any, has Dan committed? Discuss.

borbri

Simple Analysis Issue: Hypothetical #1: Diagram

Simple Analysis Issue: Hypothetical #1: Explanation

We have discussed what a simple analysis issue is: one element of the rule of law is in dispute. We also have stated that this problem involves a simple analysis issue. Let us, however, make believe that this was part of your final examination in criminal law. In such case, you would not know that this hypo involves a simple analysis issue. How then would you go about determining that this is a simple analysis issue? You would do so by using the reading and categorization approach that we discussed earlier. You read the question three times (once quickly just to get a feel for the problem) and then, after the first reading, you read again and this time isolate the key facts from the non-key facts, understanding that the key facts trigger the legal issues that you will write on. Once you spot an issue, you write it down in the margin of the exam question; then, you ask, *Are all elements of the rule applicable to that issue absolutely and clearly satisfied on the facts given?* Using this approach, this is what would happen on the exam.

After we read it through once (remember, just trying to get a general feel for the area of law), we read it through a second time, trying to isolate the key facts—which trigger the legal issues—from the non-key facts. Let us examine the facts.

First, does it matter that Charles graduated in June 2010 with a degree in accounting? Of course, it does not. He could just as easily have graduated in December 2009 with a degree in

engineering and the outcome of the hypothetical would not change. Consequently, his graduating in June 2010 with a degree in accounting is not a key fact. Rather, they are merely background facts: After we read these facts once, we can throw them away and never have need to refer to them again.

Second, does it matter that Charles owned a 2005 Dodge? Of course, it does not. It could just as easily have been a 2008 Chrysler. Consequently, Charles' owning a 2005 Dodge is also a background fact. After reading it once, we can discard it, too.

It is the same with Charles' deciding to travel across the country before he starts work: these are background facts.

What do we make of Charles' using his minivan to sleep in? Further, what is the significance of it being 10:30 PM and the stars shinning? Moreover, what is the significance of Dan breaking the glass to steal the wallet? As we read this hypo for the first time, we may not be sure. However, when we read it the second time around, we know what these facts are for: they go to the burglary issue. More specifically, all of these facts are key facts: if we change any of them or eliminate them, we change the outcome of the hypo.

So far, so good. Somewhere in the margin, we annotate the crime committed by Dan: "burglary." Most average students can get this far. What distinguishes the "A" student from the average student is what follows.

The "A" student, after having identified burglary as the issue, now talks to himself or herself: "The issue is burglary. The rule of burglary is: a breaking and entering of the dwelling house of another in the nighttime with the intent to commit a felony therein." The "A" student then asks himself the most critical question: *Are all the elements of that rule of law absolutely and clearly satisfied on the facts given?*

In order to answer this question, the student must mentally go through each and every element of the rule of burglary. Let us do just that.

1. *Was there a breaking?* A breaking is defined as the creation of a breach. There is no question that there was a breaking here: Dan accomplished this when he "broke the glass" window of the car.

2. *Was there an entering?* An entry exists if any part of the defendant intrudes. This existed when Dan put his hand through the window.

3. *Was this a dwelling house of another?*[11] BINGO! This element is not clear. It is disputable. It could go either way. Why is this the case? There is one definition of dwelling house: a place for human habitation. Charles sleeps in the car—as someone would a house—but it is not a

---

[11] Under modern statutes, one can be guilty of burglarizing a car. But read the facts carefully: the jurisdiction has codified the common law. Hence, if Dan is guilty of burglary, it must be because the car qualifies as a "dwelling house."

house. It's a machine used to transport people. Because this element can go either way (in favor of the government or Dan), it is not clearly satisfied. Thus, we will jot down "DWELLING HOUSE" in the margin of the question sheet, right next to the issue, "burglary."

4. *Was it nighttime?* Nighttime is the period between sunset and sunrise. Dan's act took place at 11:30 PM. That sure sounds like nighttime. What if this takes place is in Alaska, however, when at certain times of the year the sun could be out at 11:30 PM?[12] Is this element also in dispute? No. We are told that the stars were out and they were shining. It clearly was nighttime.

5. *Was there an intent to commit a felony?* Under the common law, all larceny was a felony. The intent to commit a felony element is met because Dan intended to take the wallet—a theft—before he broke the window.

Therefore, the only element in dispute is "dwelling house." We have a simple analysis issue.

Does this sound complicated? Well, it certainly is a lot more difficult than, "Discuss the causes of World War II"! Nevertheless, you will get quite used to this very precise way of thinking and exam taking. The key is really very simple (and it is something that I will repeat in this chapter and subsequent chapters many times): Once you spot the issue (e.g., burglary), state the rule of burglary to yourself. Then ask yourself, *Are all elements of that rule absolutely and clearly satisfied on the facts given?* In a simple analysis issue, all but one of the elements will be absolutely and clearly satisfied. That one (and only one) element will have one definition and, based on that definition, can go either way. What that means is you have a simple analysis issue to deal with.[13]

COMPLEX ANALYSIS ISSUE

Now let us proceed to the second type of issue that you will run across in your law school exams: the complex analysis issue.

Complex Analysis Issue: Overview

In a complex analysis issue, two or more elements of the rule will not be absolutely and clearly satisfied. Each of these elements will have one definition and, based on that definition,[14] the dispute could be resolved in favor of the plaintiff—as well as the defendant. The following diagram will illustrate a complex analysis issue.

---

[12] On bar exams and (most, if not all) law school exams, you are required to make "reasonable" inferences. If the facts state that the time is 11:30 PM, the reasonable inference is that it was nighttime. However, for the sake of absolute clarity, in my hypo, I make it clear that it is nighttime.

[13] We will discuss how you write and "analyze" your answer in a HIRRAC™ format later in these materials.

[14] What do we do if an element has more than one definition because there is a split of authority? We will address that later in this chapter when we cover, "Combination Issues."

Complex Analysis Issue: Diagram

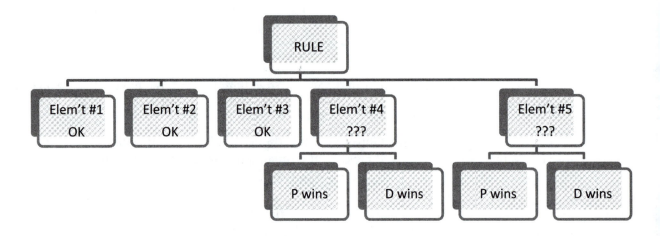

This diagram shows that Elements 1-3 of the "Rule" are absolutely and clearly satisfied on the facts given. Elements 4-5, however, are not clearly satisfied. Element #4 has one definition, and based on that definition, on the facts given, plaintiff may win or the defendant may win. Similarly, for Element #5, there is one definition for that element, and based on that definition, on the facts given, plaintiff may win or defendant may win. Thus, each of these elements can go either way. Let us now examine a hypothetical that will illustrate a complex analysis issue.

Complex Analysis Issue: Hypothetical #2

In this hypothetical, we have a real property problem, an adverse possession issue, with several elements in dispute. (I will explain this area of law after the diagram that follows. Thus, even if you have not yet had property, you will easily be able to follow the problem).

Hypothetical #2

[Complex Analysis Issue]

Oscar owns a 35-unit apartment building. There are a few cracks throughout the building, but nothing that affects a tenant's health and safety. Indeed, the building is quite sound. Oscar does not live on the premises.

In January 1988, Oscar hires Max Smith to manage the apartment house. Max does such a fine job in managing the apartment house that Oscar decides that he, Oscar, can finally take a well-deserved vacation. Oscar tells Max to continue to do the fine job that he, Max, is doing. Oscar then books a one-year cruise on the Queen Elizabeth II and sets sail on July 4, 1989.

In August 1989, Max sends out a letter to all tenants. The letter reads:

Dear Tenant:

Oscar is gone. I am in control here. You are to see me for all problems regarding your apartment. You will make your check payable to "Max Smith."

Sincerely,

Max Smith

Following receipt of the letter from Max, all of the tenants make the rent check out to "Max Smith." Max deposits the checks into his personal checking account, which he just opened.

Several months later, a vacant apartment is repainted by Max and rented out on a month-to-month basis. All other tenants have leases for a term for years for one year.

Meanwhile, Oscar loves traveling so much that he decides to stay overseas for a while after the cruise ends. In this regard, he telephones Max and lets Max know that he, Oscar, will be gone for a few more years. When Oscar asks how everything is going, Max replies, "The building is better now than when you were running it." The two then hang up. They have the same conversation twice for the duration that Oscar is overseas.

In 1999, Oscar decides that he is tired of traveling. He has also run up quite a few debts while overseas. Oscar comes back to the United States and prepares to sell the apartment house to pay off all of his debts.

The jurisdiction within which the apartment building lies provides in its Civil Code: "In any action to recover real property or the possession thereof, the state of mind of the one in possession shall be irrelevant." The Civil Code also provides that "any action to recover the possession of real property must be commenced within seven years from the time that an actual entry was made by the one in possession." Discuss.

Complex Analysis Issue: Hypothetical #2: Diagram

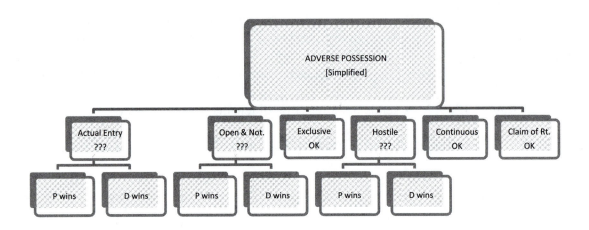

Complex Analysis Issue: Hypothetical #2: Explanation

This is a real property problem and the issue that we are dealing with is adverse possession.[15] Adverse possession is a doctrine that allows someone to acquire title to property merely by possessing it "adversely" for a number of years (which varies from jurisdiction to jurisdiction; some require as little as five years while others require twenty years). The rule of adverse possession is this: To obtain title by adverse possession, the possessor must make an actual entry, which is open and notorious, hostile, exclusive, continuous for the statutory period, and under a claim of right. (We define these terms below.)

Of course, we have let the cat out of the bag by initially categorizing the issue in this hypo as a complex analysis issue. Still, how would you arrive at that conclusion if faced with this hypo on the final exam? By reading it through once quickly (perhaps even ascertaining it is adverse possession with this first reading), and then, in the second reading, you would begin to isolate the key facts (which trigger the legal issues that you will write on) from the non-key facts.

With that introduction, let us now go through the facts. Is it a key fact that the apartment building has 35 units? No. It could have been 25 units and the outcome of the hypo would not

_____
[15] This is an actual exam, albeit somewhat modified for this text, that I gave many years ago.

have changed. Hence, that the apartment complex is 35 units is mere background. Is it significant that there are some cracks in the building? No. It is just background. Is it relevant that Oscar went on a cruise? No. He could have gone by covered wagon. This is just more background.

What is the significance of Max's letter to the tenants, painting the apartment, varying the terms of a lease from what used to be the norm, and Max's conversation with Oscar? These facts are key facts and they trigger the issue of adverse possession. We write it down on the question sheet: "adverse possession." Average students can get this far.

Now that we have identified the issue—adverse possession—let us continue. This is what the "A" student does.

We now state to ourselves the rule of adverse possession: an actual entry that is open and notorious, hostile, exclusive, under a claim of right, and continuous for the statutory period. Now we ask ourselves the most critical question: *Are all elements of that rule of law absolutely and clearly satisfied on the facts given?* Let us go through each element to determine whether the answer is "yes" or "no."

1. *Was there an actual entry by Max?* There is one definition for an actual entry, and it is this: An actual entry is a substantial occupation of the land. Painting and varying the terms of the lease for one apartment is not substantial in the classical sense of an actual entry: building roads or fences. Still, what else could any true owner do with this apartment building? Consequently, this element is not clear; it could go either way. It is in dispute. We jot down "ACTUAL ENTRY" right next to the issue, "adverse possession."

2. *Was the occupation open and notorious?* There is one definition for an open and notorious occupation. An occupation is open and notorious if the occupation is such that the true owner could have seen the occupation if he had visited the property. If Oscar, the true owner, had visited the property, he would have seen a manager doing what he was paid to do—manage the apartment house. Nonetheless, Oscar could have seen the letter to the tenants. He also could have seen the checks that the tenants made directly out to Max. If so, Oscar would have known—or should have known—that something was wrong or at least not right: The typical manager does not tell tenants to make the check out to the manager personally. Consequently, this element is also in dispute. Maybe Max would win on this issue; maybe Oscar would win on this issue. Thus, we jot down this element too: "OPEN AND NOTORIOUS."

3. *Was Max's occupation hostile?* An occupation is hostile if it is without the consent of the true owner. Max had permission to be on the property, but only in his capacity as manager—not any other capacity. On the other hand, his telephone conversations with Oscar could mean that he, Max, is claiming the property without permission from Oscar. This element is therefore in dispute. We jot down, "HOSTILE."

4. *Was Max's occupation exclusive?* An occupation is exclusive if not shared with the true owner. It was not so shared in this case. Oscar was not present. Therefore, this element is not in dispute. We need not write it down.

5. *Was the occupation under claim of right?* Claim of right goes to state of mind: bad faith or good faith.[16] Some jurisdictions require that the possessor make a good faith mistake. Other jurisdictions require (as strange as it sounds) bad faith: "I know it's not mine—but I'm taking it anyway." The facts state that, pursuant to the applicable statute, state of mind is irrelevant. This element, then, is clearly satisfied. We will not worry about it. Thus, there is no need to jot it down: we only want to make a record of those elements that are in dispute. Claim of right is not in dispute. Therefore, we will not need to jot it down.

6. *Was the occupation continuous for the statutory period?* Continuous means without interruption. Max occupied without interruption for ten years. The statute provides for a seven-year statute of limitations. Hence, this element is clearly satisfied and is not in dispute. Again, there is no need to jot this element down.

The elements that are in dispute are therefore: actual entry, open and notorious, and hostile.

A complex analysis issue does not mean that it is any harder than a simple analysis issue. What it does mean is that we have two or more elements of the rule that are in dispute. In Hypothetical #2, the elements in dispute—elements that could go either way—were: actual entry, open and notorious, and hostile.

Now let us examine the third category of issue.

RULE/COUNTER-RULE ISSUE (AKA APPLICATION ISSUE)

In the simple analysis issue, one element of the rule of law was in dispute. In the complex analysis issue, two or more elements of the rule were in dispute. With a rule/counter-rule issue, however, *all* of the elements of the rule of law are absolutely and clearly satisfied on the facts given. Still, if that is the case, if all of the elements of the rule are absolutely and clearly satisfied, how can there be a dispute between the parties (a requisite for virtually every law school exam)? To answer this, we must go back to material previously covered.[17]

Recall that in every case that you read, parties are involved in a dispute. Often the dispute revolves around an element of a rule. This runs parallel to our simple analysis (e.g., is a car a dwelling house for purposes of common law burglary) or complex analysis issue (e.g., is an occupation by an apartment building manager an actual entry; is it an open and notorious occupation; is it hostile). Sometimes, however, the parties have a dispute because they disagree, not on an element of a rule, but on the rule itself: One party wants one rule adopted to resolve the dispute while the other party wants another rule adopted. As we shall now see, this runs parallel to a rule/counter-rule issue.

---

[16] There is also another definition for claim of right (the so-called objective standard), but I choose not to go into it. My purpose here is to teach essay exam writing, not substantive property law.

[17] See Chapter 2, "How to Read Cases: The Basics."

There are three major types of rule/counter-rule issues[18]:
[1] "rule/exception to the rule" issue;
[2] "majority rule/minority rule" issue; and
[3] "rule/corollary to the rule" issue.

Irrespective of the type of rule/counter-rule issue that you have, however, there is a common characteristic: All of the elements of the rule applicable to that issue will be absolutely and clearly satisfied. All of the elements to the rule—and the counter-rule—will be satisfied on the facts given.

Now let us examine the three types of the rule/counter-rule issues. We begin with the first type: the rule/exception to the rule issue.

[1] Rule/Exception to the Rule: Overview

In the rule/exception to the rule issue, a set of key facts will trigger an issue (as is always the case). All elements of the rule applicable to that issue will be absolutely and clearly satisfied. Thereafter, the same or different key facts will trigger another issue. All of the elements of the rule applicable to that issue—the "exception" to the rule—will also be absolutely and clearly satisfied. Typically, a rule/exception to the rule issue involves a cause of action (the rule) and an affirmative defense (the exception to the rule). The following diagram illustrates the rule/exception to the rule issue (the first type of rule/counter-rule or application issue).

---

[18] The terminology here and what follows is, again, my own terminology.

[1] Rule/Exception to the Rule Issue: Diagram

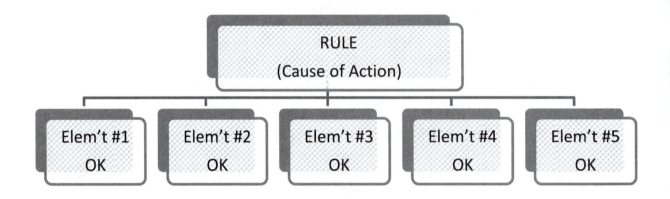

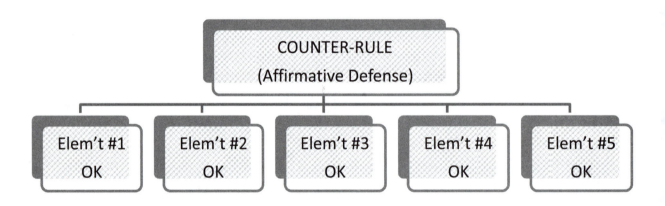

This diagram shows that all of the elements of the rule (the cause of action) are absolutely and clearly satisfied. Similarly, all of the elements of the counter-rule (the affirmative defense) are absolutely and clearly satisfied.

[1] Rule/Exception to the Rule Issue: Hypothetical #3

Hypothetical #3 illustrates this first type of rule/counter-rule issue. It is a tort problem involving negligence (the rule) and an affirmative defense to negligence (contributory negligence), terms that we will explain shortly. The point of this hypo is that it involves a cause of action (the rule) and an affirmative defense (the exception to the rule).

Hypothetical #3

[Rule/Counter-Rule: Rule/Exception to the Rule]

Lawnco is a business located in the State of Westmoreland. Lawnco's business is the renting of various kinds of gardening machines and tools. One of the machines that Lawnco rents is an electric lawn-mower, Model L-100. On all such models, there is a safety feature to prevent a certain type of injury to the user. From time to time, the safety feature on the Model L-100 will wear out because of use. Lawnco is aware of this problem but does not regularly inspect each Model L-100 to make sure that the safety feature is in good working order. Nevertheless, when Lawnco does find that a Model L-100 needs a new safety mechanism, Lawnco performs the necessary replacement. Lawnco knows that a worn out safety mechanism can result in injury to the user.

Able is a white male forty years of age who comes onto Lawnco's premises to rent a Model L-100. Throughout Lawnco's store, there are numerous signs, in large red print, that state: "ALWAYS READ OPERATING INSTRUCTIONS BEFORE USING ANY EQUIPMENT." Able is quite literate and he saw the signs. In addition, all customers of Lawnco receive a booklet of operating instructions for the machine or tool that the customer rents. Able received such a booklet for the Model L-100, but failed to read the booklet before operating the mower. Able then proceeded to use the Model L-100 in a manner not prescribed and was injured.

If the mower had a properly functioning safety feature, Able would not have been injured. Able was not aware that the safety feature was worn out. Further, even without the safety feature, if Able had read the operating instructions and used the mower in the manner prescribed, he would not have been injured.

The manufacturer is no longer in existence. You are to assume that the doctrine of strict liability does not apply on these facts in this jurisdiction. You are also to omit any discussion of the Uniform Commercial Code.

The State of Westmoreland does not recognize the doctrine of comparative negligence.

Can Able recover? Discuss.

[1] Rule/Exception to the Rule: Hypothetical #3: Diagram

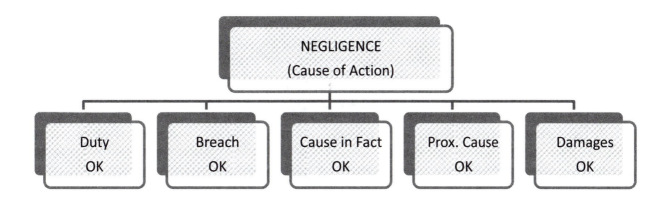

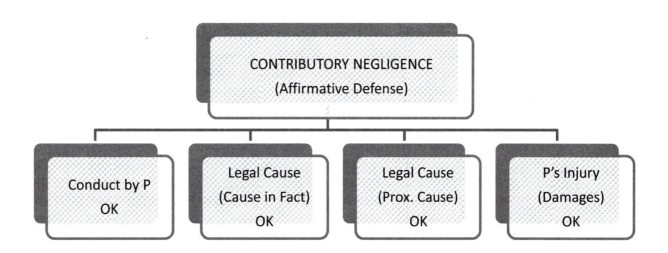

In this hypothetical, all of the elements of the cause of action, negligence (the rule) are clearly and absolutely satisfied, but all of the elements of an affirmative defense (the counter-rule) also are satisfied.

[1] Rule/Exception to the Rule: Hypothetical #3: Explanation

As in all of the other hypos that we have gone through so far, we have told you up front the category of issue that is involved. Let us now go through the hypo as though it were part of your

final exam. In such case, you would not know what category of issue is involved. We read this fact pattern the first time to simply to get a general feel for the subject matter. When we read this material through the second time, we are isolating the key facts from the non-key facts.

Let us first point out some of the non-key facts, the background facts: Able is a white male. Pure background information: Able could have been an African-American female and the outcome of the hypo would not be affected. Does it matter that Able is forty? Of course, it does not. Able could have been forty-five.[19]

Let us now look at some preclusion facts, facts that prevent us from writing on an issue. Because the manufacturer is out of business, we are precluded from discussing any cause of action against it. We are expressly told to not discuss strict liability. We also are told that this jurisdiction does not recognize the Uniform Commercial Code, again precluding us from discussing anything but common law negligence as it applies to Lawnco. Similarly, we cannot discuss the doctrine of comparative negligence.

Now let us discuss those facts that are the key facts. Recall that the key facts trigger the legal issues that we will write. What are the key facts here? Lawnco failed to inspect, knowing that injury could result from such failure. Coupled with Able's injury, these facts trigger negligence.

Nevertheless, there is another set of key facts here: Able failed to pay heed to the signs that he saw and read. He also failed to read the directions. He also used the machine in an improper manner. These facts trigger contributory negligence, and under the common law, contributory negligence bars recovery.

Are you starting to see how the rule/counter-rule issue works? In a rule/exception to the rule issue, the professor is testing you on your ability to understand that Able has a cause of action against Lawnco: negligence. Nonetheless, Lawnco also has an affirmative defense: contributory negligence. Oh, and is this not quite similar to reading cases? It certainly is![20]

To recap: We have identified negligence and contributory negligence as the issues. We annotate these issues somewhere in the margin of the question sheet: "Negligence" and "Contributory Negligence." Now let us proceed to categorizing.

---

[19] Of course, were Able ten years old, Lawnco could have been negligent for selling such a dangerous machine to a minor. Nevertheless, so long as Able is an adult, it does not matter that he was forty or twenty-one years of age.

[20] See *Li v. Yellow Cab*, discussed in Chapter 2, "How to Read Cases: The Basics." Note the minor differences: In *Li* we had a person who drove a car negligently. In Hypothetical #3, we have a person who operated a lawn-mower negligently.

The issues are negligence and contributory negligence.[21] We start with the first issue: negligence. We now state the rule of negligence to ourselves: duty, breach of duty, cause in fact, proximate cause, and damages. Now let us continue.

We ask ourselves the key question: *Are all elements of that rule of law absolutely and clearly satisfied?* We shall now think through whether each element is clearly satisfied.

1. *Did Lawnco owe a duty of care to Able?* A person owes a duty of care to anyone in the foreseeable zone of danger. Able, a purchaser and user of the machine, is clearly in the foreseeable zone of danger. This element is clearly satisfied.

2. *Did Lawnco breach the duty?* A breach occurs when the defendant's conduct is unreasonable. Failing to inspect is clearly unreasonable when Lawnco knows injury can result. This element is satisfied.

3. *Was Lawnco's failure to act the cause in fact of the injury?* An action is the cause in fact if, but for the defendant's failure, the accident would not have happened. If Lawnco had inspected, this accident would not have happened.[22]

4. *Was the failure to inspect the proximate cause of Able's injury?* Proximate cause exists when there is no superseding force or event to cut off the liability of the original actor; no such force or event exists here. This element is not in any way a problem. It is clearly satisfied.

5. *Was there injury?* Yes. The facts state there was.

Every element of negligence is absolutely and clearly satisfied. We therefore write down "ALL ELEMENTS OK," or "OK," or we put a checkmark (✓) in the margin of the question sheet, right next to the issue "negligence," letting us know that all of the elements are satisfied.

Next, we repeat these steps for the remaining issues. In this case, there is only one remaining issue: contributory negligence.[23] Let us do that now.

Once we spot the issue of contributory negligence (whether on the first, second, or third reading of the question), we write down "contributory negligence" in the margin of the question sheet. We then state the rule of contributory negligence to ourselves: conduct on the part of the plaintiff, contributing as a legal cause—cause in fact and proximate cause---to the harm he has suffered, which falls below the standard to which he is required to conform for his own protection; under the common law, it is a bar to recovery.

---

[21] You can start to categorize after you have identified all of the issues for the question, or you can categorize as you identify each issue, issue by issue. I prefer the latter approach: to categorize issue by issue, as you identify the issues. Thus, first I tackle issue #1. I identify the issue (that is, determine what legal issue is involved) and categorize it. Then, I move on to issue #2. I identify it and categorize it.

[22] There is another definition for cause in fact: the substantial factor test. I choose not to address this issue now, however. We will discuss what happens when we have an element with two or more definitions later in this chapter, when we discuss "combination issues."

[23] As stated earlier, on an actual exam, there would be many more issues than these two (negligence and contributory negligence).

Next, we ask ourselves the critical question: *Are all elements of the rule of law absolutely and clearly satisfied on the facts given?* Let us now see if all of the elements to contributory negligence are satisfied.

1. *Legal cause of Abel's injury.* Was Able's conduct a legal cause of his own injury? Able's failure to read the instructions when he sees the sign telling him to read the instructions—and he is literate—is conduct which is a legal cause of his injury. His failure was the cause in fact of the injury because if he had followed the directions he would not have been hurt (under either the "but for" test or the "substantial factor" test).[24] Moreover, his failure was the proximate cause because there was no superseding event to justify cutting off his responsibility.

2. *Unreasonable conduct.* Additionally, his failure to read the directions, when the signs that he saw stated that he should read the directions, fell below any reasonable standard, which was for his own protection.

Clearly, Able was contributorily negligent. We write down "ALL ELEMENTS OK," or "OK," or place a checkmark (✓) next to the issue of contributory negligence, the issue we wrote down in the margin of the question sheet.

Appreciate the difference between this first type of rule/counter-rule issue and any of the previous analysis issues: In the analysis issues, one or more of the elements were in dispute; we had one definition for the element and, based on that definition, on the facts given, the element(s) could have gone either way. The plaintiff could have won on the particular element—or the defendant could have won on that element. In the rule/counter-rule category of issue, however, every element of the respective rules were clearly and absolutely satisfied.

Now let us go on to the second type of rule/counter-rule issue.

[2] Majority Rule/Minority Rule: Overview

In the majority rule/minority rule issue, your professor is testing your knowledge of splits of authority—a majority approach and a minority approach. In short, your professor is testing you on a split of authority. The diagram that follows illustrates this second type of rule/counter-rule issue. Hypothetical #4, a slight variation of Hypothetical #3, illustrates this type of issue.

---

[24] As I stated earlier, we discuss in depth the approach you take when an element has two or more definitions later in this chapter, when we discuss "combination issues."

[2] Majority Rule/Minority Rule: Diagram

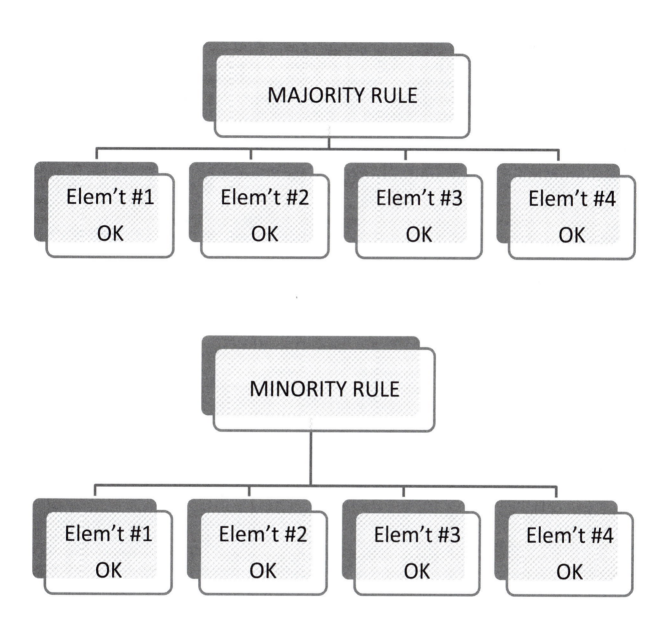

In this type of rule/counter-rule issue, all of the elements of one rule (majority rule) are satisfied, as well as all of the elements of the counter-rule (minority rule).

[2] Majority Rule/Minority Rule: Hypothetical #4

This hypo is just a slight variation of Hypothetical #3. In this hypo, we are being tested on our knowledge of two different affirmative defenses: contributory negligence (minority view) and comparative negligence (majority view). We have already explained what contributory negligence is: the plaintiff loses his cause of action. In comparative negligence, however, a plaintiff's cause of action is not destroyed if he is partly negligent in causing his own damages (unlike contributory negligence). In comparative negligence, the plaintiff's damages will be reduced proportionally, to the extent that his own conduct caused the injury. The plaintiff's cause of action is not wiped out, however.

Hypothetical #4

[Rule/Counter-Rule: Majority Rule/Minority Rule]

Lawnco is a business located in the State of Westmoreland. Lawnco's business is the renting of various kinds of gardening machines and tools. One of the machines that Lawnco rents is an electric lawn-mower, Model L-100. On all such models, there is a safety feature to prevent a certain type of injury to the user. From time to time, the safety feature on the Model L-100 will wear out because of use. Lawnco negligently fails to regularly inspect each Model L-100 to make sure that the safety feature is in good working order. A worn out safety mechanism can result in injury to the user.

Able comes onto Lawnco's premises to rent a Model L-100. Throughout Lawnco's store, there are numerous signs, in large red print, that state: "ALWAYS READ OPERATING INSTRUCTIONS BEFORE USING ANY EQUIPMENT." Able is quite literate and he saw the signs. In addition, all customers of Lawnco receive a booklet of operating instructions for the machine or tool that the customer rents. Able received such a booklet for the Model L-100, but failed to read the booklet before operating the mower. Able then proceeded to use the Model L-100 in a manner not prescribed and was injured.

If the mower had a properly functioning safety feature, Able would not have been injured. Able was not aware that the safety feature was worn out. Further, even without the safety feature, if Able had read the operating instructions and used the mower in the manner prescribed, he would not have been injured.

Lawnco was 70 % responsible for Able's injury.

The manufacturer is no longer in existence. You are to assume that the doctrine of strict liability does not apply on these facts in this jurisdiction. You are also to omit any discussion of the Uniform Commercial Code.

Can Able recover? Discuss.

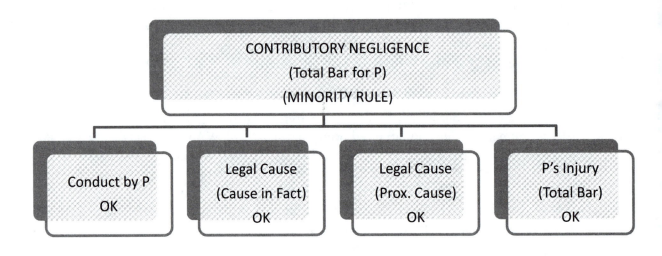

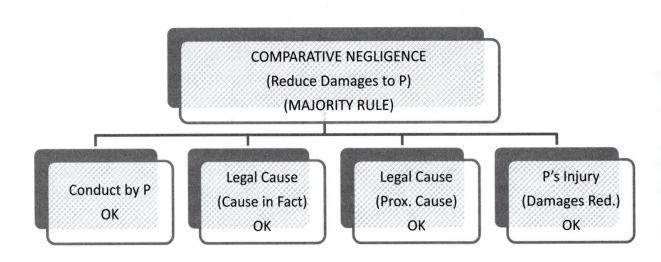

borbri

[2] Majority Rule/Minority Rule: Hypothetical #4: Explanation

Preliminarily, notice first how Hypothetical #4 differs from Hypothetical #3. In Hypothetical #4, there is a very important preclusion fact: Lawnco is negligent. Therefore, we do not have to be concerned with this issue; it is a given. Moreover, the facts also state that because of Lawnco's negligence, Lawnco is 70 percent responsible for Able's injury.[25] Able, therefore, is 30 percent responsible for his injury. Notice, too, that the facts do not preclude us from discussing comparative negligence, as we were in Hypothetical #3. Finally, we should take note that in this hypo, some of the background facts (Able is a white male) are absent. This of course is quite irrelevant to the problem.

Having stated these introductory points, let us proceed to categorize the issues.

First, after our first quick reading, we begin to read carefully and isolate the key facts from the non-key facts. What are the key facts? Again, Able's failures to heed the signs, read the instruction booklet, and properly operate the machinery. We get a sense that this involves some area of negligence. Now we go through our second reading. These same facts also trigger comparative negligence. We write down "Comparative Negligence" and "Contributory Negligence" in the margin of the question sheet. (Remember, we do not have to worry about Lawnco's negligence: It is a given in this hypothetical.) As stated earlier, even average students can do this.

Next, we ask ourselves the all-important question: *Are all elements of that rule of law absolutely and clearly satisfied on the facts given?* Are all elements of comparative negligence satisfied on these facts? Are all elements of contributory negligence satisfied on these facts?[26] Let us see.

The question actually revolves around whether Able was negligent. Able's failure to read the instructions when he sees the sign telling him to read the instructions—and he is literate—is conduct that is a legal cause of his injury. His failure was the cause in fact of the injury because if he had followed the directions, he would not have been hurt (under either the "but for" test or the "substantial factor" test). Moreover, his failure was the proximate cause because there was no

---

[25] There is a reason why the facts state that Lawnco is "70 %" responsible. In the law of comparative negligence, some jurisdictions require that the plaintiff be less than 50 percent responsible for his own injuries in order to recover. By stating that Lawnco was 70 percent responsible, assuming that the jurisdiction recognizes any type of comparative negligence, Able will be allowed to recover his damages, less 30 percent, the percentage attributable to his own negligence.

[26] Because the matter of categorization is so important, I repeat here exactly what I stated earlier: I prefer to identify an issue and then categorize, doing this issue by issue. Thus, for issue #1, I ask if all of the elements are absolutely and clearly satisfied. After I resolve this (either an analysis issue or a rule/counter-rule issue), then I move on to the next issue and do likewise. I have "lumped" comparative negligence and contributory negligence together here only because the common thread is negligence. Once I determined that Able was negligent, the only issue is whether his damages are only reduced (comparative negligence), or his cause of action is wiped out (contributory negligence). The point is this: Categorize by asking the important question : "Are all elements to the rule absolutely and clearly satisfied. You can do this issue by issue, or after you have identified all of the issues, go back and categorize. Do whatever is comfortable for you. The key is that you categorize. When you do so is not that important.

superseding event to justify cutting off his responsibility. Additionally, his failure to read the directions, when the signs that he saw stated that he should read them, fell below any reasonable standard, which was for his own protection.

Clearly, Able was negligent in causing his own injury. Thus, in a jurisdiction which recognizes comparative negligence (majority rule) in lieu of contributory negligence (minority rule), Able will merely have his damages reduced pro rata by 30 percent (Lawnco was 70 percent responsible for Able's injuries). As such, his cause of action will not be barred. We will write down "ALL ELEMENTS OK," or "OK," or place a check mark (✓) next to "Comparative Negligence and Contributory Negligence."

Do you see that the professor in this hypo was merely testing the student on his or her ability to know that there are two competing doctrines: contributory negligence (minority rule) and comparative negligence (majority rule)? Because the elements for each rule were absolutely and clearly satisfied, either rule could be adopted by the court in that jurisdiction (assuming, as is typical on exams, that this was a case of first impression in our fictitious jurisdiction).

Now let us proceed to discuss the third and last type of rule/counter-rule issue.

[3] Rule/Corollary to the Rule: Overview

In this type of rule/counter-rule issue, all of the elements to a rule will be satisfied as well as all of the elements to a "corollary" to the rule. What do I mean by a "corollary" to the rule? A corollary to the rule is a rule that is so bound up with the rule that it makes sense to discuss the two rules together. A typical "rule/corollary to the rule" issue is your cause of action (e.g., fraud) and your remedy (e.g., constructive trust or damages). The following diagram illustrates the rule/corollary to the rule issue.

[3] Rule/Corollary to the Rule: Diagram

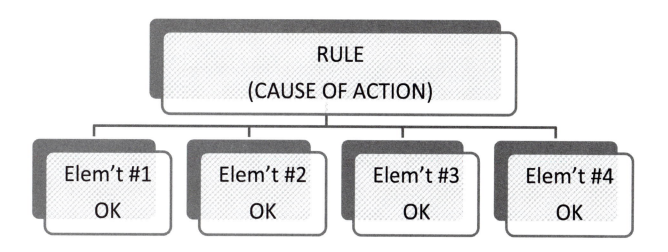

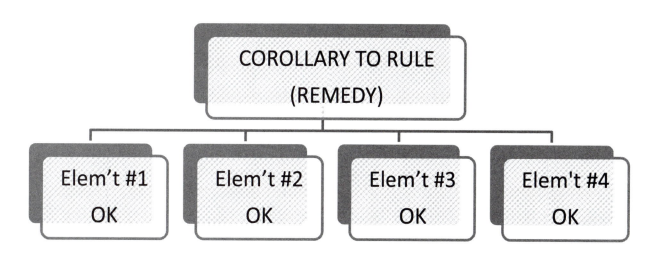

In the rule/corollary to the rule issue, all elements of a rule (a cause of action for fraud, for example) are clearly satisfied, and all elements of a counter-rule (a remedy, such as damages) also are satisfied.

[3] Rule/Counter-Rule: Hypothetical #5

Hypothetical #5 illustrates this third type of rule/counter-rule issue. In this hypo, we deal with a property issue, the implied warranty of habitability. In essence, this rule requires the landlord to maintain the premises in a habitable condition: it must be clean, safe, and fit for human habitation. The landlord will clearly breach this warranty: it is not clean; it is not safe; it is not habitable. This allows the tenant various remedies: withhold rent; repair the problem himself and deduct the cost from his rent; or sue the landlord for damages. All of these remedies clearly are available to the tenant.

Hypothetical #5

[Rule/Counter-Rule: Rule/Corollary to the Rule]

Lenore owns the Whiteacre apartment complex. The complex is rented entirely by low income tenants. Through the years, Lenore has lost interest in the building. As a result, rats and roaches are common throughout. Hot water is seldom available. Toilets regularly overflow due to old plumbing, which must be replaced. Heat in the winter is seldom available.

The tenants have repeatedly informed Lenore of this situation, but she refuses to do anything.

The tenants want to know what, if anything, they can do. Moving out, however, is not an option.

Discuss.

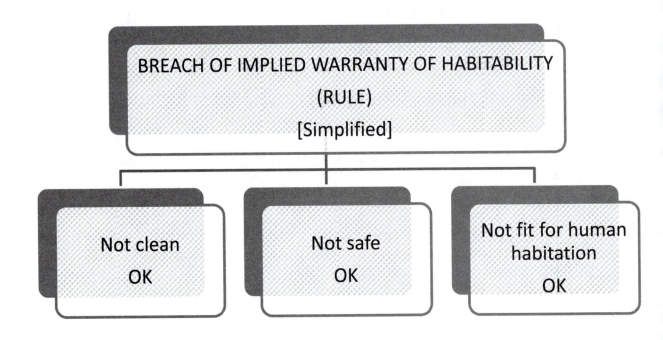

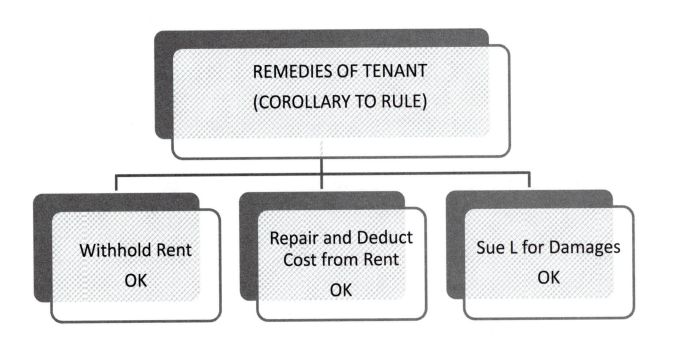

[3] Rule/Corollary to the Rule: Hypothetical #5: Explanation

We shall again tackle this problem as though it were a hypo on a final examination.

Assuming this is our second (or third) reading,[27] we identify the key facts as rats and roaches, no hot water, overflowing toilets, and no heat in the winter. These facts trigger the implied warranty of habitability. We write "implied warranty of habitability" in the margin of the question sheet.[28] We then state the rule of law to ourselves: The rule is that a landlord has a duty to deliver and maintain throughout the term of the lease, housing that is clean, safe, and fit for human habitation, and if he does not, he is in breach. We then categorize by asking the critical question: *Are all elements of that rule of law absolutely and clearly satisfied on the facts given?* The answer is a definite yes. We then write in the margin, "ALL ELEMENTS OKAY," or "OK," or put a check mark (✓) next to the issue to let us know all elements are clearly satisfied. We then move on to the next issue.

For a breach of the implied warranty of habitability, a tenant is entitled to (1) withhold rent, (2) repair the problem himself and deduct the cost from the rent for the breach; or (3) sue the landlord for damages. We write these remedies on the question sheet: "withhold rent—repair and deduct—damages." (The facts tell us that the tenants cannot move out. Thus, we are precluded from discussing constructive eviction as a remedy for breach of the covenant of quiet enjoyment.) There are rules governing when rent can be withheld, when a tenant can repair and deduct, and what type of damages are allowable. Let us stipulate for this hypo that all elements for each rule are absolutely and clearly satisfied. We would note next to each remedy (issue), "ALL ELEMENTS OK," or "OK," or put a check mark (✓) next to the remedies indicated.

We have now completed all of the rule/counter-rule issues. Now let us proceed to the fourth category of issue that you can get on your exam, the most difficult type.

COMBINATION ISSUE

A combination issue combines aspects of an analysis issue with a rule/counter-rule issue. There are two principal types of combination issues:

[1] Analysis with the Rule/Counter-Rule, and
[2] Analysis with the Rule/Counter-Rule with Analysis

Let us discuss each of them in turn.

[1] Analysis with Rule/Counter-Rule: Overview

What happens in this type of combination issue is this: After you identify the issue and ask yourself if all elements of the rule are satisfied, you will say to yourself, *No, all of the elements*

---

[27] In the first reading, we merely get a broad understanding of the problem. See preceding chapter.

[28] We omit from this discussion a traditional common law affirmative defense that the landlord could possibly invoke: "caveat lessee." Let us stipulate for purposes of this hypo that only modern law is applicable. Again, the purpose of this text is to teach essay writing; the purpose is not to teach any particular area of law.

are not absolutely satisfied; several elements are disputable. In a typical combination issue of this type, at least one element is not clearly satisfied because the element has just one definition and based on that definition, it can go either way on the facts given. This is the analysis aspect of this type of issue. This we have already covered earlier.

However, in the combination issue, there is something more: At least one additional element is in dispute because that element(s) can be *defined* in several ways.[29] For example, with respect to adverse possession in the law of property, the element "claim of right" has several different definitions, depending upon the jurisdiction. This is the rule/counter-rule aspect. The diagram that follows illustrates this first type of combination issue, the "analysis with the rule/counter-rule" issue.

---

[29] When we discussed "Simple Analysis" Issues and "Complex Analysis" Issues, we were working with only one definition of an element. Now, here, we are working with a split of authority: one element has two (or more) definitions.

[1] Analysis with Rule/Counter-Rule: Diagram

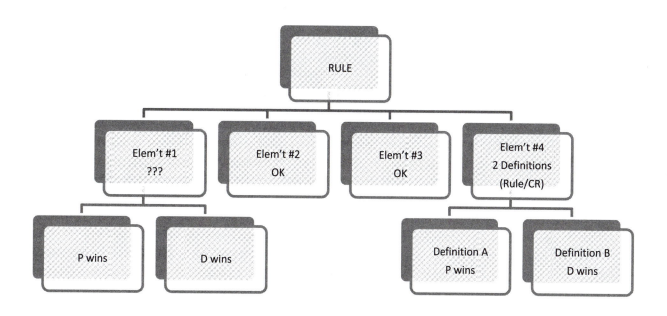

In this hypo, the rule has, for example, four elements. Elements #2 and #3 are absolutely satisfied. Element #1, which has one definition, can go either way on the facts given. Thus far, this is just like a simple analysis question. However, Element #4 has two definitions. Whether plaintiff wins or defendant wins simply depends upon which definition we use.

[1] Analysis with Rule/Counter-Rule: Hypothetical #6

Hypothetical #6, a slight variation of Hypothetical #2, the adverse possession problem, illustrates this first type of combination issue.

Hypothetical #6

[Combination Issue: Analysis with Rule/Counter-Rule]

Oscar owns a 35-unit apartment building. There are a few cracks throughout the building, but nothing that affects a tenant's health and safety. Indeed, the building is quite sound. Oscar does not live on the premises.

In January 1988, Oscar hires Max Smith to manage the apartment house. Max does such a fine job in managing the apartment house that Oscar decides that he, Oscar, can finally take a well-deserved vacation. Oscar tells Max to continue to do the fine job that he, Max, is doing. Oscar then books a one-year cruise on the Queen Elizabeth II and sets sail on July 4, 1989.

In August 1989, Max sends out a letter to all tenants. The letter reads:

Dear Tenant:

Oscar is gone. I am in control here. You are to see me for all problems regarding your apartment. You will make your check payable to "Max Smith."

Sincerely,

Max Smith

Following receipt of the letter from Max, all of the tenants make the rent check out to "Max Smith." Max deposits the checks into his personal checking account, which he just opened.

Several months later, a vacant apartment is repainted by Max and rented out on a month-to-month basis. All other tenants have leases for a term for years for one year.

Meanwhile, Oscar loves traveling so much that he decides to stay overseas for awhile after the cruise ends. In this regard, he telephones Max and lets Max know that he, Oscar, will be gone for a few more years. When Oscar asks how everything is going, Max replies, "The building is better now than when you were running it." The two then hang up. They have the same conversation twice for the duration that Oscar is overseas.

In 1999, Oscar decides that he is tired of traveling. He has also run up quite a few debts while overseas. Oscar comes back to the United States and prepares to sell the apartment house to pay off all of his debts.

The jurisdiction within which the apartment building lies provides in its Civil Code: "Any action to recover the possession of real property must be commenced within seven years from the time that an actual entry was made by the one in possession."

Discuss.

[1] Analysis with Rule/Counter-Rule: Hypothetical #6: Diagram

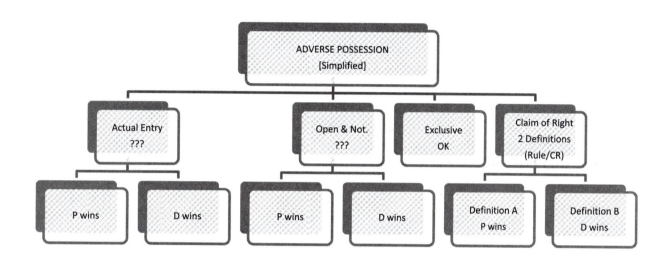

[1] Analysis with Rule/Counter-Rule: Hypothetical #6: Explanation

The only difference between Hypothetical #6 and Hypothetical #2 is that Hypothetical #6 omits the following: "In any action to recover real property or the possession thereof, the state of mind of the one in possession shall be irrelevant." Therefore, one of the elements of adverse possession, claim of right, which was not in dispute in Hypothetical #2, is in dispute in Hypothetical #6. Nevertheless, it is not in dispute in an "analysis" sense, only in a "rule/counter-rule sense." Why is this? The answer is that claim of right has several definitions. In one definition, the possessor must have had a good faith belief that the property was his. If such rule is used to define claim of right in this jurisdiction, Max must lose on this element: there could not have been good faith on his part. However, other jurisdictions define claim of right in a manner that requires the possessor to have bad faith: he knew it was not his land, but he is taking it anyway. If such is the definition used, Max must win on this element.[30]

---

[30] There is still another definition for claim of right: the so-called objective standard. As I have stated throughout this text, my purpose is to teach essay writing, not teach substantive law. As such, I omitted this definition from the answer. Still, you may easily see how that definition would merely be the third line of authority ("Definition C" in the diagram). Note, too, that in this diagram, for space-saving purposes, I have omitted the element of hostility (hence, a "simplified" version of adverse possession).

Having made these initial comments, let us now categorize. Initially, we have identified the issue (on the second or third reading) as adverse possession and we write it down in the margin of the question sheet: "adverse possession." Next, we state the rule of law to ourselves: Actual entry, open and notorious occupation; which is hostile; exclusive; under a claim of right; which is continuous for the statutory period. Finally, we ask ourselves the critical question: Are *all of the elements absolutely and clearly satisfied?* The answer is, no. As we discussed in Hypothetical #2, actual entry, open and notorious, and hostility are disputable because on the facts given, each of these elements can go in favor of Max or Oscar. (Note that each of these elements has just one definition.) This then is your "analysis" aspect of the issue. We write these elements down in the margin of the question sheet next to "adverse possession."

With respect to the element claim of right, as we discussed above, this element is also disputable, but not because it is factually unclear. Rather, it is disputable because we can define it in a number of ways. This, then, is your "rule/counter-rule" aspect of the issue. Of course, we write "CLAIM OF RIGHT" in the margin along with the other elements that are in dispute. To make it clear, you may wish to write "R/CR" (Rule/Counter-Rule) for this element to make it clear that we are dealing with a split of authority here only.[31]

The preceding was the first type of combination issue: One element(s) of the rule of law is not clearly satisfied because the element can go either way in a factual sense—a typical analysis issue aspect. The element may exist, but it may not exist, on the facts given.

With respect to another element(s), the outcome is also not clear, not because the facts are unclear, but because we can define the element in several ways.

Now let us examine the second type of combination issue. This is the toughest problem that you can get in law school. Master this and you are on your way to your "A"!

[2] Analysis with Rule/Counter-Rule with Analysis: Overview

As just stated above, this is undoubtedly the most complex type of issue that you can get. I doubt that you will see many of them during your law school career. Still, you will get some.

What happens in this type of combination issue is this: You will identify the issue. You will state the rule of law. You will ask yourself if all elements are clearly and absolutely satisfied. You will answer to yourself, "No." The reason will be that some of the elements will be in dispute. At least one element will be in dispute because on the facts given, there is one definition, and, based on that definition, the element could go in favor of the plaintiff or the defendant. This is simply the analysis part.

However, another element(s) will be in dispute because it is susceptible to several definitions. (So far, this seems just like the first type of combination issue, the "analysis with rule/counter-rule" issue.) However, with respect to this element(s) (the one which has two or more different definitions), if you ask (now a second time), *Are all elements of this rule (definition)*

---

[31] In the alternative, you may wish to diagram it out, as I have.

absolutely and clearly satisfied? your answer will be, "It's not clear." There are two definitions for this rule and based on one or both of those definitions, it can go either way on the facts given. The diagram that follows illustrates this issue.

[2] Analysis with the Rule/Counter-Rule with Analysis: Diagram

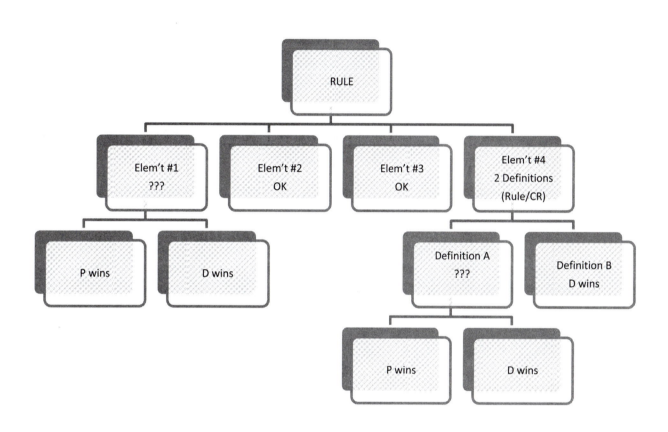

Thus, in this hypo, one element (Element #1) is just your regular analysis: we have one definition and, based on that definition, plaintiff may win or defendant may win; it is not clear on the facts given. With regard to another element (Element #4), there are two definitions. Based on one of those definitions (Definition A), it is not clear who would win. Hence, again, we have analysis. (For Definition B, defendant must win if the jurisdiction uses that definition.)

Hypothetical #7, a classical negligence problem, will illustrate this most difficult type of issue. This is as tough as you can get in law school.

[2] Analysis with Rule/Counter Rule with Analysis: Hypothetical #7

In this hypo, we have negligence (in short, careless conduct), something we have covered earlier. The elements are duty, breach of duty, cause in fact, proximate cause, and damages. The problem is that we will have two definitions for duty (and analysis for one of those definitions) and two definitions for cause in fact (and analysis for one of those definitions, too). Here is the hypo:

Hypothetical #7

[Combination Issue: Analysis with Rule/Counter-Rule with Analysis]

The day after Christmas, a group of adults knocked on the door of Yule's home and asked for the discarded Christmas tree that Yule had just placed on his porch for the trash man. Yule reluctantly agreed, although he saw in the street the large pile of similar trees, which the group had collected. In addition, Yule had read warnings in the newspaper concerning the danger faced by young neighborhood groups in burning discarded Christmas trees in large piles. He warned them to "be careful." The pile of trees was then dragged by the group to a vacant lot in the neighborhood.

One member of the group, Bob, struck a match and applied it to a corner of the pile. Bob then snapped off a burning branch and lunged toward Tiny, Bob's friend. Tiny was frightened and he dashed into the adjacent street. Tiny was injured when hit by an oncoming car without any fault on the part of the driver.

Discuss the liability of Yule.

[2] Analysis with Rule/Counter-Rule with Analysis: Hypothetical #7: Diagram

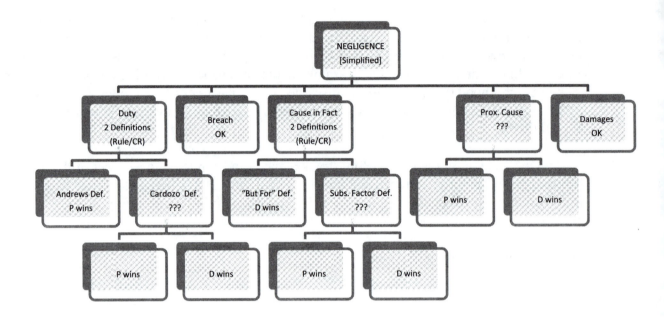

[2] Analysis with Rule/Counter-Rule with Analysis: Hypothetical #7: Explanation

Let us see how we address this problem. First, you isolate the key facts: The problem that Yule was aware of the possible danger, coupled with the warnings to the group, followed by the injury to Tiny, triggers the issue of whether Yule was negligent. We write "negligence" in the margin. Next, we state the rule of negligence: duty, breach of duty, cause in fact, proximate cause, and damages. Next, we categorize by asking, *Are all elements of the rule of law absolutely and clearly satisfied on the facts given?* The answer is, no. Why is this? Let us examine each element.

1. *Duty*. First, let us discuss duty. Did Yule owe Tiny a duty to be careful? It depends on how we define duty. Under Cardozo's view of duty, a duty is owed to those in the foreseeable zone of danger. Under Andrews' view, a duty is owed to the whole world, cut off only by the restrictive rules of proximate cause. Right off the bat, we see that this negligence issue is turning into a combination issue. But wait! There is more.

Assuming that we adopt Cardozo's view (or definition), was a duty owed on these facts? It is not clear. On the facts given, it could go either way. Yule warned the group—and you do not warn someone unless you can foresee danger. However, one can perhaps foresee danger from flying sparks—not from one friend trying to hurt another. Thus, to summarize this first issue (element), we have two definitions of duty, and using one of these definitions (Cardozo's), on the facts given, the outcome is not clear. Duty, therefore, clearly is in dispute: for rule/counter-rule reasons (Andrews' view v. Cardozo's view) and for analysis reasons (using Cardozo's view), it is not clear that all of the elements of duty are absolutely and clearly satisfied. We shall write "DUTY" in the margin next to "negligence." You can indicate "R/CR" so that you know there are two definitions or simply write ("Andrews/Cardozo"); next to "Cardozo," you can write ("Analysis"). If this gets too much, you can simply diagram this out on your scratch paper, as I have done above.

2. Breach of duty. Let us now go to the next element: breach of duty. A person breaches a duty if he or she does not act reasonably under the circumstances. Certainly if a duty was owed, Yule breached that duty by giving the tree to the group. No problem with this element: it is clearly satisfied. You can write "OK" next to this element or put a check mark (✓) next to it—or, again, just diagram it out as I have.

3. Cause in fact. The next element is cause in fact. Is this element clearly satisfied? Like duty, we have two definitions for cause in fact: the "but for" test and the "substantial factor" test. If we use the "but for" test, cause in fact does not exist: even without Yule's tree, the fire could have been set. Nonetheless, under the substantial factor test, it is not as clear. Under this test, a defendant's conduct must have been a substantial factor in producing the harm. Yule's tree was a factor—but was it a substantial one? We can argue this both ways. Consequently, this element, like the duty element, is in dispute: First, there are two definitions for the element and, second, for one of the definitions, either the plaintiff or the defendant can prevail on the facts given. We shall also write "CAUSE IN FACT" down in the margin of the question sheet and next to it put, "R/CR" or "But For" and Substantial Factor" and next to substantial factor, "analysis," to make it clear we have to do an analysis for this issue. Again, of course, if you wish, you can simply diagram it out, as I have.

4. Proximate cause. The next issue is proximate cause. Here we must be concerned with whether Bob's lunging was a superseding event: Was there anything in hindsight that, as a matter of policy, should require us to cut off liability to Yule?[32] Maybe yes, and maybe no. This element also is in dispute, analysis-wise. We will write this element down, "PROXIMATE CAUSE." Next to it, you may wish to write, "Analysis." Again, you may wish to diagram all of this as I have, so that it is clear and immediately available to you.

5. Damages. Damages are no problem. Tiny, we are told, was injured.

This is probably as tough an issue as you will get—and we have yet to discuss how to write out an answer to this! We will go over the writing of the exam in depth in the coming chapters. Right now, it is sufficient that you understand how to categorize the issues—and how the issue that we just covered is the most difficult one to categorize.

---

[32] The test that I have given here for proximate cause is the Restatement test, a hindsight approach. There also is a foreseeability test. I have chosen to not discuss this test. Yet again, I state what I have stated earlier: my purpose is to teach exam writing here and not substantive law.

One final and important point: If it is clear that causation does not exist under the "but for" test, why would we even bother to be prepared to discuss it on the exam? The answer will be found in the discussion of our last type of issue.

"NON-ISSUE" ISSUE

In this type of "issue," you really do not have an issue! Some professors use this as a testing tool, however, so I cover it here.

Non-Issue Issue: Overview

What happens in this last type of issue is this: One or more elements of the rule absolutely cannot exist on the facts given. The following diagram will illustrate this:

Non-Issue Issue: Diagram

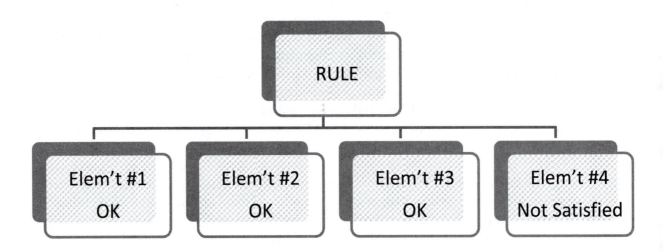

Non-Issue Issue: Explanation

For example, we might have all of the elements to common law burglary satisfied—except one element. With respect to that one element, the facts are clear: it was daytime—high noon with the sun shining. As such, there cannot be common law burglary. It is a non-issue issue. Yet some professors will want to know why there is no burglary because we are "real close" to finding one. Others do not want to know: as the saying goes, "close counts only in horseshoes." If you are in doubt with respect to what your professor wants,[33] ask your professor. If your professor is one

---

[33] For whatever it is worth, I do not test on non-issue issues.

who wants a discussion of such a "non-issue" issue, simply categorize the issue as we have discussed: identify the issue, state the rule, and for the element that does not exist, mark that element accordingly in the margin of the question sheet (for example, "NO NIGHTTIME").

We have now finished our discussion of the five categories of issues. Having done so, you should not be concerned with memorizing the names of the five categories. Indeed, I suspect that we could come up with still another category if we thought hard enough! (Moreover, ultimately, you may well conclude that there are only three types of issues: analysis, rule/counter-rule, and non-issue issues.) What you *should* be concerned with is *understanding* why we have spent so much time on categorizing. The reason that we have spent so much time on categorizing is because you must know whether you are being tested on a rule or an element of a rule. Why is that so critical? Let us now find out why.

WHY CATEGORIZE: KNOWING WHEN TO ANALYZE

Why is it not enough to just "spot the issues"? The reason that you must also categorize is this: Unless you categorize, you will not know *when* to analyze a given issue. You see, one of the great problems that students have on law school essay exams is analysis.[34] What many students do not understand is that *not every issue is an analysis issue*. Consequently, if you try to "analyze" every issue, you will be spinning your wheels.

How then do you know when to "analyze" an issue? You analyze an issue if you have an analysis issue (e.g., simple analysis) and you do not analyze if you do not have an analysis issue (e.g., a rule/counter-rule issue).

Recall that we discussed five types of issues. Those issues that are simple analysis issues, complex analysis issues, or combination issues will be "analyzed." The rule/counter-rule issues will not be "analyzed." Indeed, you cannot analyze rule/counter-rule issues. For these issues (rule/counter-rule) you just do an "application." What the difference is, you will see in the coming chapters.

SUMMARY OF CHAPTER 11

To recap this chapter, this is how you read and categorize a question: (1) Isolate the key facts to determine which issue is being tested. (2) After you spot an issue, state the rule of law applicable to that issue to yourself. (3) After you state the rule, ask yourself—*Are all elements absolutely and clearly satisfied on the facts given?* If an element has just one definition and, based on that definition, it can go either way on the facts given—it is just not clear—you have an analysis issue. If all of the elements are absolutely and clearly satisfied on the facts given, you have a rule/counter-rule issue. Do this for each issue. Also be alert for "combination issues." Depending upon your professor's preferences, you might also have a "non-issue" issue. We are almost ready to begin the actual writing of the exam. Before we do, however, we must cover how to prepare a "scratch" outline

---

[34] We have yet to define analysis. In subsequent chapters, we shall spend much time discussing what analysis is—and what it is not.

barbri®

CHAPTER 12
PREPARING A "SCRATCH" OUTLINE

You have read the question, annotated the question sheet, and identified all of the issues.[1] You also have categorized all of the issues.[2] In this chapter, we shall discuss the final step that you will need to take before you actually begin writing your exam—preparing a "scratch" outline.[3]

COURSE OUTLINES V. SCRATCH OUTLINES

A scratch outline is different from a course outline, which we previously covered in Chapter 6, "Preparing a Course Outline." A course outline synthesizes the cases, class notes, etc. A scratch outline has an entirely different purpose: it organizes your thoughts in preparation for your writing the answer to the examination.

NEED FOR A COURSE OUTLINE

Is it important for you to prepare a scratch outline? Yes. Indeed, it is very important. If you do not first outline your answer, you will find that your essay is not well organized. You will also find that if you do not first outline your answer, you can easily omit an issue. It is, you see, very easy to forget to include an issue while you are furiously writing an answer. Is it difficult to prepare a scratch outline? It is not hard at all. In fact, whether you know it or not, you have already done most of the work when you annotated the question sheet, indicating the issues and elements in dispute.[4]

COMPONENTS OF A SCRATCH OUTLINE

Let us now discuss what your scratch outline should contain. You may be surprised at how short it will be.

Parties

If the entire question deals with one party suing another, you do not need to list the parties: You know, very clearly, who is suing whom. For example, assume that you are answering a property question that deals with the law of landlord-tenant. Assume further that the question states: "Discuss the rights that the tenant has against the landlord." In such case, you know who the parties are (tenant v. landlord). Likewise, assume that you have a criminal law question. Assume further that there is only one defendant, Dan, in the fact pattern. Assume further that the question states: "Discuss the crimes for which Dan may be prosecuted." You clearly know the parties (State v. Dan). In such hypos, there is little chance that you will become confused with

---

[1] See Chapter 10, "Reading a Law School Essay Examination Question."
[2] See Chapter 11, "Categorizing the Issues."
[3] We use the term "scratch outline" to mean the brief outline that you jot down on scratch paper during a final exam to assist you in organizing your thoughts in writing the exam. We use the term to differentiate it clearly from the "course outline," which is used to synthesize an entire course.
[4] See footnotes 1 and 2, supra.

respect to the parties. However, where there are multiple parties, you will need to include the parties in your outline. You will need to know who is suing whom to make certain that you do not confuse the parties—and their causes of action. For example, assume that the question you are answering is a torts question. Assume further that Ann can sue Xavier for assault and battery; Baker can sue Yetta for intentional infliction of emotional distress; and Charles can sue Ann and Baker for negligence. In such a fact pattern, one in which there are multiple parties, you will want to include the parties as an integral part of your scratch outline. If you do not, confusion will reign and get the best of you while you are writing your exam: You may end up discussing Charles suing Yetta for negligence!

Issues (and Elements)

Your outline must include the legal issues that you are going to include in your essay. Take comfort in knowing, however, that when you are preparing your outline, you will not have to labor over finding the issues. Why is this? The answer is that you have already identified the issues and jotted them down on the question sheet.[5]

Note, however, that it is not going to be enough to merely identify the issues (e.g., battery) when you have an analysis issue (simple or complex).[6] When you have some type of analysis issue, you also will have to identify the element(s) in dispute. Is this a difficult task? It is not at all. You have previously done this when you jotted down the disputable element(s) on the question sheet.[7] Of course, for a rule/counter-rule issue, because all of the elements are absolutely and clearly satisfied, you do not have to be concerned with which element is in dispute.[8] Moreover, you also have jotted this down on the question sheet by writing "ALL ELEMENTS OK," or "OK," or placing a check-mark (✓) next to the identified issue.[9]

Key Facts

For each simple analysis issue, you will list the appropriate set of key facts next to each issue. For a rule/counter-rule issue, you will do likewise.

However, with respect to a complex analysis issue, you will list the key facts next to *each element* that is in dispute. You will do this because it is common in a complex analysis issue for one set of key facts to trigger disputable element #1 and another set of key facts to trigger disputable element #2. For a combination issue where more than one element is in dispute, also list the key facts next to each element that is in dispute.[10] A question arises, however. Why should you list the key facts at all? Why is it not enough to list just the issues or element(s)?

You should list the key facts next to each issue (for a rule/counter-rule issue or a simple analysis issue) or element (for a complex analysis issue) to make certain that an issue or element is

---

[5] See Chapter 10, "Reading a Law School Essay Examination Question."
[6] See Chapter 11, "Categorizing the Issues."
[7] *Ibid.*
[8] *Ibid.*
[9] *Ibid.*
[10] *Ibid.*

in fact a point that needs to be discussed. Indeed, students often ask, "How do I know if something is really an issue?" The answer is simple: If there are key facts to trigger the issue or element, the issue or element is real and you discuss it in your essay. However, if there are no key facts to trigger an issue or element, then there is no issue or element to discuss.[11] We shall illustrate this shortly in the hypotheticals that follow.

That is it for your scratch outline: the parties (if there are multiple parties), the legal issues (and elements for an analysis issue), and the key facts. Your outline is going to be very basic and to the point.

WHAT YOUR SCRATCH OUTLINE SHOULD NOT CONTAIN

Students often ask me, should we not also include the rules?" "Should we not include "analysis?"[12] The answer to both of these questions is, no. If you include rules and analysis in your scratch outline, you will end up writing your exam twice—once in the outline and once in your computer. You will then surely run out of time.

Keep in mind that you will get your points for what you put down in your computer or, if you handwrite, your blue book. You will not get any points for what goes into your scratch outline. Consequently, you should just list the parties, the legal issues (with the disputable elements for an analysis issue) and the key facts that trigger each legal issue or element. If you limit your outline to these matters, you will have the time to finish writing your answer.

Now you may be saying to yourself, "But I may forget the rule if I wait to state it in my computer or blue book." If this is what you are thinking, please read the next sentence very carefully: If you can remember the rule of law to put it down in your scratch outline, you can remember the rule of law to put it in your computer or blue book. DO NOT WRITE YOUR ESSAY TWICE!

SAMPLE SCRATCH OUTLINES

Let us now look at a few hypos and some sample scratch outlines. Some of the sample outlines will be good. Some will be poor. We shall discuss why the good ones are good and why the poor ones are poor. Preceding each outline is a past hypothetical.[13]

Hypothetical #1

The first outline is for the negligence problem (cause of action and affirmative defense, dealing with negligence and contributory negligence) we discussed in the previous chapter.

---

[11] Cf. the "non-issue" issue, discussed in Chapter 11, "Categorizing the Issues."

[12] We have yet to discuss the meaning of "analysis." See Chapter 14, "Using HIRRAC™ to Answer a Simple Analysis Issue."

[13] So that the student does not have to flip back to the previous chapter to reread the underlying exam hypo, I reproduce the hypos here, again.

Hypothetical #1

[Rule/Counter-Rule Issue: Rule/Exception to the Rule: Negligence/Contributory Negligence]

Lawnco is a business, located in the State of Westmoreland. Lawnco's business is the renting of various kinds of gardening machines and tools. One of the machines that Lawnco rents is an electric lawn-mower, Model L-100. On all such models, there is a safety feature to prevent a certain type of injury to the user. From time to time, the safety feature on the Model L-100 will wear out because of use. Lawnco is aware of this problem but does not regularly inspect each Model L-100 to make sure that the safety feature is in good working order. Nevertheless, when Lawnco does find that a Model L-100 needs a new safety mechanism, Lawnco performs the necessary replacement. Lawnco knows that a worn out safety mechanism can result in injury to the user.

Able comes onto Lawnco's premises to rent a Model L-100. Throughout Lawnco's store, there are numerous signs, in large red print, that state: "ALWAYS READ OPERATING INSTRUCTIONS BEFORE USING ANY EQUIPMENT." Able is quite literate and he saw the signs. In addition, all customers of Lawnco receive a booklet of operating instructions for the machine or tool that the customer rents. Able received such a booklet for the Model L-100, but failed to read the booklet before operating the mower. Consequently, Able then proceeded to use the Model L-100 in a manner not prescribed and was injured.

If the mower had a properly functioning safety feature, Able would not have been injured. Able was not aware that the safety feature was worn out. Further, even without the safety feature, if Able read the operating instructions and used the mower in the manner prescribed, he would not have been injured.

The manufacturer is no longer in existence. You are to assume that the doctrine of strict liability does not apply on these facts in this jurisdiction. You are also to omit any discussion of the Uniform Commercial Code.

The State of Westmoreland does not recognize the doctrine of comparative negligence.

Can Able recover? Discuss.

Sample Scratch Outline #1A : A Good Outline

A v. L: Negligence: Known danger/L failed to inspect

L v. A: Contributory Negligence: Failure to heed signs and read/Improper use of equipment
....

Let us examine why this outline is a good outline. There are two parties and two issues: negligence and contributory negligence. All of the elements are satisfied for each issue (we have a rule/counter-rule issue.) The key facts that trigger negligence are that Lawnco knew of the danger and still failed to inspect. The key facts that trigger the contributory negligence are Able's failure to heed the signs and read the instructions and his improper use of the equipment.

You will notice that the rule of negligence is not written out. Neither is the rule of contributory negligence. Why is this so? Because your outline will not contain full rules of law: We write out exams only once—in your computer or in the blue book.

Now let us look at another outline. This sample is not as good as Sample Scratch Outline #1A. Let us read the sample and then discuss why it is not as good.

Sample Scratch Outline #1B: A Poor Outline

A v. L: Negligence: L failed to inspect

      Plaintiff is owed a duty of care; defendant breaches that duty; the breach was the cause in fact and the proximate cause of the plaintiff's damages.

L v. A: Contributory Negligence: Failure to read/Improper use of equipment

      Conduct on the part of the plaintiff, contributing as a legal cause to the harm he has suffered, which falls below the standard to which he is required to conform for his own protection; under the common law, it is a bar to recovery.

···

      The problem with this outline is that the student has included rules of law. There is no reason to do so.[14] 1f you can remember to write the rule in your outline, you can remember to write it in your computer or blue book—the only place where you get points.

      Now let us look at still another sample outline.

---

[14] There is certainly no reason to include rules of law when you have a rule/counter-rule issue (all of the elements are satisfied). When you have an analysis issue, however, there is a situation where you might want to list all of the elements of the rule. We cover that situation in Sample Scratch Outlines #2B and #3B.

Sample Scratch Outline #lC: A Weak Outline

A v. L: Negligence

L v. A: Contributory Negligence

....

On its face, this outline looks very similar to Sample Scratch Outline #1A. But there is one big difference between Sample Scratch Outline #1A and 1C: The latter has no key facts.

You may be saying to yourself, "What is the big deal with leaving out the key facts?" Remember that there is a reason why you want to include the key facts in your outline: to make certain that you do not write on non-issues. If you do not force yourself to list the key facts, you will run the risk of writing on non-issues. Sample Scratch Outline #1D is a prime illustration of a common occurrence on law school exams.

Sample Scratch Outline #1D: A Self-Made Trap

A v. L: Negligence

               Intentional Infliction of Emotional Distress

L v. A: Contributory Negligence

....

     Students often struggle with whether an issue or element is a point that he or she needs to raise. In Sample Scratch Outline #ID, the student is not certain if intentional infliction of emotional distress is an issue. Still, the answer is clear: Intentional infliction of emotional distress is not an issue. Why is it not an issue? The reason is that there are no key facts to trigger that issue. If there are no key facts to trigger the issue, do not write on it.

     Now let us move from outlining a rule/counter-rule issue to outlining a simple analysis issue. The hypo that we shall use is the burglary issue that we previously studied in chapter 11.

Hypothetical #2

The next hypothetical is the simple analysis problem dealing with the college student and the burglary of his minivan.

Hypothetical #2

[Simple Analysis Issue]

In June 2010, Charles graduated from college with a B.S. degree in accounting. Prior to beginning work in September for an accounting firm, Charles decided to travel across the United States in his 2005 Dodge minivan, seeing small towns and just enjoying himself. Not being financially well off, however, Charles felt he could economize by sleeping in the back of his minivan. In this way, he would not have to pay for a motel room nightly.

While traveling through State X, Charles pulled over from the public highway to catch a few hours of sleep. It was a cool night so Charles rolled up all of the windows of his car. For safety reasons, he also locked all of the doors of his car. By 10:30 PM, with the nighttime stars shining brightly, Charles fell asleep.

An hour later, Dan walked by. Dan saw Charles' wallet lying next to Charles. Being low on funds, Dan decided that it would be easy to take Charles' wallet. Dan then broke the glass nearest Charles with the intent of snatching Charles' wallet; Dan put his hand into the car and succeeded in taking the wallet. Charles' person, however, was not harmed in any way.

Assuming that State X's Penal Code codifies the common law, what crimes, if any, has Dan committed? Discuss.

Sample Scratch Outline #2A: A Good Outline

State v. Dan: Burglary: Dwelling House: Charles Sleeps in Car

....

There is of course a larceny issue, which comes from taking Charles' wallet. Let us, however, focus our attention on the burglary issue. Recall that all of the elements of common law burglary are clearly satisfied except one: dwelling house. The question sheet is annotated, "Burglary: Dwelling House."[15] Consequently, the outline is also, "Burglary: Dwelling House," along with the key facts. By making the outline as clear as it is, the student, when he or she writes the exam, will not have any problem in remembering what the heart of the discussion is with respect to burglary: dwelling house.

Nonetheless, what if the student has a professor who wants each and every element discussed: If an element is clearly satisfied, the professor wants the student to state why it is clearly satisfied.

In such case, the student has two ways of handling the situation. In the first, the student can prepare the outline in the same manner as it is prepared in Sample Scratch Outline #2A, above, and trust to his or her memory that although the major problem in the burglary issue is "dwelling house," the student will also have to address the other elements, albeit in more summary nature.[16] In the second, the student can make a brief notation on the outline to indicate that the other elements, although satisfied, need to be discussed. Sample Scratch Outline #2B illustrates this point.

---

[15] See Chapter 11, "Categorizing the Issues."

[16] We shall discuss how to do this when we cover exam writing, later in these materials.

Sample Scratch Outline #2B : Another Good Outline

State v. Dan: Burglary: Dwelling House: Charles Sleeps in Car

    Elements satisfied:
                Breaking
                Entering
                Nighttime
                Intent to commit felony therein

....

    In this outline, the student clearly lays out all of the elements that he or she must cover: the "big" issue of dwelling house, as well as the "small" issues of breaking, entering, nighttime, and intent to commit a felony.

    Now let us look at an outline which will present grave problems for the student.

Sample Scratch Outline #2C: An Outline with Grave Problems

State v. Dan: Burglary: Charles Sleeps in Car

....

     The problem with this outline is that the student has identified the issue ("burglary") but has not categorized the issue and focused in on the element that is in dispute ("dwelling house"). This is a "cardinal sin." Why is this a major problem? When the student starts to write his or her exam, the student will not consciously know which particular element is in dispute. As a result, the student will probably ramble. Indeed, the student may even believe in the heat of writing the exam that no element is in dispute and answer the entire issue as though it were a rule/counter-rule issue (without any analysis whatsoever). In fact, from the looks of this outline, it appears that all of the elements are absolutely and clearly satisfied. The result: the student will get no credit for "analysis" (which we will cover in the next chapter), and rightfully so, as none would have been done.

     The point that we are making is this: When you have a simple analysis issue, make sure that you focus in with precision on the element that is in dispute. Further, when you have a complex analysis issue, make sure that you focus in on the elements that are in dispute.

Hypothetical #3

This next hypothetical is the complex analysis issue—the adverse possession issue that we covered in chapter 11.

Hypothetical #3

[Complex Analysis Issue]

Oscar owns a 35-unit apartment building. There are a few cracks throughout the building, but nothing that affects a tenant's health and safety. Indeed, the building is quite sound. Oscar does not live on the premises.

In January 1988, Oscar hires Max Smith to manage the apartment house. Max does such a fine job in managing the apartment house that Oscar decides that he, Oscar, can finally take a well-deserved vacation. Oscar tells Max to continue to do the fine job that he, Max, is doing. Oscar then books a one-year cruise on the Queen Elizabeth II and sets sail on July 4, 1989.

In August 1989, Max sends out a letter to all tenants. The letter reads:

Dear Tenant:

Oscar is gone. I am in control here. You are to see me for all problems regarding your apartment. You will make your check payable to "Max Smith."

Sincerely,

Max Smith

Following receipt of the letter from Max, all of the tenants make the rent check out to "Max Smith." Max deposits the checks into his personal checking account, which he just opened.

Several months later, a vacant apartment is repainted by Max and rented out on a month-to-month basis. All other tenants have leases for a term for years for one year.

Meanwhile, Oscar loves traveling so much that he decides to stay overseas for awhile after the cruise ends. In this regard he telephones Max and lets Max know that he, Oscar, will be gone for a few more years. When Oscar asks how everything is going, Max replies, "The building is better now than when you were running it." The two then hang up. They have the same conversation twice for the duration that Oscar is overseas.

In 1999, Oscar decides that he is tired of traveling. He has also run up quite a few debts while overseas. Oscar comes back to the United States and prepares to sell the apartment house to pay off all of his debts.

The jurisdiction within which the apartment building lies provides in its Civil Code: "In any action to recover real property or the possession thereof, the state of mind of the one in possession shall be irrelevant." The Civil Code also provides that "any action to recover the possession of real property must be commenced within seven years from the time that an actual entry was made by the one in possession."

Discuss.

Sample Scratch Outline #3A: A Good Outline

Max v. Oscar: Adverse Possession

     Actual Entry: Letter to tenants, new lease/checks deposited in Max's name/repainting

     Open and Notorious: Letter to tenants, new lease/checks deposited in Max's name/repainting

     Hostile: Conversation with Oscar, checks deposited

....

This is a good outline because the elements, which the student feels that he or she has to discuss, are clearly delineated. Moreover, the key facts, which trigger the elements, also are indicated.[17] Again, if the student has a professor who also wants a discussion of those elements that are not in dispute (e.g., claim of right), the student can either rely on memory to discuss those elements, or make a notation as part of the outline, as is indicated in Sample Scratch Outline #3B.

---

[17] The student has also indicated the parties, although this is not necessary: There is only one set of parties.

Sample Scratch Outline #3B: Another Good Outline

Max v. Oscar: Adverse Possession

Actual Entry: Letter to tenants, new lease, checks deposited in Max's name, repainting

Open and Notorious: Letter to tenants, new lease, checks deposited in Max's name, repainting

Hostile: Conversation with Oscar, checks deposited

Elements satisfied: Continuous, Exclusive, Claim of Right.

....

Here, the student lists all of the elements that he or she will discuss and these elements include not just the questionable elements, but all of them. Again, this is because of the professor's preference.

Hypothetical #4

Now let us outline one more problem: a combination issue. The problem which we shall use is the tort question—the "Christmas tree" problem—which we discussed in the previous chapter.

Hypothetical #4

[Combination Issue: Analysis with Rule/Counter-Rule with Analysis]

The day after Christmas, a group of adults knocked on the door of Yule's home and asked for the discarded Christmas tree that Yule had just placed on his porch for the trash man. Yule reluctantly agreed, although he saw in the street the large pile of similar trees which the group had collected. In addition, Yule had read warnings in the newspaper concerning the danger faced by young neighborhood groups in burning discarded Christmas trees in large piles. He warned them to "be careful." The pile of trees was then dragged by the group to a vacant lot in the neighborhood.

One member of the group, Bob, struck a match and applied it to a corner of the pile. Bob then snapped off a burning branch and lunged toward Tiny, Bob's friend. Tiny was frightened and he dashed into the adjacent street. Tiny was injured when hit by an oncoming car without any fault on the part of the driver.

Discuss the liability of Yule.

Sample Scratch Outline #4A: A Good Outline

Tiny v. Yule: Negligence

Duty: Cardozo Approach: Warnings given; Newspaper account; Reluctant agreement; Bob's lunging

Duty: Andrews Approach: Warnings given; Newspaper account; Reluctant agreement; Bob's lunging

Cause in fact: Substantial Factor Test: Match applied to corner of pile[18]

Proximate cause: Bob's lunging

....

This is a good outline because the elements that are in dispute are clearly laid out along with the key facts. The elements not in dispute are not mentioned (e.g., damages), although, as we have indicated above in Scratch Outlines #2B and #3B, there is nothing wrong with appropriately indicating in the outline those elements that are clearly satisfied. The main point that you should come away with at the conclusion of this chapter is that your outline simply lists the issues in the order that you are going to address them on the exam. As such, make your outline brief: no rules and no analysis.

CHOOSING THE ORDER IN WHICH TO ADDRESS THE ISSUES

One important point: in what order do you list the issues? What if you have a criminal law question and you have five issues: burglary, robbery, murder, voluntary manslaughter, and larceny? Which issue goes first? Which issue goes second? Which one is third? And so on.

Tackle the "Big" Issues First

Some professors will tell you to start with the "big issue" first. If you know what the "big issue" is, then by all means, start with that issue. For example, if you know that one issue is going to be worth 40 percent of an entire question, you should absolutely start with that issue. Unfortunately, during the exam, most students do not know which issue is the "big issue."

Follow Your Teacher's Advice

Assuming that you do not know what the "big issue" is, then you should do what your professor says: Some will tell you to organize your issues by transaction (which is especially true

---

[18] Recall from our discussion in Chapter 11, "Categorizing the Issues," that under the "but for" test, cause in fact is not satisfied here: even without Yule's tree, the fire could have been set. Therefore, cause in fact, using the "but for" test, is not in dispute. However, cause in fact, using the "substantial factor" test, is in dispute. Hence, it is included in the scratch outline.

in contracts questions). Others will tell you to organize your issues by parties. Still others will have different advice. Follow your professors' advice—they are grading your final exam.

That is all fine and good, but what do you do if your professors do not give you any advice, or if they do, you still find yourself "stuck" on the exam? In such case, I have a plan for you to use—an assured plan. The plan is comprised of a basic rule, subject to only one exception.

The Rule to Follow When You Are Stuck

First the rule: If you are not sure of the order for tackling the issues, tackle the issues in the order that you see them in the fact pattern. For example, assume that the first paragraph of the question contains a battery issue, the second paragraph contains an intentional infliction of emotional distress issue, and the third paragraph contains a negligence issue. Would it not make sense if your first issue were battery, your second issue intentional infliction of emotional distress, and your third issue negligence? After all, if your professor thinks that he or she is very clever for making battery the first issue, intentional infliction of emotional distress the second issue, and negligence the third issue, how wrong can you go if you follow suit?

The One Exception to the Rule: Follow the Interrogatories

Now the exception to the rule: Irrespective of the order of the issues in the fact pattern, if the interrogatories at the end of the fact pattern force you to tackle the issues in a different order, follow the order called for by the interrogatories. For example, assume that the order of the issues in the fact pattern is battery, intentional infliction of emotional distress, and negligence. Assume further that there are three interrogatories (questions) at the end of the fact pattern. Assume further that the first interrogatory is, "What rights, if any, does Charles have against Ann and Bill?" Assume further that the only cause of action that Charles has against Ann and Bill is negligence—the issue that appeared in the very *last* paragraph of the fact pattern. Nevertheless, in such case, the first issue that you would discuss is negligence: The issues raised by the interrogatories override the general rule that you discuss the issues in the order that they appear in the fact pattern.

TIMING MATTERS

I make one last point here: Time. How much time should you spend on reading the fact pattern,[19] annotating it, categorizing the issues,[20] and outlining your answer? For a question to be answered in one hour, your reading, annotating, categorizing, and outlining should take no more than twenty minutes (and with practice, you can get it down to fifteen).[21]

Some of your professors—my colleagues—will tell you to spend at least half the time reading, annotating and outlining. I disagree, however. Remember: You will get your points for what you write and download or put in your blue book. You will get no points for what is in your

---

[19] See Chapter 10, "Reading a Law School Essay Examination Question."
[20] See Chapter 11, "Categorizing the Issues."
[21] If you have only one question, to be answered in three hours, extrapolate accordingly.

outline. Further, if you do the things that I have suggested (no rules and no analysis in your outline), you will have ample time to think, annotate, outline, and write.

SUMMARY OF CHAPTER 12

To summarize this chapter: Limit your outline to the parties, the issues, and the key facts. Omit any rules or analyses. When in doubt, tackle the issues in the order that you see them arise in the fact pattern. There is one exception to this rule: if the interrogatories at the end of the question dictate otherwise.

Now let us learn how to write a law school essay exam.

CHAPTER 13
ESSAY WRITING: AN OVERVIEW OF THE "IRAC" (AND HIRRAC™) METHOD

For you to write your exams in a well organized and thoughtful manner, you need to be introduced to the so-called "IRAC" method—and this author's variation of IRAC—HIRRAC™.

AN INTRODUCTION

IRAC stands for ISSUE, RULE, ANALYSIS/APPLICATION,[1] and CONCLUSION. HIRRAC™, this author's version, stands for HEADING, ISSUE, RULE, RULE, ANALYSIS/APPLICATION,[2] and CONCLUSION. You should know, however, that neither HIRRAC™ nor IRAC is a substitute for learning and thinking. Rather, HIRRAC™ (or IRAC) is merely an organizational tool. Using the HIRRAC™ method will allow you to have a tightly knit essay. If you know the law, HIRRAC™ will allow you to demonstrate it.

IRAC BROADLY EXPLAINED

Now let us explain the IRAC method in a very broad manner. Later on in this chapter, we shall explain the HIRRAC™ method, also in a very broad manner. In the chapters that follow, we shall discuss HIRRAC™ in much detail. We will not spend as much time on IRAC, however. This is because, as you will soon see, IRAC is simply inferior to HIRRAC™. Nonetheless, before you can appreciate the attributes of the HIRRAC™ method, you will need to understand the IRAC method.

Let us preliminarily assume that you have identified negligence as one of the issues on your torts exam. You will recall from previous chapters[3] that after you have identified an issue, you will jot it down on the question sheet next to the appropriate set of key facts. Let us assume that you do this and that you have jotted down, "negligence." Thereafter, you determine that all but one of the elements of negligence are absolutely and clearly satisfied. That one element, the element that is in dispute, is damages. You have therefore written "damages" next to "negligence."[4] Now how do you go about writing an answer—in a lawyer-like manner—to this simple analysis issue?[5]

In college, you would probably have started with the history of negligence. Then you would have repeated all of the facts that the professor stated. Then you would have discussed everything that you knew about the law of negligence. That is how you would have done it in

---

[1] Most, if not all, of your professors may use the terms "analysis" and "application" interchangeably. We do not. As you will see in subsequent chapters, when we use the term "analysis" we mean something clearly different from "application."

[2] See footnote 1, supra.

[3] See Chapter 10, "Reading a Law School Essay Examination Question" and Chapter 11, "Categorizing the Issues."

[4] See Chapter 11, "Categorizing the Issues."

[5] See Chapter 11, "Categorizing the Issues," for a discussion of a "simple analysis" issue.

college. That is not how you will do it in law school, however. Let us now see how you will do it in law school—using the IRAC method.

The first thing that you will do is to identify the problem (issue) that you are dealing with: negligence. Second, you will state the doctrine (rule) that is applicable to the problem and which can be used to solve the problem: duty, breach, cause in fact, proximate cause, and damages. Third, you will "analyze" the doctrine that you just stated.[6] Fourth, you will reach a conclusion. Issue. Rule. Analysis. Conclusion. This is IRAC. It is a good method. It is not the best method, however, as you will now learn.

HIRRAC™ BROADLY EXPLAINED

When you use the HIRRAC™ method, you will get an answer that is even more precise and tightly knit. The first thing that you will do in using HIRRAC™ is to write a heading, which will be the legal issue involved. This will give you a proper and clear focus and hit your teacher over the head with your knowledge. (Already, by using a heading to give focus, you see why HIRRAC™ is superior to IRAC.) Next, you will identify the problem, negligence, in a formal manner; this is the issue statement. This is identical to the IRAC method. The next step also is identical to IRAC—you state the doctrine (rule) of negligence: duty, breach, cause in fact, proximate cause, and damages. The third thing that you will do—here is the big difference—is *isolate the element* that is in dispute, and the typical way that you will isolate the element in dispute is by *defining the element*.[7] (This is the second "R" of HIRRAC™.) Next, you will "analyze" the element. Because you know *exactly* what part of the rule you are analyzing, you have a more precise answer using the HIRRAC™ method than if you had used the IRAC method. Lastly, you will reach your conclusion. Heading. Issue. Rule(1). Rule(2). Analysis. Conclusion.

After you HIRRAC™[8] this issue (the damages element of negligence), you will go on and HIRRAC™ each issue on the exam until you finish the exam.[9] Thus, for a one-hour essay, you might HIRRAC™ six or seven issues.

CONVINCING YOU TO USE HIRRAC™

HIRRAC™ makes for a well-structured and flowing answer. It makes sense to use HIRRAC™. In fact, as a lawyer and professor, I do not know any other way of answering a law school exam, writing a brief, or authoring a book (if you pay close attention, even this book is in HIRRAC™ format).

---

[6] We discuss what "analysis" is in the next chapter.

[7] If the element that is in dispute is a term of art, such as "duty," you will always isolate it by defining it. Sometimes, however, the element in dispute will not be a term of art. In such case, you cannot isolate the element by defining it. Rather, you will isolate it simply by telling the professor, "The element in dispute is X." We cover this point in detail in the next chapter.

[8] Because HIRRAC™ is superior to IRAC, we shall henceforth seldom refer to IRAC.

[9] To introduce you to HIRRAC™, we have explained it in a very broad manner with respect to a simple analysis issue. In the chapters that follow, we will explain the HIRRAC™ method in great detail and how it is used in conjunction with a simple analysis issue, a complex analysis issue, a rule/counter-rule issue, and a combination issue.

Still, in the beginning, first year students often resist HIRRAC™. If you are one of these students, I shall now convince you to use HIRRAC™.

If you think that HIRRAC™ does not make sense, how else do you want to answer a law school exam? Do you think that it would make sense if you started first with analysis and then gave a rule of law? If you try this, your answer will simply not make any sense. The same is true if you start first with a conclusion and finish with the issue.

The point that we are making is this: There is no other way of solving any legal problem (which is what a law school exam is all about) except by: identifying the problem, stating the doctrine that may be used to solve the problem, and solving the problem. I guess we can have an acronym, "PDS" (Problem, Doctrine, Solution). A rose by any other name is still HIRRAC™.

Some students feel uncomfortable using HIRRAC™ because it gets to the point quickly. This is quite true. It does. Yet, what is wrong with getting to the point quickly? If you use HIRRAC™, you will not be "messing around." You will be getting to the significant part of the problem and get there fast. That is what good lawyers do.

As beneficial as it is for you to get to the point, the contrary is also true: You will not get good results for "beating around the bush." A "stream of consciousness" approach may have been what the professor wanted in English 101 or Sociology 101. That will not work, however, in law school. Legal writing, which includes essay exam writing, requires precision. (Remember the "ambiguity with precision" dictum we discussed earlier in this text.) The HIRRAC™ method will help you to achieve that precision. It will enable you not only to hit the target; it will allow you to hit the "bull's eye."

FINAL THOUGHTS ON THIS CHAPTER

A few closing thoughts are appropriate before we proceed to the next chapter. First, your professors know the term, "IRAC." However, the term "HIRRAC™" is this author's own terminology. Consequently, your professor, unless he or she reads these materials, may not understand what HIRRAC™ is and how it differs from IRAC.

Second, you may get a professor who will tell you that he or she does not want you to use the IRAC or HIRRAC™ method. What this professor probably means, as we shall illustrate in the next chapter, is that he or she does not want the essay labeled with the words: *issue, rule, analysis,* and *conclusion*. If this is what your professor means, do not be concerned. In the chapters that follow, you will learn how to write using the HIRRAC™ method—but without ever using the terns: *issue, rule, analysis,* and *conclusion*.

However, if your professor sincerely means that he or she does not want you to use IRAC or HIRRAC™, you *must* speak with your professor and find out what he, or she, wants. I personally do not know of any other way of answering a law school exam. In any type of legal writing, we have to identify the issue, state some doctrine or rule, and analyze/apply the rule. If your professor knows of another way, then he or she needs to disclose it.

CHAPTER 14
USING HIRRAC™ TO ANSWER A SIMPLE ANALYSIS ISSUE

We have previously discussed the characteristics of a simple analysis issue.[1] You will recall that in a simple analysis issue, only one element of the rule of law is in dispute; all other elements are absolutely and clearly satisfied on the facts given.

HYPOTHETICAL #1

Hypothetical #1 presents a simple analysis issue. We have previously studied this hypo, the burglary of Charles' minivan.[2] For purposes of review, we reproduce the diagram as well as a good scratch outline, which we also discussed in a previous chapter.[3] We also do this to give you a feel for the entire flow that you would experience in an actual exam.[4]

---

[1] See Chapter 11, "Categorizing the Issues."

[2] *Ibid.*

[3] See Chapter 12, "Preparing a 'Scratch' Outline."

[4] Keep in mind that we are addressing only one issue in the hypothetical. On the actual exam, you would have to address six or seven issues in one hour. Entire exams are covered in Chapter 19, "Sample Exams."

Hypothetical #1

[Simple Analysis Issue]

In June 2010, Charles graduated from college with a B.S. degree in accounting. Prior to beginning work in September for an accounting firm, Charles decided to travel across the United States in his 2005 Dodge minivan, seeing small towns and just enjoying himself. Not being financially well off, however, Charles felt he could economize by sleeping in the back of his minivan. In this way, he would not have to pay for a motel room nightly.

While traveling through State X, Charles pulled over from the public highway to catch a few hours of sleep. It was a cool night so Charles rolled up all of the windows of his car. For safety reasons, he also locked all of the doors of his car. By 10:30 PM, with the nighttime stars shining brightly, Charles fell asleep.

An hour later, Dan walked by. Dan saw Charles' wallet lying next to Charles. Being low on funds, Dan decided that it would be easy to take Charles' wallet. Dan then broke the glass nearest Charles with the intent of snatching Charles' wallet; Dan put his hand into the car and succeeded in taking the wallet. Charles' person, however, was not harmed in any way.

Assuming that State X's Penal Code codifies the common law, what crimes, if any, has Dan committed? Discuss.

Diagram

Sample Scratch Outline #1

State v. Dan: Burglary: Dwelling House: Charles Sleeps in Car

....

Common law burglary is the issue. The rule of law for burglary is: a breaking and entering of the dwelling house of another in the nighttime with the intent to commit a felony therein. The only element that is in dispute (the element can "go either way") is, "dwelling house." On the facts given, it is not clear if the car is a dwelling house (a place of human habitation). How are we going to write a lawyer-like answer for this issue? We will use the HIRRAC™ method.

This is what we are going to do: First, we will identify the problem via a heading and issue statement—the issue. Second, we will state the rule of law that is applicable to the problem—the rule. Third, we will isolate the element in dispute by defining it—the second rule. Fourth, we will discuss whether the element in dispute exists on the facts given—analysis. Finally, we shall reach a resolution—the conclusion. H-I-R-R-A-C. HIRRAC™.

Sample Exam Answer #1A: A Great Answer

Sample Exam Answer #1A is a great answer. It is in HIRRAC™ format. Let us carefully read it. Then we shall discuss why it is a great answer.

Sample Exam Answer #1A

<u>State v. Dan: Burglary: Dwelling House</u>
Can the State convict Dan of burglary on the ground that the car was a dwelling house because Charles was sleeping in it while on his trip?

A burglary is the breaking and entering of the dwelling house of another in the nighttime with the intent to commit a felony therein. A dwelling house is a place of human habitation.

Although Dan broke into Charles' car while Charles was sleeping in it, the car would not qualify as a dwelling house because a car is typically not thought of as being something used for habitation; it is used for travel. Moreover, even though Charles was sleeping in the car at the time, this should not make a car a dwelling because every time a person would take a nap in his car, that would transform the car into a dwelling, not the intent of the common law, which was to protect a person in his home. Finally, sleeping in a car even for a few months should not change the characterization of the car because Charles still used it for travel around the country; he did not use it exclusively as a place to sleep, wash, and entertain, as homes are typically used.

On the other hand, although he used the car for travel, it should be deemed a house because it was also used as a place for sleeping, a characteristic of a place for human habitation. Indeed, when Dan broke into the car, it was stationary with Charles sleeping in it. As such, the car took on more of the characteristics of a home than a car. Additionally, even though the car went from being a car to a dwelling for the two months that Charles was on the road and then back again to a car, this is no different than a structure that is used as a store, then transformed into a residential apartment for two months, and then back to a store again upon the tenant vacating the premises. The focus should be on the time that humans use it for habitation-like purposes.

Therefore, the car was a dwelling house.

<u>Breaking</u>
A breaking is the creation of a breach, which Dan accomplished when he "broke the glass" window of the car.

<u>Entering</u>
An entry exists if any part of the defendant intrudes; this existed when Dan put his hand through the window.

<u>Nighttime</u>
It was nighttime, the period between sunset and sunrise, since it took place at 11:30 PM.

<u>Intent to Commit Felony</u>
The intent to commit a felony element is met because Dan intended to take the wallet before he broke the window and, under common law, all larceny was a felony.

Therefore, Dan committed a burglary.

Sample Exam Answer #1A: Dissecting the Answer

Let us now examine why this is a great answer.

1. *Heading.* We start with the "H" of HIRRAC™. The first thing that the professor sees while reading this answer is a heading. The heading has the parties, broad legal issue (burglary), and the precise element that is in dispute (dwelling house). This gives the professor a focus. Right from the start, the professor knows what he or she is going to read. It serves as a roadmap for the professor. Importantly, the heading gives the student a focus, too. The student clearly knows that all that he or she is going to write on at this point is the dwelling house element.

2. *Issue Statement.* We next go to the "I" of HIRRAC™, the issue. You will notice that the issue statement ("Can the State convict Dan of burglary on the ground that the car was a dwelling house because Charles was regularly sleeping in it while on his trip?") is composed of four parts. First, it contains the parties (State and Dan). Second, it has the legal issue (burglary). Third, it contains the element of burglary that is in dispute (dwelling house). Fourth, it has the key facts that are triggering this element (Charles slept in his car). It is not coincidental that the issue statement comes directly from the scratch outline. You, therefore, see how critical the scratch outline is. It will not only organize your thoughts; it will also allow you effortlessly to state the issue.

Why do you want to include these four parts (parties; legal issue; element in dispute; and key facts) in your issue statement? There are a number of reasons. (1) As you proceed to write your answer using the HIRRAC™ format, you will consciously be aware of what is the so-called big picture: burglary. (2) You will also be aware of the particular problem—the element—that you will have to discuss with precision-like manner: dwelling house. (3) By framing the issue with great precision, you will be able to write and "analyze" with great precision, a trademark of all good law students and lawyers. (4) Your professor will know immediately what you are discussing and not have to wonder what you are going to discuss. In effect, you will have given your professor a blueprint.

3. *Rule.* Now let us discuss the next section of HIRRAC™, the first "R." This is our rule of law. If the issue is negligence, the applicable rule will be the rule of negligence. If the issue is "X", the applicable rule will be the rule of "X." If the issue is burglary, the applicable rule will be the rule of burglary: the breaking and entering of the dwelling house of another in the nighttime with the intent to commit a felony therein.

4. *Second Rule.* We shall now discuss the next section of HIRRAC™, the second "R." What we are going to do here is isolate the element that is in dispute. The element that is in dispute (it could go "either way") is "dwelling house." How do you isolate this element? Whenever you have an element in dispute, and that element is a term of art (it has a particular meaning in law), the best way of isolating that element is to define it. Hence, "a dwelling house is a place of human habitation." In this way, both you and your professor know exactly what the real problem is—whether the car is a dwelling house. Let us spend a few moments discussing why this is the real problem.

Let us suppose that you were the defense attorney representing Dan on appeal. What would you emphasize in your brief? Would you devote most of the pages in your brief to arguing that the act took place during "daylight" hours? Of course, you would not. The facts state that it was nighttime. As an attorney, you must represent your client with zeal, but you cannot change the facts. Similarly, would you contend that what Dan did, did not constitute a "breaking and entering?" No. In whatever jurisdiction you are in, Dan did "break and enter." The same is true for all of the other elements. How then is Dan's attorney going to proceed?

Dan's counsel is going to do his or her best to convince the court that the prosecution's case fails, because whatever Dan did, it was not a burglary because a car is not a dwelling house.

Likewise, if you were the state's attorney, what are you going to spend most of your time on? The answer is the "dwelling house" problem: All of the other elements of the crime are clearly established.

One last point on the second "R" of HIRRAC™: What do you do if the element that is in dispute is *not* a term of art? If it were not a term of art, it would be silly to define it. Consequently, when the disputable element is not a term of art, you will isolate it by simply stating: "The element that is in dispute is [state the element]." This sentence, in such case, will be your second "R" of the HIRRAC™. As a practical matter, most of the elements that you will have to isolate will be terms of art. Still, just in case you get an element that is not a term of art, you now know how to proceed.

5. *Analysis.* We will now discuss the "A" of HIRRAC™—analysis. Many students do not understand analysis. Indeed, if I were to ask you to define it, I know that the overwhelming majority of students would not have an easy time of it—and through no fault of your own. Students hear professors use the word "analysis" all the time. Seldom, however, do professors define "analysis." This, by itself, accounts for much of the confusion.

In any event, there is still another reason why students get confused: Professors also use the term "analysis" within the context of discussing the material from the casebook. For example, at the beginning of a torts class, your professor might say, "Let us now analyze the case of *Li v. Yellow Cab* on page 325 of the casebook." As a result, students reasonably think that analysis of a case is the same as the analysis of an issue on a final exam.[5]

Importantly, "case analysis" and "exam analysis" are not the same. Indeed, they have different meanings. However, unless you know that "case analysis" is different from "exam analysis," you will end up with disastrous results on your examinations.

Let us first discuss the meaning of "case analysis." Then we shall discuss the meaning of "exam analysis." When we finish the discussion, you will clearly see the differences—and you will never have trouble with "analysis" again.

Although you did not know it at the time, we covered "case analysis" in Chapter 7, "I Don't Understand What's Going On in Class." You may recall from chapter 7 that professors will

---

[5] That is why in my classroom and in this text, I limit the term, "analysis," to the context of essay writing, unless I qualify it as, "case analysis." See below.

often lead the class in a discussion to determine whether a case is "correct" from a moral, economic, or internal perspective. This is case analysis. When we "analyze" a case, we are examining the case to see if the case makes sense from a number of different positions. Now that you know what "case analysis" is, let us proceed to discuss "exam analysis."

Once you have identified the element that is in dispute and defined it (if it is a term of art), you take the key facts that you are given and add to the key facts a creative argument for proving that the element exists. What is a creative argument? It is an argument that comes from your own head. You cannot find it on the four corners of the question sheet. In short, it is something that is creative and original. The argument that you make may be based on logic, economic policy, social policy, etc. It also may be based on precedent. For example, if you covered an important case in class (not just "any" case but, for example, a United States Supreme Court case), you may wish to argue that the case covered in class (*A v. B*) should be applied to the hypo (*and* why it should not be, as discussed in the paragraph immediately below). But be warned: the key facts in *A v. B* will almost certainly not be on "all fours" (identical) to the facts in the exam hypo. Thus, even here you will have to make a bridge between *A v. B* and the exam hypo. How will you make that bridge? You will make it by creative argument: logic, social policy, economic policy, etc.

Immediately after you argue that the element exists, you make an argument for "the other side." You take the key facts that you are given (which may be the same or different key facts) and add to the key facts a different creative argument to prove that the element does *not* exist.[6]

This is "exam analysis."[7]

Because law—and law school exam writing—is both art and a science,[8] you may find the following "scientific formula" helpful in understanding what analysis is:

KEY FACTS GIVEN + CREATIVE ARGUMENT = DISPUTABLE ELEMENT DOES EXIST

AND[9]

KEY FACTS GIVEN + DIFFERENT CREATIVE ARGUMENT = DISPUTABLE ELEMENT DOES NOT EXIST

The diagrams on the next two pages will illustrate what we have just discussed. It is not anything new; it is merely presented in diagram format (different people learn differently). The first diagram illustrates analysis. The second diagram illustrates creative argument.

---

[6] Of course, it does not matter if you want to reverse the order—first prove that the element does not exist and then prove that it does exist. We shall spend more time on this point later in this chapter.

[7] For the balance of these materials, unless otherwise stated, the term "analysis" will mean "exam analysis."

[8] This is the "ambiguity with precision" we discussed in Chapter 3, "More on Cases: The Importance of Facts (and How They Trigger the Legal Issues.")

[9] The "AND" here is very important: Each time you do an analysis, you must argue both sides, i.e., why the element exists *and* why the element does not exist on the facts given.

Diagram: Exam Analysis

Diagram: Creative Argument

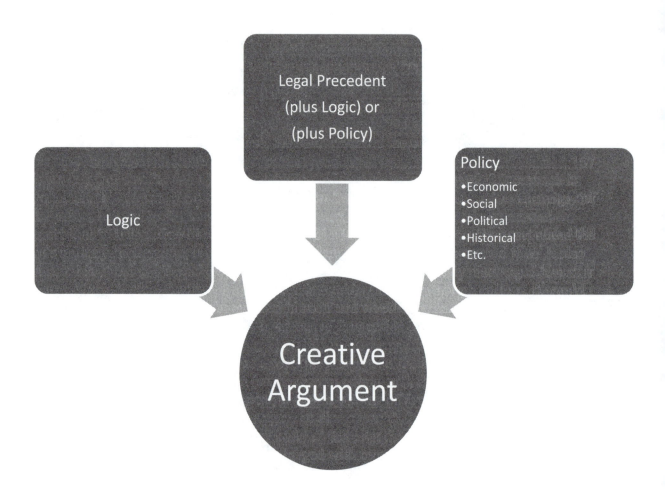

Let us now discuss the "analysis" of Sample Exam Answer #1A.

The pivotal problem is whether the car is a dwelling house for purposes of burglary. After we define what a dwelling house is, we must take the key facts that we are given, and build on to those facts a creative argument (something original) to establish that the car was not a dwelling—that the element does not exist. Immediately after doing this, we must again take the key facts that we are given, and build on to those facts another creative argument to establish that the car was a dwelling—that the element does exist.[10]

We start with the key facts that are given: "Dan broke into Charles' car while Charles was sleeping in it." We must then build onto those facts a creative argument to establish that the car was not a dwelling.[11]

On these facts, why was the car not a dwelling? There are several *reasons* (your *reasons* are the heart of your analysis; more about this three paragraphs down): (a) One typically thinks of a car as something for traveling in, not living in. (b) Just because Charles did sleep in it, that should not transform it into a "dwelling." To say that sleeping transforms a car into a dwelling means that every time someone takes a nap in a car, the car then becomes a house—a result that the law could not have intended since the purpose of the common law rule was to protect people in their homes. (c) Charles did not use the car exclusively as a place to sleep, wash, entertain—characteristics of a home or dwelling.

Now let us explore the reasons why, on the facts given, the car is a dwelling: (a) The car was used to sleep in and so it takes on the characteristics of a home. (b) It does not matter that sometimes it was used as a means of travel while at other times it was used as a place of habitation. This is no different than a structure that is used as a store, then transformed into a residential apartment for two months before reverting back to being used as store again upon the tenant's vacating the premises; the focus is on the time that it is used for habitation-like purposes.

What we have stated in the two preceding paragraphs is the analysis in Sample Exam Answer #1A: it takes the key facts and uses those facts to create an argument (1) why the car is not a dwelling and, alternatively, (2) why the car is a dwelling.

Put another way (we are really saying the same thing that we have said in the paragraphs above), analysis represents your *reasons* why the element exists and does not exist—your original reasons.

Let us focus for a moment on this last point—"Your original reasons." A number of you are probably saying to yourselves, "I can think of two additional reasons why the car is not a dwelling." If so, that is great! That is what makes law school exams so challenging and, in some respects, enjoyable. Ten people can each come up with ten different reasons why the car is not a dwelling—and all ten can get a final grade of "A." Why is this? The reason is simple: There is no one absolute final answer to this question. The issue raised in Hypothetical #1 (or any simple analysis issue for that matter) is what I call an "open-ended" question. There is no one definitive

---

[10] See footnote 6, supra.
[11] See footnote 6, supra.

answer to the question of whether the car is a dwelling. There are perhaps many answers—and this is what first year students have such a hard time understanding. (Again, this is the ambiguity with precision that we discussed in chapter 3.)

So there you have it. You now know what "analysis" is.[12] To repeat, analysis is your *reasons* why a particular element exists/does not exist.

Here is a test that you can give yourself to see if you have actually performed an analysis: After you have performed what you think is an analysis, ask yourself the question, "Why?" If you think you have performed an analysis and you can intelligently ask this question, "Why?" then you have not performed an analysis. On the other hand, after you have performed a true analysis, you will not be able to ask yourself this question, "Why?" intelligently. To help you answer the question "why," and if you want to virtually assure yourself that you are doing an analysis (giving your reasons), work in the word, "because" after the key facts. If you use the word "because," you force yourself to follow up with reasons. If you take a close look at Sample Exam Answer #1A, you will see the word "because" sprinkled throughout.

Let us now illustrate this test. Look at the analysis in Sample Exam Answer #1A. In the paragraph that deals with why the car is not a dwelling, ask yourself the question, "Why?" If you do, the question, "Why?" will not make any sense. This is because the question is fully answered. You can do the same with the paragraph that deals with why the car was a dwelling.

Later in this chapter, we shall examine essays that purport to contain analysis. However, when we will ask, "Why?" the question will make absolute sense. That is because no analysis exists.

We need to discuss one last point on analysis. Many students are needlessly concerned about which part of the analysis goes first: the "winning side" or the "losing side." You should not be concerned about this. It does not make any substantial difference which side goes first because there is no winning side, per se. Because the element is in dispute, it is not certain who would prevail. While you will have to reach a conclusion (a discussion of which follows), that is not significant, as you will soon come to understand.

Nevertheless, I do offer a suggestion with respect to which side should go first: The side that you think is the "weaker side" is the side with which you should begin. The reason that I suggest that you begin with the "weaker side" is for purposes of closure: You will state the argument for the "weaker side," then you will state the argument for the "stronger side," and then you will conclude with the "stronger side." It flows nicely.

On the other hand, if you start with the stronger side (why the element exists), then go to the weaker side (why the element does not exist), and then conclude on the stronger side (the element exists), your analysis may be technically correct but it will not flow well for purposes of closure.

---

[12] Later on in this chapter, we shall explore what analysis is *not*.

borbri

To illustrate this point, just reverse the two paragraphs of analysis in Sample Exam Answer #1A. If you do, you will see that the analysis, in conjunction with the conclusion ("Therefore the car was a dwelling house") will not flow.

6. *Conclusion.* We are now about to conclude the discussion on the element that we have analyzed: "Therefore, the car was a dwelling house." It is short and to the point. Brevity often troubles many first year students. After all, should not the conclusion be a little longer? Should it not state reasons for why the car is a dwelling? The answer to these questions is, no.

You will recall that your "reasons" make up your "analysis." If your reasons were stated in the analysis section, there is no need to repeat yourself in the conclusion. Indeed, you will not get additional points for discussing the same point twice. However, if you did not give your reasons with your "analysis" (where your reasons belong), you will lose points. Reasons belong in your "analysis," not in your "conclusion."

To summarize, your conclusion is just that: an ending. It lets your professor know that one thought is finished. That is its only purpose.

7. *Rule Mop-Up.* This is not technically part of HIRRAC™. That is because your professor may not require it. Let us explain the meaning of this "rule mop-up."[13]

We have determined that the only element that was in dispute in Hypothetical #1 was "dwelling house." The rule mop-up summarily disposes of those elements of the rule that are not in dispute because they are absolutely and clearly satisfied. In the rule mop-up, we are letting the professor know that the elements remaining are clearly satisfied on the facts given in summary format.

How do we let the professor know that the remaining elements are clearly satisfied? For each such element, we first identify the element by using a heading (you will note that we do not have a formal issue statement). Then we define it if it is a term of art. Then we match definition, to the facts to let the professor know that the element is clearly satisfied.[14]

By way of illustration, let us look at the "breaking" element. We identified the element ("A breaking"). We defined it ("is the creation of a breach"). We matched up the definition to the facts to let the professor know that the element is clearly satisfied on the facts given ("which Dan accomplished when he broke the glass window of the car"). You will notice that there is no analysis here because the breaking element is not disputable. Nor is there anything creative about our use of the facts. We are just letting the professor know what a breaking is and that it clearly exists on the facts given.

After we do this with the breaking element, we do the same with the other elements.

Will you always have a rule mop-up? The answer all depends upon your professor. Most professors will want you to discuss all elements of a rule, even those absolutely satisfied (i.e., they

---

[13] This is a term created by the author of this material.
[14] It sounds a little like HIRRAC™, does it not?

want a rule mop-up). On the other hand, I am in a minority on this. I tell my students that for my exams they do not need a rule mop-up: For an analysis issue, I only want discussed those elements that are in dispute. If your professor wants a rule mop-up, you now know how to handle those elements. (Remember that the term "rule mop-up" is my own terminology. If you are not sure if your professor wants a rule mop-up, ask the professor whether you need to discuss those elements that are absolutely and clearly satisfied.)

Finally, we have an overall conclusion: There was a burglary.

Because this is really just one issue of an examination (you might have four or five or six more to go), you would then continue to HIRRAC™ the remaining issues.[15]

Sample Exam Answer #1A: Observations

We have gone through HIRRAC™ in some depth. At this point, it will be helpful to make some observations about the format of Sample Exam Answer #1A.

Observation #1: The answer is in an HIRRAC™ format without stating it is in an HIRRAC™ format. You will notice that this answer is clearly in HIRRAC™ format. Yet, we do not once use the word "issue," "rule," "analysis" or "conclusion." Some students (not those who get the "A") will state: "The issue here is. . . . The rule of law is . . . . The analysis for the plaintiff is . . . ." Do not do this. Never do this!

Observation #2: The style is simple but correct and to the point. You do not have to write in a "flowery" style. This is not English 101. Being a good legal writer requires only that you be able to string together a subject, noun and verb.

Observation #3: Paragraphs are used regularly. For each part of the HIRRAC™ formulation, there is a separate paragraph. Thus, after the heading, the first paragraph contains the issue statement. The next paragraph contains the two rules of law. The next paragraph is the analysis for one side. The next paragraph is the analysis for the other side, etc. There is a lesson in this: paragraph regularly. If you do, it will be easy for your professor to read. Remember, you will want to make your professor's life easy—the professor is grading your exam. That is just common sense.

Observation #4: There is no underlining. Underlining is used to give emphasis. However, with the exception of the heading, there is no underlining in this answer. The reason is that every word in this answer is important. Consequently, there is nothing to emphasize. You should strive to train yourself to write so that every word is important. When you write, do not include

---

[15] You may be thinking that if Sample Exam Answer #1A is just one issue, you will never finish in time. To that, let me respond: I did not write this answer under any time constraints and I have been doing this for many years. I am using it for teaching purposes; your exam answer will necessarily not be as good. This is not because I am smarter than you are. It is only because, and I repeat this because it is important, I have been doing this for many years—and am not working with a time limit. To summarize, practice and experience is important. Do not be too hard on yourself. Indeed, it will surprise you how relatively "easy" it is to get an "A" on your exam if you follow the tips and guidelines in this text.

surplusage. Again, practice makes perfect. Nevertheless, some good students like to underline certain important words. Used sparingly (and I mean sparingly!), underlining can allow the professor to follow you more easily. If you wish to underline for this purpose, remember to underline sparingly. If you underline every other word, you will defeat your purpose. That said, Sample Exam Answer #1A has no underlining (again, except for the headings).

Observation #5: The use of policy can come into play in analysis. You will notice that policy is part of the analysis for "Dan's side": a car is not a dwelling.

> Moreover, even though Charles was sleeping in the car at the time, this should not make a car a dwelling because every time a person would take a nap in his car that would transform the car into a dwelling, not the intent of the common law, which was to protect a person in his home.

You may recall that policy can influence the rule that a court adopts or the definition that a court gives to an element of a rule.[16] Professors do not typically test on policy per se on an exam. Nevertheless, you see from Sample Exam Answer #1A that policy may be used as part of our analysis: It is a reason why the element ("dwelling house") does not exist in this case.

Observation #6: Transitional words are used in the analysis. You will notice that when we change sides in the analysis we have a nice flow. How do we get that flow? We use a transitional phrase: "on the other hand." Some students will state, "The defendant will argue . . ." "The State will argue . . . ." If you do this throughout your exam, the reader (your professor) will get bored and annoyed. You, therefore, should use transitional words. Each time you have an analysis issue and you want to let the professor know that you are "switching sides," use transitional words to lead into the other side's argument. Use words such as: alternatively; in the alternative; nevertheless; however; nonetheless; regardless; yet; notwithstanding. And remember to never state, "The Defendant will argue…." It is not necessary. Just state the argument without prefacing it with those trite words.

Observation #7: Key facts are the foundation of analysis. Key facts create the parties' legal dispute. We saw that in our earlier discussion of cases.[17] We have also seen that key facts create the parties' legal dispute in the exam scenario. But key facts also serve another purpose: they are the foundation for your analysis. Although the heart of the analysis is your creative argument, the analysis cannot exist without facts to support the argument. Consequently, the same facts which are part of your issue statement (Charles sleeping in his car), will also become the foundation for your analysis.

Now do you understand why we earlier spent so much time on key facts?[18] It was to teach you the importance of key facts since without understanding what key facts are, you would not be able to formulate an issue statement—or perform an analysis.

---

[16] See Chapter 5, "Case Briefing: What to Do—And What Not to Do." See also Chapter 7, "I Don't Understand What's Going on in Class."

[17] See Chapter 3, "More on Cases: The Importance of Facts."

[18] See, for example, Chapter 3, "More on Cases: The Importance of Facts."

Now let us examine some variations of Sample Answer #1A.

Sample Exam Answer #1B: Good but not Great

This answer is good, but not as good as Answer #1A. The reason will be obvious when you see it.

Sample Exam Answer #1B

Can the State convict Dan of burglary on the ground that the car was a dwelling house because Charles was sleeping in it while on his trip?

A burglary is the breaking and entering of the dwelling house of another in the nighttime with the intent to commit a felony therein. A dwelling house is a place of human habitation.

Although Dan broke into Charles' car while Charles was sleeping in it, the car would not qualify as a dwelling house because a car is typically not thought of as being something used for habitation; it is used for travel. Moreover, even though Charles was sleeping in the car at the time, this should not make a car a dwelling because every time a person would take a nap in his car, that would transform the car into a dwelling, not the intent of the common law, which was to protect a person in his home. Finally, sleeping in a car even for a few months should not change the characterization of the car because Charles still used it for travel around the country; he did not use it exclusively as a place to sleep, wash, and entertain, as homes are typically used.

On the other hand, although he used the car for travel, it should be deemed a house because it was also used as a place for sleeping, a characteristic of a place for human habitation. Indeed, when Dan broke into the car, it was stationary with Charles sleeping in it. As such, the car took on more of the characteristics of a home than a car. Additionally, even though the car went from being a car to a dwelling for the two months that Charles was on the road and then back again to a car, this is no different than a structure that is used as a store, then transformed into a residential apartment for two months, and then back to a store again upon the tenant vacating the premises. The focus should be on the time that humans use it for habitation-like purposes.

Therefore, the car was a dwelling house.

A breaking is the creation of a breach, which Dan accomplished when he "broke the glass" window of the car.

An entry exists if any part of the defendant intrudes; this existed when Dan put his hand through the window.

It was nighttime, the period between sunset and sunrise, since it took place at 11:30 PM.

The intent to commit a felony element is met because Dan intended to take the wallet before he broke the window and, under common law, all larceny was a felony.

Therefore, Dan committed a burglary.

Sample Exam Answer #1B: Dissecting the Answer

You will notice that Sample Exam Answer #1B is identical to Answer #1A, but with one difference: Answer #1B has no headings. Thus, we can say that while the student used "IRRAC," the student did not use HIRRAC™. Which would you rather read? You can clearly see that when a student does not use headings, the job of reading the essay is necessarily harder. Do not make your professor's job harder! Use headings!

Sample Exam Answer #1C: Another Good Answer

Now let us look at Sample Exam #1C. It also uses a heading, although it is in an abbreviated format. In all other respects, Sample Exam Answer #1C is identical to Answer #1A.

Sample Exam Answer #1C

<u>State v. Dan: Burglary</u>

Can the State convict Dan of burglary on the ground that the car was a dwelling house because Charles was regularly sleeping in it while on his trip?

* * *

………………………………………………………………………………………………......

Sample Exam Answer #1C: Dissecting the Answer

This answer omits "Dwelling House" from the heading. In all other respects, it is identical to Sample Exam Answer #1A. The reason that we include Sample Exam Answer #1C is to show you that there is no *single* way to write a good exam. There are a number of ways. However, all good exams will in some way or another state the issues, the relevant rules and analyze the rules. Whichever way you slice it, all good exams must have these attributes. Everything else is just the wrapping.

Sample Exam Answer #1D: Yet Another Good Answer

Sample Exam Answer #1D is another illustration of the preceding point.

Sample Exam Answer #1D

<u>State v. Dan: Burglary: Dwelling house: Car used for sleeping purposes</u>

A burglary is the breaking and entering of the dwelling house of another in the nighttime with the intent to commit a felony therein. A dwelling house is a place of human habitation.

* * *

....

Sample Exam Answer #1D: Dissecting the Answer

Answer #1D is identical to #1A with one exception: In lieu of a full-blown issue statement, the student uses only a heading, with the key facts in the heading. Again, there are a number of ways to get the job done.

We next continue with another example.

Sample Exam Answer #1E: Another Great Essay (Maybe the Best)

Sample Exam Answer #1E is as great an answer as is Sample Exam Answer #1A. Let us examine it and then dissect the answer, below.

Sample Exam Answer #1E

<u>State v. Dan: Burglary</u>
Is Dan guilty of burglary of Charles' car?

A burglary is the breaking and entering of the dwelling house of another in the nighttime with the intent to commit a felony therein.

Breaking

A breaking is the creation of a breach or opening. This was accomplished when Dan broke the glass window.

Entering

The entry exists if any part of the defendant's body intruded. This element was met when Dan reached into the auto.

Dwelling

The problem is whether a car that is slept in is a dwelling. A dwelling is a place of human habitation.

Although Dan broke into Charles' car while Charles was sleeping in it, the car would not qualify as a dwelling house because a car is typically not thought of as being something used for habitation; it is used for travel. Moreover, even though Charles was sleeping in the car at the time, this should not make a car a dwelling because every time a person would take a nap in his car, that would transform the car into a dwelling, not the intent of the common law, which was to protect a person in his home. Finally, sleeping in a car even for a few months should not change the characterization of the car because Charles still used it for travel around the country; he did not use it exclusively as a place to sleep, wash, and entertain, as homes are typically used.

On the other hand, although he used the car for travel, it should be deemed a house because it was also used as a place for sleeping, a characteristic of a place for human habitation. Indeed, when Dan broke into the car, it was stationary with Charles sleeping in it. As such, the car took on more of the characteristics of a home than a car. Additionally, even though the car went from being a car to a dwelling for the two months that Charles was on the road and then back again to a car, this is no different than a structure that is used as a store, then transformed into a residential apartment for two months and then back to a store again upon the tenant vacating the premises. The focus should be on the time that humans use it for habitation-like purposes.

Therefore, the car was a dwelling house.

Nighttime

It was nighttime, the period between sunset and sunrise, since it took place at 11:30 PM.

Intent to Commit Felony

The intent to commit a felony element is met because Dan intended to take the wallet before he broke the window and, under common law, all larceny was a felony.

Therefore, Dan committed a burglary.

Sample Exam Answer #1E: Dissecting the Answer

You will note that Sample Exam Answer #1E is an excellent answer (as was Sample Exam Answer #1A). Indeed, Answer #1E is substantively the exact same as Answer #1A. The only substantial differences are (1) the initial broadness of the issue statement, (2) the order of the rule mop-up, and (3) the fact that all of the elements are indented to make it clear that all of these elements come under the broad issue of burglary. We will now explore each of these points in greater depth.

The initial issue statement is broad, but the student knows which element is in dispute. This is evidenced by the thorough discussion of "dwelling house." Why did this student tackle the "dwelling house" element where he did? The reason is this: The fictitious student apparently has a professor who wants each element of an analysis issue discussed, even if a particular element(s) is absolutely and clearly satisfied (just as in Sample Exam Answer #1A). However, Sample Exam Answer #1A tackles the problematical element (dwelling house) first; Sample Exam Answer #1E tackles each element in the order that they arise in the rule. Which way is better? It depends.

If you are running low on time, get to the problematical element first (Sample Exam Answer #1A). You will get more points for discussing "dwelling house" than "breaking." However, if you have plenty of time and you like to tackle the elements in the order that they appear in the rule, feel free to do just that (Sample Exam Answer #1E).

You may also want to check with your professor. If he or she has a certain preference, you would want to tackle the issue consistent with that preference.

What I personally like about this answer #1E is that all of the elements are clearly delineated and indented under the broad issue of burglary. For this single reason, I do like this answer (Sample Exam Answer #1E) the best.

Nevertheless, the bottom line, again, is that these differences are minor. Again, note that all good answers will identify the element ("dwelling house"), define the element, and analyze the element within the context of the facts given.

Now let us look at some other sample answers. These samples will not be as well written as the ones that we have discussed so far. Let us begin with Sample Exam Answer #1F.

Sample Exam Answer #1F: Lacking Analysis

This answer will show you what does not constitute an analysis. As such, it is important to read and study. Knowing what a "bad" analysis is will reinforce what a "good" analysis is.

Sample Exam Answer #1F

Can Dan be convicted of burglary on the ground that the car was a dwelling house because Charles regularly slept in it while on his trip?

A burglary is the breaking and entering of the dwelling house of another in the nighttime with the intent to commit a felony therein. A dwelling house is a place of human habitation.

Because Dan broke into Charles' car, the car would not qualify as a dwelling house.

On the other hand, because Charles was sleeping in the car, it would qualify as a dwelling house.

A breaking is the creation of a breach, which Dan accomplished when he "broke the glass" window of the car.

An entry exists if any part of the defendant intrudes; this existed when Dan put his hand through the window.

It was nighttime, the period between sunset and sunrise, since it took place at 11:30 PM.

The intent to commit a felony element is met since Dan intended to take the wallet before he broke the window and, under common law, all larceny was a felony.

Therefore, Dan committed a burglary.

Sample Exam Answer #1F: Dissecting the Answer

The issue statement for Sample Exam Answer #1F is perfect. Indeed, it is identical to the issue statement found in Answer #1A. The same is true for the two rules of law ("burglary" and "dwelling house"). What then is the problem with this answer? The problem is two-fold. First, this answer has no headings. That is clear. That alone makes it a weaker answer, but there is more. This answer has a problem with analysis. In short, there is none.

Remember what we stated about analysis and how to perform an analysis on the exam: You take the key facts that you are given and build onto those facts a creative argument to prove/disprove that the element in question exists/does not exist. Remember, too, that while your key facts will be the foundation of your analysis, the heart of your analysis (and the professor's grade) is going to be your creative argument (reasons). In Sample Exam Answer #1F, however, there is no creative argument. Let us examine this point more closely.

Let us first examine the "analysis" for why the car is not a dwelling. The student starts with the facts ("Because Dan broke into Charles' car"). Now the next part of the sentence should begin the creative argument. Remember our formula for analysis: KEY FACTS GIVEN + CREATIVE ARGUMENT = DISPUTABLE FACT DOES NOT EXIST. However, we have no creative argument here. Rather, immediately after the facts ("because Dan broke into Charles' car"), the student writes, "the car would not qualify as a dwelling house." This is a mere conclusion. It is not analysis.

Remember also that we stated there is a test to see if you have in fact performed an analysis: Ask yourself the question, "Why?" If you can intelligently ask yourself this question, then you have not performed an analysis: You have not given your reasons or a creative argument *why* the element exists.

If we ask ourselves the question "Why?" in Sample Exam Answer #1F, we will notice that we *can* intelligently ask this question—and we can because there is no reasoning. There is no creative argument. It is merely a statement of the facts ("Because Dan broke into Charles' car") plus a conclusion ("the car would not qualify as a dwelling house"). When a professor reads this, he or she will write in the margin of the exam, "Conclusory!"[19]

If we look at the "analysis" for the other side, we see that the same problem exists. We have only a restatement of the key facts ("On the other hand, because Charles was sleeping in the car") plus a conclusion ("the car would qualify as a dwelling house"). There is no creative argument. The "analysis" does not tell us *why* Charles' sleeping in the car makes it a dwelling house. Consequently, there is no "analysis." Of course, professors do not award points for conclusions.

---

[19] Many students have heard the term, "conclusory," but few understand it. Now you do. It is when you have the facts and a mere conclusion without the supporting creative argument—your reasons.

Sample Exam Answer #1G: No Analysis (Redux)

Now let us examine a look at another sample answer, Sample Exam Answer #1G. This answer, too, has a problem and for the same reason Sample Exam Answer #1F was a problem: no analysis. However, Sample Exam Answer #1G's weakness is more pronounced than the problem of Sample Exam Answer #1F.

Sample Exam Answer #1G

Can Dan be convicted of burglary on the ground that the car was a dwelling house because Charles regularly slept in it while on his trip?

A burglary is the breaking and entering of the dwelling house of another in the nighttime with the intent to commit a felony therein. A dwelling house is a place of human habitation.

The facts state that in June 2010, Charles graduated from college with a B.S. degree in accounting. Prior to beginning work in September for an accounting firm, Charles decided to travel across the United States in his 2005 Dodge minivan, seeing small towns and just enjoying himself. Not being financially well off, however, Charles felt he could economize by sleeping in the back of his station wagon. In this way, he would not have to pay for a motel nightly. While traveling through State X, Charles pulled over from the public highway to catch a few hours of sleep. It was a cool night so Charles rolled up all of the windows of his car. For safety reasons, he also locked all of the doors of his car. By 10:30 PM, with the nighttime stars shining brightly, Charles fell asleep. An hour later, Dan walked by. Dan saw Charles' wallet lying next to Charles. Being low on funds, Dan decided that it would be easy to take Charles' wallet. Dan then broke the glass nearest Charles with the intent of snatching Charles' wallet; Dan did put his hand into the car and succeeded in taking the wallet. Charles' person, however, was not harmed in any way.

On these facts, the car was a dwelling house.

Sample Exam Answer #1G: Dissecting the Answer

Putting aside the lack of headings, I think that you will agree that this is a very poor analysis of the element, "dwelling house." Indeed, there is no analysis. We have only a repetition of facts, many of which are pure background facts (such as Charles getting his bachelor's degree).

If you want to do well in the analysis phase of HIRRAC™, memorize the following statement: NEVER HAVE A SENTENCE OF PURE FACTS IN YOUR ANALYSIS. The reason that you should never have a sentence of pure facts is because to perform an analysis, you need the key facts as your foundation BUT YOU MUST BUILD ONTO THOSE FACTS A CREATIVE ARGUMENT. Remember, it is the creative argument that is the heart of your analysis. Without that, you have nothing.

Sample Exam Answer #1H: "Clearing Your Throat"

Now let us look at still another sample answer. Sample Answer #1H is typical of what many first year students write. We can call this, "clearing your throat."

borbri

Sample Exam Answer #1H

The facts state that in June 2010, Charles graduated from college with a B.S. degree in accounting. Prior to beginning work in September for an accounting firm, Charles decided to travel across the United States in his 2005 Dodge minvan, seeing small towns and just enjoying himself. Not being financially well off, however, Charles felt he could economize by sleeping in the back of his station wagon. In this way, he would not have to pay for a motel nightly. While traveling through State X, Charles pulled over from the public highway to catch a few hours of sleep. It was a cool night so Charles rolled up all of the windows of his car. For safety reasons, he also locked all of the doors of his car. By 10:30 PM, with the nighttime stars shining brightly, Charles fell asleep. An hour later, Dan walked by. Dan saw Charles' wallet lying next to Charles. Being low on funds, Dan decided that it would be easy to take Charles' wallet. Dan then broke the glass nearest Charles with the intent of snatching Charles' wallet; Dan did put his hand into the car and succeeded in taking the wallet. Charles' person, however, was not harmed in any way.

State v. Dan: Burglary: Dwelling House
Can Dan be convicted of burglary on the ground that the car was a dwelling house because Charles regularly slept in it while on his trip?

A burglary is the breaking and entering of the dwelling house of another in the nighttime with the intent to commit a felony therein. A dwelling house is a place of human habitation.

* * *

Sample Exam Answer #1H: Dissecting the Answer

Many students feel that they have to be "apologetic" for writing their exams. Don't be. Just get in there and start to HIRRAC™ your answer. No "introduction" is necessary.[20]

Sample Exam Answer #1I: Failing to HIRRAC™

Now let us peruse still another answer. Sample Answer #1I presents several problems, common among first year students. See if you can identify what the problems are before we discuss it.

---

[20] You may give a synopsis of what you are going to discuss, however. For example, you may have six crimes that you wish to HIRRAC™. You may initially tell your professor: "The defendant can be prosecuted for burglary, robbery, extortion, murder in the first degree, murder in the second degree, and kidnapping." Thereafter, you do a HIRRAC™ for each issue. Some professors like this. (I do not.) Others do not care one way or the other. If you are in doubt, ask your professor.

Sample Exam Answer #1I

The problem here is whether a burglary has been committed. A burglary is the breaking and entering of the dwelling house of another in the nighttime with the intent to commit a felony. The underlying purpose of criminalizing this type of conduct is to protect one in one's house. There is probably a burglary here. It was nighttime and Dan broke and entered. The car is used by Charles for sleeping. The other elements are also met.

....

Sample Exam Answer #1I: Dissecting the Answer

Sample Exam Answer #1I has an obvious core problem. The student does not HIRRAC™ the answer. Importantly, if an answer is not in HIRRAC™ format, there will not be a proper focus. As a result, the entire discussion just barely touches on the elements of burglary—but without discussing whether the car is a "dwelling house."

The moral of this sample answer is clear: If you do not consciously and affirmatively know which element is in dispute, you will wander and be conclusory. To prevent this from happening, you must always remember to ask yourself the all-important question after identifying the issue: *Are all elements of the rule applicable to the issue absolutely and clearly satisfied?* If the answer is no, identify those elements which are in dispute and HIRRAC™ those elements. Sample Answer #1I did not do this—and it shows.

There is still another problem with this answer: no paragraphs. You must remember to have a separate paragraph for each part of the HIRRAC™ formula for each issue. You always want to make the professor's job of reading the essay as easy as possible.

Sample Exam Answer#1J: A Common Problem

We now look at another sample answer. It too reveals a common mistake.

Sample Exam Answer #1J

State v. Dan: Burglary: Dwelling House

Can the State convict Dan of burglary on the ground that the car was a dwelling house because Charles regularly slept in it while on his trip?

A burglary is the breaking and entering of the dwelling house of another in the nighttime with the intent to commit a felony therein. A dwelling house is a place of human habitation.

Although Dan broke into Charles' car while Charles was sleeping in it, the car would not qualify as a dwelling house because a car is typically not thought of as being something used for habitation; it is used for travel. Moreover, even though Charles was sleeping in the car at the time, this should not make a car a dwelling because every time a person would take a nap in his car, that would transform the car into a dwelling, not the intent of the common law, which was to protect a person in his home. Finally, sleeping in a car even for a few months should not change the characterization of the car because Charles still used it for travel around the country; he did not use it exclusively as a place to sleep, wash, and entertain, as homes are typically used.

Therefore, the car was a dwelling house.

Breaking

A breaking is the creation of a breach, which Dan accomplished when he "broke the glass" window of the car.

Entering

An entry exists if any part of the defendant intrudes; this existed when Dan put his hand through the window.

Nighttime

It was nighttime, the period between sunset and sunrise, since it took place at 11:30 PM.

Intent to Commit Felony

The intent to commit a felony element is met since Dan intended to take the wallet before he broke the window and, under common law, all larceny was a felony.

Therefore, Dan committed a burglary.

Sample Exam Answer #1J: Dissecting the Answer

The problem with this answer is that while at first it seems to be identical to Sample Exam Answer #1A (a great answer), it does not give both sides of the argument. When you have an analysis issue, you must argue both sides: Why the car was a dwelling *and* why the car was not a dwelling. Remember, when you have an analysis issue: argue both sides.

Nevertheless, that is not to say that you should play "ping-pong." What is "ping-pong"? Ping-pong is where first you give one reason why the car is a dwelling; then you give a reason why the car is not a dwelling. Next, you give a reason why the car is a dwelling; then you give another reason why the car is not a dwelling. Then you give a reason why the car is a dwelling…...

I think that you get the idea. The point is this: Unless your teacher tells you to do otherwise, give *all of your reasons* why the car is a dwelling and then, in the next paragraph, give *all of your reasons* why the car is not a dwelling. Do not, however, play "ping-pong."

HYPOTHETICAL #2

Now let us examine one more hypothetical. This hypo is a property question. We have chosen this subject to show you that any subject fits into the HIRRAC™ format. We follow the hypo with a diagram and a scratch outline.

Hypothetical #2

[Simple Analysis Issue]

Anna deposited her coat with a fur piece hidden in the sleeve in Baker's coat-room, a business that Baker operates. The fur piece was subsequently lost while the coat was in Baker's possession. Baker did not know that the fur was hidden in the coat. Anna sues Baker. Will Anna prevail? Discuss.

Diagram

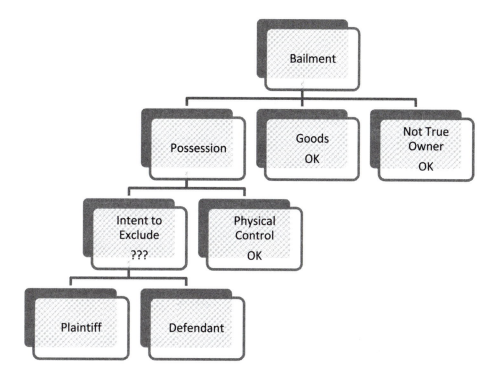

Bailment is the possession of goods by one not the true owner. Possession requires an intent to exclude others and physical control. There is one element in dispute: intent to exclude others. The resolution of this element is just not clear from the facts given, as the first sample answer will explain.

You will note that it seems that we have a "sub-element" in dispute here. Bailment, per the diagram, has three elements: possession, goods, and not the true owner. Possession has two elements (or sub-elements): intent to exclude and physical control. The sub-element in dispute, as you will see, is intent to exclude. Do we have a problem because we are dealing not with an "element," but a "sub-element"? The answer is, no. Whether we have to deal with an element or sub-element, the key is to isolate the element (or sub-element) that is in dispute, and isolate that element (or sub-element) by defining it if it is a term of art. If it is not a term of art, just isolate it by telling the professor that the element (or sub-element) in dispute is *element x*. We do all this in a HIRRAC™ format, as the answer that follows explains.

Sample Scratch Outline #2

Anna v. Baker: Bailment: Possession: Fur hidden and unknown to coat-room owner

………..

There are a number of issues here: (1) Was a bailment created? (2) If so, what kind of bailment was it? (3) Depending upon the type of bailment, what was the standard of care? For purposes of this exercise, however, we shall focus solely on the first issue. Was a bailment created?[21]

A bailment is the rightful possession of goods by one who is not the owner. We have only one element that is in dispute: possession. Consequently, the issue is a simple analysis issue.[22]

The heart of the controversy is whether Baker had possession of the fur. The scratch outline is testimony to the student's clear understanding of the problem.

Sample Exam Answer #2A: A Great Answer

Let us now look at Sample Exam Answer #2A. It is thoughtful and well written in the HIRRAC™ format.

---

[21] We discuss only the first bailment issue (was a bailment created?) here because the purpose of this chapter is to give you a feel for handling a simple analysis issue. We cover complete examinations later in these materials.

[22] See Chapter 11, "Categorizing the Issues."

borbri

Sample Exam Answer #2A

<u>Bailment: Possession</u>[23]

When Anna checked her coat with Baker, a coat-room operator, and a fur piece was hidden in the coat's sleeve and Baker did not know of the hidden fur, did Baker have possession of the fur so that a bailment existed between Anna and Baker with respect to the fur piece?

A bailment is the rightful possession of goods by one who is not the owner. Possession consists of physical control of the chattel with an intent to exercise that control.

As the fur was hidden and its existence was not known to Baker, Baker could not have had the intent to exercise control because intent requires a state of mind; one cannot have that state of mind when one does not know in fact that something exists.

However, because Baker owned the coat-room, Baker's knowledge of the fur could be implied in law. It is reasonable to believe that people may leave property in coats and one who is in the business of checking coats can better absorb the loss by way of insurance or slightly increasing his fees for his service.

<u>Physical Control</u>
Physical control, dominion, exists because the coat and the fur were in Baker's coat-room.

<u>Goods</u>
Further, the coat and fur are goods in that they are chattels or personal property.

<u>Rightful</u>
Finally, Baker's possession was rightful since Anna checked the property with Baker.

Therefore, a bailment was created.

---

[23] You may be asking yourself, "Should not the heading include the sub-element, so that the heading reads, "Bailment: Possession: Intent to Exclude"? Perhaps it should. Still, I am not going to become so bogged down in this that I run out of time or drive myself crazy. It really is that simple. The fact is that you will rarely have to get into sub-elements. I put this hypo here to show you that you do not need to become "stressed out" over elements and sub-elements. This is an excellent answer and we have no need to keep delving deeper and deeper. You have a finite amount of time to answer this one issue. You cannot spend one hour on one issue. Stop ruminating over whether the heading is "perfect." This sample answer illustrates this point clearly. Get in and out, and do not stress out over the format. Put it in a HIRRAC™ format (that is, a logical format) and be done with it. Remember, perfection implies improvement is impossible. Nothing that humans do is perfect. A car can be made safer. A book can be more concise. A brief can always be better. An exam can always be more precise. You can get your "A" by using HIRRAC™ while recognizing that you can always improve. That is the human equation of life itself. In short, this sample answer is quite good, but not perfect. So it is with life.

Sample Exam Answer #2A: Dissecting the Answer

This is a great answer. Initially, it is in HIRRAC™ format and it mirrors Sample Exam Answer #1A.[24] The student's answer has a heading and the student has identified bailment as the issue. Consequently, the next paragraph[25] is the rule of bailment. In that same paragraph, the student isolates the element that is in dispute by defining it because "possession" is a legal term, a term of art.

In the next paragraph, the student begins with the analysis. Recall what analysis is: We take the key facts that we are given and add on to those facts a creative argument to prove that the element in dispute exists; then we take the key facts that are given and, with a different creative argument, prove that the element in dispute does not exist.[26]

The fictitious student who wrote Sample Answer #2A believes that the weaker side is Baker's view. The student believes that a bailment was not created because Baker did not have possession of the fur piece.[27] Consequently, the student takes the key facts that are given ("a fur piece was hidden in the coat's sleeve and Baker did not know of the hidden fur"). The student then adds on to those facts a creative argument ("Baker could not have had the intent to exercise control since intent requires a state of mind; one cannot have that state of mind when one does not know in fact something exists"), to prove that a bailment was not created.

The student has stated *why* a bailment could not exist: the student has given a *reason* why Baker did not have possession. The student has performed a proper analysis for one side.

Is this the only argument available? Of course, it is not. Can you think of others? I am certain that you can. Remember that if five students come up with five different reasons, each of the five students can get an "A" grade.

In the next paragraph, the student performs the analysis for the "other side." The student gives us a reason why possession, for purposes of bailment, exists on these facts. Again, can you think up a different reason(s)? I am certain that you can. Again, if five students come up with five different reasons, each of the five students can get an "A" grade. Such is the beauty of law.

The student then proceeds with the rule mop-up, each element given its own heading to give both teacher and student focus. Remember to ask your professor if he or she even wants a rule mop-up (most do).[28] Finally, there is the conclusion.

---

[24] Of course, we easily could have made it just even a little better by mirroring Sample Exam Answer #1E. My purpose here was to show you a great answer, not the best. You can, of course, easily take this answer and make it mirror Sample Exam Answer #1E (where you do not start with the problematic issue, but with the first element in the order it appears in the rule). Remember, however, the differences between Sample Exam Answer #1A and Sample Exam Answer #1E are minor.

[25] Remember: we always paragraph regularly to make it easier for the professor to read.

[26] Remember that it does not matter which side you start with. However, for purposes of closure, you may wish to start out with the side that you think is the weaker side. See footnote 6, supra.

[27] See preceding footnote.

[28] Recall that the term, "rule mop-up," is this author's creation.

Sample Exam Answer #2B: A Common Error

Sample Exam Answer #2B addresses a very important point. Read the answer and see if you can figure out how this answer differs from answer #2A. To help you figure it out, let us stipulate that the professor wants a rule mop-up.

Bailment: Possession

When Anna checked her coat with Baker, a coat-room operator, and a fur piece was hidden in the coat's sleeve and Baker did not know of the hidden fur, did Baker have possession of the fur so that a bailment existed between Anna and Baker with respect to the fur piece?

A bailment is the rightful possession of goods by one who is not the owner. Possession consists of physical control of the chattel with an intent to exercise that control.

Because the fur was hidden and its existence was not known to Baker, Baker could not have had the intent to exercise control because intent requires a state of mind; one cannot have that state of mind when one does not know in fact that something exists.

Being that I have concluded that Baker did not have possession, a bailment cannot exist. Therefore, a discussion of the other elements, although satisfied, is irrelevant.

Sample Exam Answer #2B: Dissecting the Answer

Preliminarily we should note that this student made a grave error: The student had an analysis issue and did not argue both sides of the element that was in dispute. That would be bad enough, but the student compounded his or her mistake. The student then went on to "conclude himself or herself out of points." The student concluded that there was no possession. The student then went on to state that without possession the other elements are irrelevant. True—but why deprive yourself of points (remember that we stipulated that for this sample answer, the professor wants a rule mop-up)?

How do you proceed if you conclude that the element in dispute does not exist? Sample Exam Answer #2C is illustrative.

Sample Exam Answer #2C: No Common Error Here

In this sample answer, the student does not conclude himself or herself out of points. See how the student accomplishes this.

Sample Exam Answer #2C

Bailment: Possession

When Anna checked her coat with Baker, a coat-room operator, and a fur piece was hidden in the coat's sleeve and Baker did not know of the hidden fur, did Baker have possession of the fur so that a bailment existed between Anna and Baker with respect to the fur piece?

A bailment is the rightful possession of goods by one who is not the owner. Possession consists of physical control of the chattel with an intent to exercise that control.

Because Baker owned the coat-room, Baker's knowledge of the fur could be implied in law. It is reasonable to believe that people may leave property in coats and one who is in the business of checking coats can better absorb the loss by way of insurance or slightly increasing his fees for his service.

However, because the fur was hidden and its existence was not in fact known to Baker, he could not have had the intent to exercise control; intent requires a state of mind and one cannot have that state of mind when one does not know in fact that something exists. Moreover, to impute knowledge simply on the basis of who can best afford the loss is arbitrary. Indeed, any given customer may be many times more wealthy than Baker. In such case, the customer should absorb the loss.

Consequently, Baker should not be deemed to have had possession.

Physical Control

Assuming, however, that Baker did have possession, physical control, dominion, existed because the coat and the fur were in Baker's coat-room.

Goods

Further, the coat and fur are goods in that they are chattels or personal property.

Rightful

Finally, Baker's possession was rightful because Anna checked the property with Baker.

Nevertheless, because possession did not exist, there was no bailment.

Sample Exam Answer #2C: Dissecting the Answer

In Sample Answer #2C, the student argued both sides of the possession element. Moreover, even though the student concluded that there was no possession, the student went on to discuss the existence of the other elements. The student did not conclude himself or herself out of additional points.

Sample Exam Answer #2D: No Analysis

Now let us examine Sample Exam Answer #2D. Although we discussed earlier what analysis is not, it is such an important aspect of exam writing (and an area that many students have problems with), that we cover it again.

Sample Exam Answer #2D

<u>Bailment: Possession</u>

When Anna checked her coat with Baker, a coat-room operator, and a fur piece was hidden in the coat's sleeve and Baker did not know of the hidden fur, did Baker have possession of the fur so that a bailment existed between Anna and Baker with respect to the fur piece?

A bailment is the rightful possession of goods by one who is not the owner. Possession consists of physical control of the chattel with an intent to exercise that control.

The facts state that Anna deposited her coat with a fur piece hidden in the sleeve in Baker's coat-room, a business that Baker operates. The fur piece was subsequently lost while the coat was in Baker's possession. The facts further state that Baker did not know that the fur was hidden in the coat. Therefore, Baker did not have possession.

* * *

Sample Exam Answer #2D: Dissecting the Answer

The problem with this answer is that the student does not analyze the issue: whether Baker had possession (the requisite intent). All that the student does is to repeat the facts. Recall what we stated earlier: analysis requires creative argument. All that we have here is a repetition of facts plus a conclusion. A professor would state that this answer is, "conclusory."

Sample Exam Answer#2E: Several Problems

The student here makes several mistakes. One is a "cardinal sin" of exam writing. See if you can determine what the mistakes are.

Bailment

When Anna checked her coat with Baker, a coat-room operator, and a fur piece was hidden in the coat's sleeve and Baker did not know of the hidden fur, did a bailment exist between Anna and Baker with respect to the fur piece?

A bailment is the rightful possession of goods by one who is not the true owner.

Baker had rightful possession of the coat because Anna voluntarily checked it with Baker. Once it was in Baker's possession, Baker can be deemed to be a bailee for the mutual benefit of Baker and Anna. In determining whether Baker used ordinary care, we must look to the totality of the circumstances to determine why the fur was lost. Indeed, maybe it was not lost. Maybe it was stolen. In such case, it would not be fair to make Baker responsible. Moreover, maybe Anna is insured. If she is, she should not be complaining since she will not have any monetary loss.

* * *

Sample Exam Answer #2E: Dissecting the Answer

There are two problems in Sample Exam Answer #2E. (1) The student does not focus on the element in dispute. As a result, the student wanders. (2) The student makes unwarranted assumptions in the "analysis." Let us discuss these points in depth.

First, we shall discuss the lack of focus. The student jumps from "rightful possession" to "mutual bailment,"[29] to the standard of care, "ordinary care." Why does this student wander? This is all because the student has not consciously, and affirmatively, categorized the issue as a simple analysis issue.[30] The student is not aware that the element that is the problem is "possession." This is evident from the heading and the issue statement. Both the heading and the issue statement mention the "big picture" of bailment, but neither mentions the element that is the problem: possession.

Always direct your attention to the element that is the subject of the dispute: possession. Deal with that issue. Thereafter, you can move on to HIRRAC™ what type of bailment existed (mutual benefit bailment or some other type), followed by another HIRRAC™ to discuss the standard of care.

Now let us discuss the next problem: making assumptions. The student makes several assumptions: "Maybe it was stolen. . . . Maybe Anna is insured." The problem with this, however, is that the facts do not tell us it was stolen. Nor are there any facts available for us to make the inference that maybe the fur piece was stolen. Similarly, there are no facts present to allow us to state "Maybe Anna is insured."

Never make an assumption if there are no underlying facts to support that assumption. Can you ever make an assumption? Yes, you can, but only if there are underlying facts. Moreover, in such case, you will have to make the assumption favorable for the plaintiff and, in the alternative, favorable for the defendant.[31]

SUMMARY OF CHAPTER 14

We have covered a lot of material in this chapter. To summarize:

1. When you have a simple analysis issue, isolate the element in dispute, and then analyze it: facts plus creative argument to prove that the element exists/does not exist.

2. Never repeat facts.

3. Never lose sight of the element that is the subject of the parties' dispute.

4. HIRRAC™ your answers.

---

[29] This is a separate issue and, hence, we need a separate HIRRAC™.
[30] See Chapter 11, "Categorizing the Issues."
[31] We cover when to make assumptions in Chapter 20, "Making Assumptions."

5. Be confident: Ten students can have ten different arguments—and all ten can be correct.

6. HIRRAC™ is merely an organizational tool. Feel free to modify it to make yourself comfortable (e.g., use headings instead of an issue statement).

7. All good answers will have headings, issues, rules, and analyses.

8. If your professor does not want HIRRAC™, ask what it is that he or she wants (because all good answers have to have issues, rules, and analyses).

Now let us examine how to answer a complex analysis issue.

CHAPTER 15
USING HIRRAC™ TO ANSWER A COMPLEX ANALYSIS ISSUE

In this chapter, we shall discuss how to answer a complex analysis issue. We have previously discussed what a complex analysis issue is.[1] In short, in a complex analysis issue, two or more elements of the rule of law will be in dispute. Complex analysis issues present substantial organizational problems for many students. In this chapter, we shall learn how you can successfully attack any complex analysis issue.

HYPOTHETICAL #1

Hypothetical #1 deals with adverse possession. We have visited this problem earlier.[2] Consistent with what we did in the last chapter, we have included a diagram and a good scratch outline immediately following Hypothetical #l.

---

[1] See Chapter 11, "Categorizing the Issues."
[2] See Chapter 11, "Categorizing the Issues," and Chapter 12, "Preparing a 'Scratch' Outline."

Hypothetical #1

[Complex Analysis Issue]

Oscar owns a 35-unit apartment building. There are a few cracks throughout the building, but nothing that affects a tenant's health and safety. Indeed, the building is quite sound. Oscar does not live on the premises.

In January 1988, Oscar hires Max Smith to manage the apartment house. Max does such a fine job in managing the apartment house that Oscar decides that he, Oscar, can finally take a well-deserved vacation. Oscar tells Max to continue to do the fine job that he, Max, is doing. Oscar then books a one-year cruise on the Queen Elizabeth II and sets sail on July 4, 1989.

In August 1989, Max sends out a letter to all tenants. The letter reads:

Dear Tenant:

Oscar is gone. I am in control here. You are to see me for all problems regarding your apartment. You will make your check payable to "Max Smith."

Sincerely,

Max Smith

Following receipt of the letter from Max, all of the tenants make the rent check out to "Max Smith." Max deposits the checks into his personal checking account, which he just opened.

Several months later, a vacant apartment is repainted by Max and rented out on a month-to-month basis. All other tenants have leases for a term for years for one year.

Meanwhile, Oscar loves traveling so much that he decides to stay overseas for awhile after the cruise ends. In this regard, he telephones Max and lets Max know that he, Oscar, will be gone for a few more years. When Oscar asks how everything is going, Max replies, "The building is better now than when you were running it." The two then hang up. They have the same conversation twice for the duration that Oscar is overseas.

In 1999, Oscar decides that he is tired of traveling. He has also run up quite a few debts while overseas. Oscar comes back to the United States and prepares to sell the apartment house to pay off all of his debts.

The jurisdiction within which the apartment building lies provides in its Civil Code: "In any action to recover real property or the possession thereof, the state of mind of the one in possession shall be irrelevant." The Civil Code also provides that "any action to recover the possession of real property must be commenced within seven years from the time that an actual entry was made by the one in possession." Discuss.

Diagram

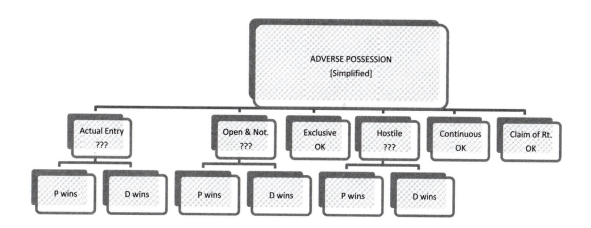

Sample Scratch Outline #1

Max v. Oscar: Adverse Possession

    Actual Entry: Letter to tenants/new lease; checks deposited in Max's name; repainting

    Open and Notorious: Letter to tenants; new lease; checks deposited in Max's name; repainting

    Hostile: Conversation with Oscar; checks deposited

....

The elements of adverse possession are: actual entry; open and notorious; hostile; under a claim of right; exclusive; and continuous for the statutory period. In this adverse possession issue, three elements are in dispute: actual entry; open and notorious; and hostility. The other elements, claim of right, exclusivity, and continuous for the statutory period are not in dispute. Claim of right deals with whether the possessor had a good faith or bad faith intent. Some jurisdictions require a good faith mistake while others require bad faith ("It's not mine but I am taking it anyway"). Claim of right is not in issue in this hypo because the statute states that intent is not relevant.

Exclusivity is also not in dispute. This element requires that the adverse possessor not share the occupation with the true owner. Since Max occupied the land while Oscar was away, Max did not share possession with Oscar.

Continuous for the statutory period is not in dispute. This element requires that the possessor occupy the land without interruption for the statutory period. In the hypo, the statutory period is seven years; Max substantially exceeded that period of time.

Thus, three elements are in dispute and three elements are not.[3]

How then do we tackle this adverse possession issue?[4] The answer should be obvious by now: by using the HIRRAC™ method. When you have a complex analysis issue, each element will in effect become a separate issue. In short, you will HIRRAC™ each element.

Sample Exam Answer #1A: A Great Answer

Sample Exam Answer #1A is a good answer. After you study it, we shall discuss why it is a good answer.

---

[3] In some jurisdictions, the possessor must also pay the property taxes. We do not address that here.

[4] We point out again, as we did in the previous chapter, that the hypothetical discussed in this chapter would not constitute an entire one-hour examination (although it could constitute as much as one-half or maybe a bit more of an hour-long examination). In Chapter 19, "Sample Exams," we discuss entire examinations.

borbri

Sample Exam Answer #1A

<u>Adverse Possession</u>
Can Max prevent Oscar from selling the apartment building because Max in fact is the new owner under the doctrine of adverse possession?

To obtain title by adverse possession, there must be: an actual entry that is open and notorious, hostile, exclusive, under claim of right and continuous for the statutory period.

<u>Actual Entry</u>
Did Max make an actual entry of Oscar's apartment house when he sent a letter to all the tenants stating that he was in control and all checks were to be made out to him, he entered into a new lease with a tenant and had the apartment painted, and deposited checks into his own account?

An actual entry is a substantial physical occupation of the land.

By repainting the apartment, entering into a month-to-month lease with a new tenant while others have leases for a term for years, and ordering the tenants to pay him personally, Max was occupying the land in a substantial manner because, although at first blush it seems that Max is not doing much, in fact no true owner could do more. Indeed, the month-to-month lease was a break with tradition and, in this regard, Max again was doing what any owner would do: conveying the type of lease that he chooses to convey without being concerned about tradition or prior conduct.

On the other hand, although Max did all these things, that is what he was hired to do—be the agent for Oscar, especially while Oscar is gone. Under such circumstances, it would be reasonable for Max to exercise his independent judgment. Further, a variance of one lease for one apartment is not an act that is so unusual that it could be deemed to be outside the scope of the duties of Max. After all, managers are charged with getting new tenants. Finally, even the checking account in Max's name is consistent with his employment-related duties: with Oscar away, Max must reasonably be expected to pay for expenses of the apartment house and an account solely in his name would facilitate such payments.

Thus, Max did not make an actual entry.

<u>Open and Notorious</u>
Assuming that Max did make an actual entry, was his occupation also open and notorious because of his letter to the tenants, the execution of the new lease, the repainting, and the deposit of the checks into his own checking account?

An occupation is open and notorious if the true owner, upon visiting the premises, would have been made aware that another is occupying the premises.

* * *

Therefore, the occupation was not open and notorious.

<u>Hostile</u>

* * *

Max's occupation, therefore, was hostile.

For the foregoing reasons, Max did not acquire the property by adverse possession.

Sample Exam #1A: Dissecting the Answer

Let us now examine this answer in depth. Of course, it is in HIRRAC™ format.

1. *Heading: "Adverse Possession."* As we discussed in the previous chapter, it is always good to have a brief heading precede the issue statement: It gives the professor a crisp and clear preview of what you are going to discuss. A heading will also help you keep your focus and prevent you from wandering.

2. *Issue statement: "Can Max prevent Oscar from selling the apartment . . . under the doctrine of adverse possession?"* You will notice that this issue statement contains (1) the parties (Max and Oscar) and (2) the legal issue (adverse possession). Contrast this issue statement with the issue statement for a simple analysis issue, where we have: (1) the parties; (2) the legal issue; (3) the element that is in dispute; and (4) the key facts that are triggering that element.[5] Why does the issue statement for a complex analysis issue include only the parties and the legal issue?

The reason is this: When we deal with a complex analysis issue, we will necessarily have two or more elements of the rule that will be in dispute. Consequently, an issue statement that includes *all* of the disputable elements and *all* of the respective key facts will be totally unwieldy. For example, in Hypothetical #1, we have three elements that are in dispute. As you can see from Scratch Outline #1, there are far too many different key facts triggering too many elements to have one clearly articulated issue statement. Indeed, an issue statement that would include all three elements and all of the key facts would be extremely difficult to follow, if not unintelligible.

Consequently, when you are dealing with a complex analysis issue, your issue statement will be broad: You will state the "big picture" (adverse possession). However, you will not even attempt to indicate the disputable elements (actual entry, open and notorious, hostile). Nor will you attempt to state the corresponding key facts (letter to the tenants, repainting, etc.).

2. *Rule: ". . . there must be an actual entry that is open and notorious, hostile, exclusive, under claim of right and continuous for the statutory period."* This is the rule for adverse possession. What do we do after stating the rule? What we will do is just what we did for a simple analysis issue: We are going to isolate each element that is in dispute, define it, and analyze it.[6] Each element effectively becomes an issue and each element will be tackled in the HIRRAC™ format. If you wish, we can refer to the HIRRAC™ of each element as a "sub-HIRRAC™".

Let us now, therefore, HIRRAC™ (or sub-HIRRAC™) each element. So that you clearly understand that everything that we are discussing is all part of the overall issue of adverse possession, we have decided to indent the explanatory material that follows (just as we have indented the headings of each of the elements that we will discuss). You will then be able to see clearly how all of the parts fit together.

---

[5] See Chapter 14, "Using HIRRAC™ to Answer a Simple Analysis Issue."
[6] *Ibid.*

(i) *Sub-Heading: "Actual Entry."* This is a good heading (or, sub-heading, if you will). As we have previously discussed, headings are like a road map for your professors. This sub-heading allows the professor to see at a glance that you are going to discuss "actual entry." By indenting the heading,[7] the student makes it clear to the professor that this element is part of the greater problem of "adverse possession."

(ii) *Issue statement: "Did Max make an actual entry of Oscar's apartment house when he sent a letter to all the tenants . . . and deposited checks into his own account?"* The issue statement (or, again, the sub-issue statement), includes the parties (although this is not necessary because there is only one set of parties in this hypo),[8] the element that is in dispute (actual entry), and the key facts that are triggering that element.

Of course, if the student had wanted to, he could have used an underlined clause (including the element in dispute and the key facts that triggered the element) in lieu of the issue statement.[9]

(iii) *Rule: "An actual entry is a substantial physical occupation of the land."* This is, of course, the rule of law, the definition of the element. Of course, this is the second "R" of HIRRAC™.

Now some of you may be asking yourselves, "The second "R" of HIRRAC™? Where is the first rule, the first "R" of HIRRAC™?" The answer to the question is this: You have already stated the first "R" of HIRRAC™ when you defined adverse possession: an actual entry, which is open and notorious, hostile, under claim of right, etc.

To further explain the matter, let us compare what we are doing here in a complex analysis issue with what we would do in a simple analysis issue. Let us suppose that we had a simple analysis issue that dealt with adverse possession. Let us also suppose that every element of adverse possession was clearly satisfied, with one exception: actual entry. What would we do?

First, we would have a heading (the parties and "Adverse Possession: Actual Entry"); an issue statement which would include (1) the parties (*A v. B*); (2) the legal issue (adverse possession); (3) the element that is in dispute (actual entry); and (4) the key facts that are triggering the element (X). Second, we would state the rule of adverse possession. *This is the first "R" of HIRRAC™.* Third, we would isolate the element that is in dispute (actual entry) by defining what an actual entry is (a substantial physical occupation of the land).[10] *This is the second "R" of HIRRAC™.* Fourth, we would analyze the element: prove that there was/was not a substantial physical occupation of the land.

---

[7] Indent only the heading. Do not indent the body of text that follows the heading. See Sample Exam Answer #1A (the heading of adverse possession has a .5 inch indentation; the sub-heading for each of the elements has a 1 inch indentation).

[8] See also Chapter 12, "Preparing a 'Scratch' Outline."

[9] See Chapter 14, "Using HIRRAC™ to Answer a Simple Analysis Issue," Sample Exam Answer #1D.

[10] See Chapter 14, "Using HIRRAC™ to Answer a Simple Analysis Issue," Sample Exam Answer #1A; compare with Sample Exam Answer #1E (where we attack the elements in the order they show up in the rule).

Notice that in a simple analysis issue we give the rule of adverse possession (the first "R") and then we define what an actual entry is (the second "R"). That is exactly what we have done above in Sample Exam Answer #1A, a complex analysis issue.

The point that we are making is this: whether you have a simple analysis issue or a complex analysis issue, the element will have to be defined (if it is a term of art).[11]

         (iv) *Analysis: "By repainting the apartment, entering into a month-to-month lease ...."* This analysis is very good. Before we examine why this is so, let us recall that whenever you have an analysis issue, it is because the element has only one definition and, based on that definition, the element can go "either way" on the facts given. It is just not clear if the element is satisfied. Thus, there is no "right" answer. You must argue both sides. You will recall, as a suggestion, I think it is good if you start with the side that you think is the "weaker" side.[12]

The fictitious student who wrote Sample Exam Answer #1A believes that Oscar has the "stronger" argument: that Max did not make an actual entry. As such, the student begins with the "weaker" side: Max did make an actual entry.

The student performs an analysis in the manner that we previously discussed:[13] The student takes the facts that are given (the letter to tenants; the new lease; the checks deposited; and the repainting) and builds onto these facts a creative argument to prove that Max's occupation was substantial. That is, (a) no true owner could do more than what Max did; (b) the month-to-month lease was a break with tradition and, in this regard, Max again was doing what any owner would do: convey the type of lease that he chooses to convey without being concerned about tradition or prior conduct. Note, too, the importance of using the word, "because." As stated in the previous chapter, if you work in this magical word, you will almost certainly assure yourself of doing an analysis and not merely repeating facts.

In the next paragraph, the student prefaces the argument for the "stronger side" with words of transition: "On the other hand." Remember always to use words of transition to introduce the "other side" of the analysis.[14]

After letting the reader know that "the other side" is going to be discussed, the student restates the facts in a shorthand-like manner—"although Max did all these things. . . ." The student then begins the creative arguments. That is, (a) he acted like an agent; (b) as such, he would be expected to exercise independent judgment; (c) varying the terms of just one lease is not inconsistent with his duties; (d) neither is having a bank account in his own name: With Oscar away, it would be necessary for payment of expenses of the building.

---

[11] It is unlikely that you would have a complex analysis issue where an element in dispute is not a term of art. However, should that happen, after you have given your issue statement for the disputable element, immediately go to the analysis of the element. There is no rule because there is nothing to define: The element is not a term of art. Moreover, you do not have to tell the professor that the element is in dispute (as in a simple analysis issue) because you have already clearly isolated it: The element is already set out as a separate issue.

[12] See Chapter 14, "Using HIRRAC™ to Answer a Simple Analysis Issue."

[13] *Ibid.*

[14] *Ibid.*

(v) *Conclusion: "Thus, Max did not make an actual entry."* This is the conclusion for *this* element; it is not your overall conclusion for the entire issue of adverse possession. As we previously discussed,[15] conclusions are short and to the point, as is this one.

We have finished the HIRRAC™ of the first element that is in dispute. Having finished the HIRRAC™ of that element, we would next move on to HIRRAC™ the second element: open and notorious.

As we employed HIRRAC™ for the actual entry element, we would do the same for the open and notorious element. We would (i) give a brief heading ("Open and Notorious"); (ii) state the issue in a manner that includes the key facts; (iii) define what open and notorious means; (iv) analyze the element: facts plus creative argument to prove that the element exists/does not exist; and (v) conclude for that element.

We should take this time to point out again[16] that you must not "conclude" yourself out of points. In Sample Exam Answer #1A, the student concluded that Max did not make an actual entry. As such, as a matter of law, Max cannot obtain title to the apartment house by adverse possession.

Nevertheless, the student continues to discuss the other elements, beginning with "open and notorious." Notice how the student handles the apparent contradiction between the conclusion (Max did not make an actual entry) and the discussion of the next element (which would be moot if in fact there was no actual entry): The student prefaces the issue statement with, "Assuming that Max did make an actual entry . . . ." Of course, in this context, you not only may "assume," but you must—otherwise you will miss points.[17]

After we do a HIRRAC™ for open and notorious, we do a HIRRAC™ for hostility. After we state our conclusion for hostility ("Max's occupation, therefore, was hostile"), we give our overall conclusion: "For the foregoing reasons, Max did not acquire the property by adverse possession."

As I stated earlier, you may, if you wish (and if this helps you understand the process more easily) refer to the HIRRAC™ of each element in a complex analysis issue as a "sub-HIRRAC™" because it is all part of one main issue (in this hypo, adverse possession). In any case, however you wish to think of it, it is critical that you recognize that the only way to effectively deal with each disputable element is to HIRRAC™ each one of them.

---

[15] *Ibid.*

[16] See Chapter 14, "Using HIRRAC™ to Answer a Simple Analysis Issue," Sample Exam Answers #2B and #2C and relevant text.

[17] We discuss making assumptions in Chapter 20.

What do you do for those elements that are not in dispute? As we previously discussed, if your professor wants you to discuss those elements of the rule that are not in dispute (those elements which are absolutely satisfied), you will summarily dispose of those elements in a "rule mop-up."[18] Thus, because claim of right is satisfied, you would (if you needed to have a rule mop-up) state what claim of right is and why it is clearly satisfied on these facts. Then you would do the same for exclusivity and continuous for the statutory period.

In summary, when you have to deal with a complex issue, simply approach the issue as several separate simple analysis issues: HIRRAC™ each element. If you do that, you can handle anything your professor throws at you on the exam. Indeed, even a negligence issue (which first year students often find troubling from an organizational perspective) can be handled very readily. How is this so? You have a separate HIRRAC™ for each of the elements of negligence (duty, breach of duty, cause in fact, proximate cause, and damages) that are in dispute.

Now let us examine other sample answers. As we progress through the remaining sample answers in this chapter, we shall find all of them have certain weaknesses—common weaknesses.

Sample Exam Answer #1B: Analysis Problems

In Sample Exam Answer #1B, the student thinks that she is analyzing actual entry, but in fact, there is no analysis.

---

[18] See Chapter 14, "Using HIRRAC™ to Answer a Simple Analysis Issue," Sample Exam Answer #1A and relevant text; compare with Sample Exam Answer #1E.

Sample Exam Answer #1B

Adverse Possession

Can Max prevent Oscar from selling the apartment building because Max in fact is the new owner under the doctrine of adverse possession?

To obtain title by adverse possession, there must be an actual entry that is open and notorious, hostile, exclusive, under claim of right, and continuous for the statutory period.

Actual Entry

Did Max make an actual entry of Oscar's apartment house when he sent a letter to all the tenants stating that he was in control and all checks were to be made out to him, he entered into a new lease with a tenant and had the apartment painted, and deposited checks into his own account?

An actual entry is a substantial physical occupation of the land.

By repainting the apartment, entering into a month-to-month lease with a new tenant while others have leases for a term for years, and ordering the tenants to pay him personally, Max was occupying the land in a substantial manner.

On the other hand, although Max did all these things, they may not qualify as a substantial occupation.

Thus, Max did not make an actual entry.

Open and Notorious

Assuming that Max did make an actual entry, was his occupation also open and notorious by his letter to the tenants, the execution of the new lease, the repainting, and the deposit of the checks into his own checking account?

An occupation is open and notorious if the true owner, upon visiting the premises, would have been made aware that another is occupying the premises.

* * *

Sample Exam Answer #1B: Dissecting the Answer

All that we have in the preceding sample answer is a set of facts ("By repainting the apartment, entering into a month to month lease with a new tenant while others have leases for a term for years and ordering the tenants to pay him personally") and a conclusion ("Max was occupying the land in a substantial manner"). There is no creative argument. As stated earlier, a professor would call this, "conclusory."

If we were to apply the "test" to this purported analysis and ask the question, "Why?"[19] it would become quite apparent that the student did not analyze actual entry.

As such, the "analysis" in Sample Exam Answer #1B is nothing more than a conclusion and it will receive little, if any, credit.

Sample Exam Answer #1C: Never Do This!

Now let us examine Sample Exam Answer #1C. In this answer, the student does not HIRRAC™ each issue. Study what the student does.

---

[19] See Chapter 14, "Using HIRRAC™ to Answer a Simple Analysis Issue."

Sample Exam Answer #1C

The issue in this matter is whether Max has adversely possessed Oscar's apartment building, thus preventing Oscar from selling his building to meet his debts.

In order to prove that he has adversely possessed Oscar's apartment building, Max must prove each of the following:

1.   Actual entry, i.e., an actual physical occupation of the land.

2.   Open and notorious occupation, i.e. an occupation that would give visible evidence.

3.   Hostility: Without the consent of the owner.

4.   Exclusive: Not shared with the owner.

* * *

As to the first element, actual entry: By repainting the apartment, entering into a month-to-month lease with a new tenant while others have leases for a term for years, and ordering the tenants to pay him personally, Max was occupying the land in a substantial manner, because, although at first blush it seems that Max is not doing much, in fact no true owner could do more. Indeed, the month-to-month lease was a break with tradition and, in this regard, Max again was doing what any owner would do: convey the type of lease that he chooses to convey without being concerned about tradition or prior conduct.

On the other hand. . . .

Thus, Max did not make an actual entry.

As to the second element, the open and notorious occupation . . . .

* * *

Sample Exam Answer #1C: Dissecting the Answer

In Sample Exam Answer #1C, the student states *all* of the rules first (with numbers, yet!) and then gives an analysis of each element. Although the rules and analyses are technically correct, the format will require the professor to turn the pages back to make certain, for example, that the analysis of the "third element" matches up with the rule of the "third element." This is too burdensome for a professor. Ultimately, the professor gets lost and the student pays the price.

In short, *never, never* list all of the rules first. Rather, you must HIRRAC™ each element, element by element. After you state the definition of the first element that is in dispute, analyze that first element. After you have totally finished discussing the first element, proceed to the second element and HIRRAC™ that element.[20]

Sample Exam Answer #1D: Combining Issues Spells Trouble

Sample Exam Answer #1D is a result of the student getting flustered and not doing a HIRRAC™ for each element, element by element.

---

[20] There is one additional problem in Sample Answer #1C: the rules are not stated in complete sentences. In all cases (with the exception of a heading), you should write in complete sentences; do not write in clauses. You should be formal in your exam writing. As I tell my own students, you are writing an exam for a professor; you are not texting a friend.

Sample Exam Answer #1D

Adverse Possession

The elements of adverse possession are: an actual entry; open and notorious; hostile; exclusive; under claim of right; and continuous for the statutory period.

Actual Entry and Open and Notorious

Was Max's sending out the letter, repainting the apartment, entering into a new lease and depositing the rents into his own account an actual entry and an open and notorious occupation?

An actual entry is a substantial occupation of the land. An occupation is open and notorious if the true owner, upon visiting the premises, would have been made aware that another is occupying the premises.

By repainting the apartment, entering into a month-to-month lease with a new tenant while others have leases for a term for years, and ordering the tenants to pay him personally, Max was occupying the land in a substantial manner, because, although at first blush it seems that Max is not doing much, in fact no true owner could do more. Indeed, the month-to-month lease was a break with tradition and, in this regard, Max again was doing what any owner would do: convey the type of lease that he chooses to convey without being concerned about tradition or prior conduct.

On the other hand, doing these things would not qualify as an open and notorious occupation since, if Oscar had visited the premises, he only would have seen Max engage in conduct for which he had been hired: to run an apartment house. Moreover, visiting the apartment would not be enough to allow Oscar to see the letter that Max wrote to the tenants; for that, Oscar would need to get into Max's private premises.

Therefore, there was no open and notorious occupation.

* * *

Sample Exam Answer #1D: Dissecting the Answer

By discussing two disputable elements within one HIRRAC™, the student gives only a partial analysis for each element. For the actual entry element, the student states why there was an actual entry—but does not discuss why there was not an actual entry. For the open and notorious element, the student states why there was no open and notorious occupation—but does not discuss why there was an open and notorious occupation.

Why did this happen? To answer this it will be necessary for you to recall what you do in a simple analysis issue. In a simple analysis issue, you will write one paragraph for each "side"—a total of two paragraphs of analysis for each element that is in dispute.[21] The fictitious student who wrote the analysis in Sample Exam Answer #1D said to himself, "I have two paragraphs for analysis," and thought, therefore, that everything was okay. However, during the heat of the exam, the student forgot that she combined two issues into one HIRRAC™, which would necessitate four paragraphs of analysis—not two. Never, ever combine issues when you have analysis issues.

The moral—and summary of this chapter—is HIRRAC™ each element when you have a complex analysis issue. We now move on to answering combination issues.

---

[21] See Chapter 14, "Using HIRRAC™ to Answer a Simple Analysis Issue."

CHAPTER 16
USING HIRRAC™ TO ANSWER A RULE/COUNTER-RULE ISSUE

We have previously discussed the "rule/counter-rule" issue.[1] You will recall that in a rule/counter-rule issue, all of the elements of the rule of law are absolutely and clearly satisfied.[2]

THREE TYPES OF RULE/COUNTER-RULE ISSUES

We have learned that there are three principal types of rule/counter-rule issues. The first is the "rule/exception to the rule" issue. An example of this would be negligence/contributory negligence. The second is the "majority rule/minority rule" issue. An example of this would be comparative negligence/contributory negligence. The third is the "rule/corollary to the rule." An example of this would be breach of contract/damages.[3]

ANSWERING A RULE/COUNTER-RULE ISSUE

How do we answer any kind of rule/counter-rule issue? We do so by the HIRRAC™ method, of course. Nevertheless, the HIRRAC™ for a rule/counter-rule issue is going to be much different from the HIRRAC™ for an analysis issue. Let us now see why this is so.

Application and Not Analysis

When you HIRRAC™ an analysis issue, you have learned that the "A" in HIRRAC™ stands for "analysis." On the other hand, when you HIRRAC™ a rule/counter-rule issue, the "A" will *not* stand for analysis; instead, the "A" will stand for "application." What is the difference between "analysis" (in an analysis issue) and "application" (in a rule/counter-rule issue)?

Analysis versus Application

We have learned that in an analysis issue, one or more elements of the rule are in dispute.[4] This means that there is one definition for the element and, based on that definition, it is not clear if the elements exists on the facts given. (In the next chapter, we discuss combination issues, when the element will have more than one definition.) Further, when you perform an analysis, you take the facts that you are given and build on to those facts an argument—a creative argument—to prove that the element exists/does not exist.[5]

Importantly, in a rule/counter-rule issue, all of the elements of the rule are absolutely and clearly satisfied.[6] As such, there is nothing to analyze. Rather, in a rule/counter-rule issue, you will

---

[1] See Chapter 11, "Categorizing the Issues."

[2] This is to be contrasted with an analysis issue, where one or more elements of the rule are in dispute. See Chapter 11, "Categorizing the Issues."

[3] See Chapter 11, "Categorizing the Issues."

[4] *Ibid.*

[5] *Ibid.* See also Chapter 14, "Using HIRRAC™ to Answer a Simple Analysis Issue.

[6] See Chapter 11, "Categorizing the Issues."

simply establish for the professor that on the facts given, all of the elements are satisfied.[7] Put another way, in a rule/counter-rule issue, you will merely *apply* the rule to the facts.

Not a Test of Analytical Skills

In a rule/counter-rule issue, the professor is not testing analytical skills—there is no analysis involved. Why then would a professor include a rule/counter-rule issue on an exam? The reason is that the professor simply wants to test whether the student knows that there are competing rules or doctrines that are applicable to the issues that are triggered by the key facts.[8]

To highlight the differences between analysis and application, we can state that analysis requires originality and is not easy to do. Application, on the other hand, does not require originality; indeed, in an application, creativity is simply irrelevant. Moreover, application is quite easy, as you will see.[9]

You are probably just now starting to understand why doing a HIRRAC™ for an analysis issue is totally different from doing a HIRRAC™ for a rule/counter-rule issue, at least from the "A" perspective of HIRRAC™ (analysis versus application). As we go through the hypotheticals in this chapter, your understanding will grow exponentially.

HYPOTHETICAL #1: RULE/EXCEPTION TO THE RULE

Let us look at Hypothetical #1. This hypo deals with the first type of rule/counter-rule issue: rule/exception to the rule.[10] Immediately preceding Sample Exam Answer #1A, a very good answer, we include a diagram of the problem and a good scratch outline.

One final point is in order before we begin studying Hypothetical #1 and the sample answers that follow. When you study Sample Exam Answer #1A, you will think that we are using the "HIRAC" method, not the HIRRAC™ method.[11] The reason that you will think that we are using HIRAC (and not HIRRAC™) is because you will see only one rule of law—one "R"—and not two.

---

[7] In this respect, the "application" for a rule/counter-rule issue is identical to the "rule mop-up" section of an analysis issue. See Chapter 14, "Using HIRRAC™ to Answer a Simple Analysis Issue." You will clearly understand "application" (and see how it differs from analysis) when we go over the hypotheticals in the present chapter.

[8] Rule/counter-rule issues are especially common on so-called "racehorse" exams. In a racehorse exam, the student has to grapple with a dozen *or more* issues in an hour. By contrast, if the exam has analysis issues only, the student can expect approximately six to seven issues. In your typical racehorse exam, the professor is not interested in testing analytical skills; the professor is only interested in knowing if the student can identify the issue, state the rule, and "apply the rule" to the facts. We discuss "application" in the hypos that follow.

[9] As I have stated earlier in this text, the student should be aware that many professors use the terms "analysis" and "application" interchangeably. I do not. I use the term "analysis" in the context of an analysis issue (requiring creative arguments) and the term "application" in the context of a rule/counter-rule issue (not requiring creative arguments).

[10] The student should note that each of the hypotheticals covered in this chapter would be the equivalent of one to two issues on a one-hour examination. Complete examinations are discussed in Chapter 19, "Sample Exams."

[11] See Chapter 13, "Essay Writing: An Overview of the "IRAC" (and "HIRRAC™") Method," for a discussion of the differences between IRAC and HIRRAC™.

Nevertheless, we are in fact using HIRRAC™ and not HIRAC. You will see this very clearly—but only *after* you study the explanatory text to both Sample Exam Answers #1A *and* #1B.

Now let us proceed to read Hypothetical #1, a negligence problem. It should look familiar to you: We previously covered this hypo in another section of this text.[12]

---

[12] See Chapter 11, "Categorizing the Issues," Hypothetical #3.

Hypothetical #1

[Rule/Counter-Rule: Rule/Exception to the Rule]

Lawnco is a business located in the State of Westmoreland. Lawnco's business is the renting of various kinds of gardening machines and tools. One of the machines that Lawnco rents is an electric lawn-mower, Model L-100. On all such models, there is a safety feature to prevent a certain type of injury to the user. From time to time, the safety feature on the Model L-100 will wear out because of use. Lawnco is aware of this problem but does not regularly inspect each Model L-100 to make sure that the safety feature is in good working order. Nevertheless, when Lawnco does find that a Model L-100 needs a new safety mechanism, Lawnco performs the necessary replacement. Lawnco knows that a worn out safety mechanism can result in injury to the user.

Able is a white male forty years of age who comes onto Lawnco's premises to rent a Model L-100.[13] Throughout Lawnco's store, there are numerous signs, in large red print, that state: "ALWAYS READ OPERATING INSTRUCTIONS BEFORE USING ANY EQUIPMENT." Able is quite literate and he saw the signs. In addition, all customers of Lawnco receive a booklet of operating instructions for the machine or tool that the customer rents. Able received such a booklet for the Model L-100, but failed to read the booklet before operating the mower. Able then proceeded to use the Model L-100 in a manner not prescribed and was injured.

If the mower had a properly functioning safety feature, Able would not have been injured. Able was not aware that the safety feature was worn out. Further, even without the safety feature, if Able had read the operating instructions and used the mower in the manner prescribed, he would not have been injured.

The manufacturer is no longer in existence. You are to assume that the doctrine of strict liability does not apply on these facts in this jurisdiction. You are also to omit any discussion of the Uniform Commercial Code.

The State of Westmoreland does not recognize the doctrine of comparative negligence.

Can Able recover? Discuss.

---

[13] As we discussed in Chapter 11, "Categorizing the Issues," Able could have been an African-American female, aged fifty-five. These are not key facts. This is just background information. Do not let it confuse you on the exam.

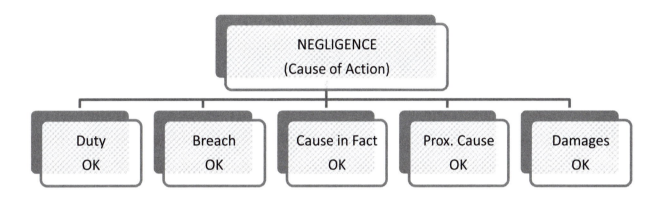

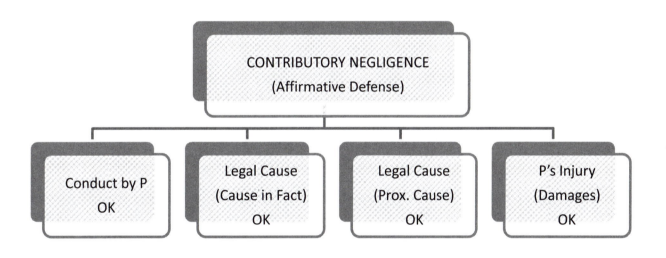

Sample Scratch Outline #1

A v. L: Negligence: Known danger; L failed to inspect.

L v. A: Contributory Negligence: Failure to heed signs and read; Improper use of equipment.

....

Sample Exam Answer #1A: An Excellent Answer

The answer that follows is exceptionally well written and clear. Take note that there is application, but no analysis.

borbri

Sample Exam Answer #1A

Negligence
Can Able recover from Lawnco in negligence because Lawnco failed to inspect the Model L-100 for wear while knowing that a worn safety feature can result in injury to the user?

Liability for negligence exists when the plaintiff proves that a duty was owed to him, that the defendant breached the duty, and that the defendant's act was the cause in fact and proximate cause of the plaintiff's injury.

A duty is owed to all foreseeable plaintiffs. Able was a foreseeable plaintiff: Able was a user and Lawnco had actual knowledge that a worn out safety mechanism can result in injury to the user.

A breach of duty is found when the defendant's conduct was unreasonable, as it was here when Lawnco failed to inspect some Model L-100s, while knowing that the safety mechanisms wear out and knowing that an improper safety can cause injury.

Cause in fact is established when, but for defendant's conduct, plaintiff would not have suffered the injury. Here, if the safety mechanism had been working properly, Able would not have been injured.

Proximate cause exists when there is no external intervening and superseding force to cut off liability; no such force is found here.

The injury required is also stated.

Thus, Lawnco was negligent.

Contributory Negligence
Will Lawnco be able to avoid liability to Able on the ground that Able was contributorily negligent in failing to read the instructions and use the mower properly?

Contributory negligence is conduct on the part of the plaintiff, contributing as a legal cause—cause in fact and proximate cause—to the harm he has suffered, which falls below the standard to which he is required to conform for his own protection; under the common law, it is a bar to recovery.

Able's failure to read the instructions and operate the machinery in the prescribed manner was a legal cause of the injury: if he had read the instructions and operated the mower in the prescribed manner, he would not have been injured.

The warning signs ("ALWAYS READ OPERATING INSTRUCTIONS BEFORE USING ANY EQUIPMENT") and the booklet of instructions which he was given were for his own

protection. His failure to take heed of the signs and read the booklet was conduct which fell below the standard that he should have conformed to for his own safety.

Therefore, Able was contributorily negligent and will be barred from recovering damages.

Sample Exam Answer #1A: Dissecting the Answer

In Hypothetical #1, the professor is simply testing the student on his understanding of two rules: (1) a cause of action, negligence and (2) an affirmative defense, contributory negligence. As you have seen, there is no analysis. There is no creativity. Yet, it is in HIRRAC™ format.

Now let us examine Sample Exam Answer #1 in detail.

1. *Heading: "Negligence."* A heading that is limited to the legal issue can help the professor know immediately what you are going to discuss.

2. *The issue statement: "Can Able recover from Lawnco in negligence because Lawnco failed to inspect . . . knowing that a worn safety feature can result in injury to the user?"* This is a good issue statement. As we have previously discussed,[14] an issue statement for an *analysis* issue (not a rule/counter-rule issue) should include four parts: (a) the parties; (b) the legal issue; (c) the element that is in dispute;[15] and (d) the key facts that are triggering that element.

However, in a rule/counter-rule issue, no elements are in dispute; all of the elements are absolutely and clearly satisfied. Therefore, in a rule/counter-rule issue, the issue statement will include only three parts: (a) the parties (Able v. Lawnco); (b) the legal issue (negligence); and (c) the key facts that are triggering that legal issue (Lawnco's failure to inspect, knowing that there is a danger).

The issue statement in Sample Exam Answer #1 includes all of these parts. It is therefore a good issue statement.[16]

3. *Rule of law: "Liability for negligence exists when the plaintiff proves . . . duty . . . [breach] . . . cause in fact and proximate cause . . . injury."* This is the rule of negligence.

4. *Application.* The next five paragraphs make up our application. What we are going to do is simply let the professor know that all of the elements to the rule are absolutely and clearly satisfied. We shall now establish that all of the elements are clearly satisfied.

(i) *Duty: "A duty is owed to all foreseeable plaintiffs."* After we have defined what a duty is, we then let the professor know that on the facts given, a duty was absolutely and clearly satisfied. The facts plainly tell us that Lawnco knew that a worn out safety mechanism can result in injury to the user. Hence, "Able was a foreseeable plaintiff: Able was a user and Lawnco had actual knowledge that a worn out safety mechanism can result in injury to the user."

---

[14] See Chapter 14, "Using HIRRAC™ to Answer a Simple Analysis Issue" and Chapter 15, "Using HIRRAC™ to Answer a Complex Analysis Issue."

[15] But see Chapter 14, "Using HIRRAC™ to Answer a Simple Analysis Issue," Sample Exam Answer #1A with Sample Exam Answer #1E (where each element is broken out separately in the order it comes up in the rule). But note that any difference between these two answers is really quite minor, as explained in those materials.

[16] Of course, we could have eliminated the issue statement and the brief heading ("Negligence") in favor of a more complete heading: one that has the parties, legal issue, and key facts. See, for example, Chapter 14, "Using HIRRAC™ to Answer a Simple Analysis Issue," Sample Examination Answer #1D.

Do you see how this "application" of the rule to the facts is totally different from an "analysis"? In analysis, we have to *prove* by an original argument that a duty exists. In an "application," we do not have to *prove* that a duty exists. The facts are so clear that there is no room for debate whether a duty exists: it does.

There is also something else to understand. The reason that we spent so much time on categorizing the issues was to enable you to know when you must "analyze" an element—and when you should not "analyze." You see, if you tried to "analyze" duty in this hypothetical, it would be frustrating. Indeed, it would be fruitless: there is nothing to analyze with respect to duty. Whether you like it or not, a duty exists.

Through the years, I have taught and counseled many students. One of the biggest problems for students is understanding that analysis is not necessarily performed on every single issue on an exam. Once the student realizes this and the difference between analysis on the one hand and application on the other, the student finds law school exams to be smooth sailing (or, if not smooth, at least the student is no longer in the middle of a storm).

(ii) *Breach: "A breach of duty is found when the defendant's conduct was unreasonable . . . ."* After we define what a breach is, we inform the professor that on the facts given, there was definitely a breach, "as was here when Lawnco failed to inspect some Model L-100s, knowing that the safety mechanisms wear out and knowing that an improper safety can cause injury."

Again, it is not possible to analyze "breach of duty." Lawnco acted unreasonably and it is not possible to argue, "Maybe it did and maybe it didn't." Lawnco *did* act unreasonably. Further, if you try to argue that it "may have acted reasonably," you will be spinning your wheels (just like if you tried to argue that maybe Lawnco did not owe a duty to Able).

The key to all of this is relatively easy: categorize the issues. Ask yourself, *Are all of the elements absolutely and clearly satisfied?*[17]

(iii) *Cause in fact: "Cause in fact is established when but for defendant's conduct, plaintiff would not have suffered the injury."* It is absolutely clear that Lawnco's acts were the cause in fact of Able's injury: the fact pattern actually states that such is the case. Hence, the application: "Here, if the safety mechanism had been working properly, Able would not have been injured."

Again, there is no analysis to be done. We are simply applying the rule to the facts that we are given to show that all of the elements of the rule are clearly satisfied.

(iv) *Proximate cause: "Proximate cause exists when there is no external intervening and superseding force . . ."* It is clear that there is no such force here. This element, too, is clearly satisfied. This element, too, cannot be analyzed.

---

[17] See Chapter 11, "Categorizing the Issues."

(v) *Damages: "The injury required is also stated."* The facts tell us that Able was injured. This element is satisfied. Again, it would be pointless to "analyze this element."

5. *Conclusion: "Thus, Lawnco was negligent."* This is our conclusion to the issue of negligence.

Now that we have done the HIRRAC™ for negligence, we shall HIRRAC™ the next issue: contributory negligence.[18]

1. *Heading: "Contributory negligence."* As discussed above, headings are good: it helps the professor to zero in on what the student is going to discuss—and anything that helps the professor can only help the student.

2. *Issue statement: "Will Lawnco be able to avoid liability to Able on the ground that Able was contributorily negligent in failing to read the instructions and use the mower properly?"* As we have discussed above, an issue statement for a rule/counter-rule issue should have (1) the parties (Lawnco v. Able); (2) the legal issue (contributory negligence); and (3) the key facts that trigger the legal issue (failing to read the instructions and using the mower improperly). We have all of these components in this issue statement.

3. *Rule of law: "Contributory negligence is conduct on the part of the plaintiff, contributing as a legal cause—cause in fact and proximate cause—to the harm he has suffered, which falls below the standard to which he is required to conform for his own protection; under the common law, it is a bar to recovery."* If the issue statement deals with contributory negligence, the rule of law must deal with contributory negligence.

4. *Application.* The next two paragraphs are the application. We are going to apply the rule to the facts (no "analysis").

(i) *Legal cause: "Able's failure to read the instructions and operate the machinery in the prescribed manner was a legal cause of the injury: if he had read the instructions and operated the mower in the prescribed manner, he would not have been injured."* The facts tell us that if he had complied with the instructions, he would not have been injured.

(ii) *Unreasonable conduct: "The warning signs ("ALWAYS READ OPERATING INSTRUCTIONS BEFORE USING ANY EQUIPMENT") and the booklet of instructions which he was given were for his own protection. His failure to take heed of the signs and read the booklet was conduct which fell below the standard that he should have conformed to for his own safety."* The signs and booklet were for his protection; his failure to read the instructions was unreasonable.

---

[18] As we discussed earlier on in this chapter, you are probably saying to yourself that this is not HIRRAC™, but rather HIRAC: there is only one rule that we are dealing with (negligence) and none of the elements are in dispute. However, after we finish our discussion of Sample Exam Answer #1B, you will see why this is really HIRRAC™ (two rules).

5. *Conclusion: "Therefore, Able was contributorily negligent and will be barred from recovering damages."* That ends the discussion of this issue.

Sample Exam Answer #1A was a great answer. However, as we indicated earlier in this chapter, you are probably thinking that we have used the "HIRAC" method of answering the hypo: We have an issue, *a* rule of law (not two rules as we have in the HIRRAC™ of an analysis issue) and an application. All this is true. Still, let us see how Sample Exam Answer #1A can easily be turned into a HIRRAC™ (two rules) and, in the process, made even "tighter."

Sample Exam Answer #1B: Another Great Answer

With Sample Exam Answer #1B, you will see how we can easily transform Sample Exam Answer #1A into a "true" HIRRAC™ format.

Sample Exam Answer #1B

<u>Negligence/Contributory Negligence</u>

Can Able recover from Lawnco in negligence because Lawnco failed to inspect the Model L-100 for wear while knowing that a worn safety feature can result in injury to the user, or will Lawnco be able to avoid liability to Able on the ground that Able was contributorily negligent in failing to read the instructions and using the mower improperly?

Liability for negligence exists when the plaintiff proves that a duty was owed to him, that the defendant breached the duty, and that the defendant's act was the cause in fact and proximate cause of the plaintiff's injury. Contributory negligence is conduct on the part of the plaintiff, contributing as a legal cause—cause in fact and proximate cause—to the harm he has suffered, which falls below the standard to which he is required to conform for his own protection; under the common law, it is a bar to recovery.

A duty is owed to all foreseeable plaintiffs. Able was a foreseeable plaintiff: Able was a user and Lawnco had actual knowledge that a worn out safety mechanism can result in injury to the user. A breach of duty is found when the defendant's conduct was unreasonable, as here when Lawnco failed to inspect some Model L-100s, knowing that the safety mechanisms wear out and knowing that an improper safety can cause injury. Cause in fact is established when but for defendant's conduct, plaintiff would not have suffered the injury. Here, if the safety mechanism had been working properly, Able would not have been injured. Proximate cause exists when there is no external intervening and superseding force; no such force is found here. The injury required is also stated.

Thus, Lawnco was negligent.

However, Able's failure to read the instructions and operate the machinery in the prescribed manner was a legal cause of the injury: if he had read the instructions and operated the mower in the prescribed manner, he would not have been injured. The warning signs ("ALWAYS READ OPERATING INSTRUCTIONS BEFORE USING ANY EQUIPMENT") and the booklet of instructions which he was given were for his own protection. His failure to take heed of the signs and read the booklet was conduct which fell below the standard that he should have conformed to for his own safety.

Therefore, Able was contributorily negligent and will be barred from recovering damages.

Sample Exam Answer #1B: Dissecting the Answer

Let us look at Sample Exam Answer #1B.

This sample answer is identical to Sample Exam Answer #1A. The only difference is that the two issues (negligence and contributory negligence) have been combined into one HIRRAC™. Why have we done this? Whenever you have a rule/counter-rule issue,[19] the rule and the counter-rule are so related to each other that it makes absolute sense to discuss the rule (negligence) and the counter-rule (contributory negligence) together—in one HIRRAC™.

Must you combine the two issues into one HIRRAC™ when you have a rule/counter-rule issue? Of course, you need not. Feel free to tackle the rule (negligence) and then separately tackle the counter-rule (contributory negligence) in the manner that we have illustrated in Sample Exam Answer #1A. (In law school, that was my own preference. I like to keep matters simple, and doing a separate HIRRAC™ for each issue is simple.) However, if you wish, you certainly can combine the two issues into one HIRRAC™, as we have done here in Sample Exam Answer #1B.[20]

Sample Exam Answer #1B also shows you (again) that there are indeed many ways of writing a correct answer.[21] You should read these sample answers not with the idea of memorizing an answer. Rather, you should study these samples so that you understand what good answers always have: issues, rules, applications/analyses.

Now let us examine Sample Answer #1B in detail.

1. *Heading: "Negligence/contributory negligence."* We combine the two headings from the two separate issues into one.

2. *Issue statement: "Can Able recover from Lawnco in negligence . . . or will Lawnco be able to avoid liability to Able on the ground that Able was contributorily negligent. . . ?"* This is where we clearly and plainly combine the two issues. Nevertheless, remember why we can do this: because the two issues are so intertwined with each other that it makes sense to discuss the two together. DO NOT DO THIS WHEN YOU HAVE ANALYSES ISSUES.

---

[19] Recall that there are three types of rule/counter-rule issues, as is discussed earlier in this chapter and in Chapter 11, "Categorizing the Issues."

[20] Although you can combine two issues into one HIRRAC™ when you have a rule/counter-rule issue, *never* do this when you have an analysis issue. When you have an analysis issue (especially a complex analysis issue), you should/must tackle each element in a HIRRAC™ format, element by element. After you HIRRAC™ one element, you go on to HIRRAC™ the next element, and so forth. Remember this: If you try to combine several analyses issues into one HIRRAC™, you will get confused—and write a confusing answer.

[21] See for example Chapter 14, "Using HIRRAC™ to Answer a Simple Analysis Issue" and sample answers therein.

3. *(Two) Rules:* *"Liability for negligence exists when . . . duty . . . [breach] . . . and that the defendant's act was the cause in fact and proximate cause of the plaintiff's injury. Contributory negligence is conduct on the part of the plaintiff, contributing as a legal cause—cause in fact and proximate cause—to the harm he has suffered, which falls below the standard to which he is required to conform for his own protection; under the common law, it is a bar to recovery."*

The first sentence, the rule of negligence, is the first rule, the first "R" of HIRRAC™. The second sentence, the rule of contributory negligence, is the second rule, the second "R" of HIRRAC™. Do you now understand why this is the HIRRAC™ (and not HIRAC) method?

4. *Application:* The first paragraph of application is the application for negligence; the second paragraph of application is the application for contributory negligence.

5. *Conclusion:* We have two conclusions. The first is that Lawnco was negligent; the second is that Able was contributorily negligent.

There you have it. Now you know how to use HIRRAC™ for a rule/counter-rule issue. Again, it is necessary to point out that if you feel more comfortable tackling one issue at a time (as we did in Sample Exam Answer #1A), that is okay and there is absolutely nothing wrong with such an approach. However, if you want to look perhaps just a little more "sophisticated," consider the approach that we used in Sample Exam Answer #1B and combine the two issues.[22]

Sample Exam Answer #1C: Running Low on Time

Sample Exam Answer #1C follows. This sample answer is a good answer and should be considered, especially if you are running short on time. Let us study Sample Answer #1C. Thereafter we shall discuss its pros—and cons.

---

[22] Sample Answer #1B is clearly in HIRRAC™ format because we clearly have two rules. Still, we also consider Sample Answer #1A to be in HIRRAC™ format because we still have two rules (negligence and contributory negligence). We, therefore, will refer to either format (#1A or #1B) as being in the HIRRAC™ format.

Sample Exam Answer #1C

<u>Negligence/Contributory Negligence</u>

Can Able recover from Lawnco in negligence because Lawnco failed to inspect the Model L-100 for wear while knowing that a worn safety feature can result in injury to the user, or will Lawnco be able to avoid liability to Able on the ground that Able was contributorily negligent in failing to read the instructions and use the mower properly?

Liability for negligence exists when the plaintiff proves that a duty was owed to him, that the defendant breached the duty, and that the defendant's act was the cause in fact and proximate cause of the plaintiff's injury. Contributory negligence is conduct on the part of the plaintiff, contributing as a legal cause—cause in fact and proximate cause—to the harm he has suffered, which falls below the standard to which he is required to conform for his own protection; under the common law, it is a bar to recovery.

A duty was owed to Able since Able was a user and Lawnco had actual knowledge that a worn out safety mechanism can result in injury to the user. There was a breach of duty when Lawnco failed to inspect some Model L-100s, knowing that the safety mechanisms wear out and knowing that an improper safety can cause injury. Cause in fact was established because Able would not have been injured if Lawnco inspected. Proximate cause exists since there was no superseding force to cut off liability. The injury required is also stated.

Thus, Lawnco was negligent.

However, if Able had read the instructions and operated the mower in the prescribed manner, he would not have been injured. The warning signs ("ALWAYS READ OPERATING INSTRUCTIONS BEFORE USING ANY EQUIPMENT") and the booklet of instructions which he was given were for his own protection.

Therefore, Able was contributorily negligent and will be barred from recovering damages.

Sample Exam Answer #1C: Dissecting the Answer

You will note that the only difference between Sample Exam Answer #1B and #1C is the application: the application in #1C is significantly shorter. The reason for this is because we have omitted the rules for each of the elements. Is this a "wise" thing to do? It depends.

The issues require us to discuss two problems: negligence and contributory negligence.[23] How much time is available to do this? If these (negligence/contributory negligence) issues are the last points we are going to discuss on the exam and we have plenty of time available, we would follow the model of Sample Exam Answer #1A or #1B: We would define the elements of the rule. Failure to do so may cost us points. However, if our time is running out and we still have an analysis issue to get to, we would probably follow the approach of Sample Answer #1C. The moral is never to lose sight of your common sense: use your time smartly.

Sample Exam Answer #1D: A Qualified Great Answer

Sample Exam Answer #1D is yet another answer, demonstrating how several people can answer a question somewhat differently, and all can get an "A" grade. Still, I qualify it somewhat, as you will see when we dissect the answer.

---

[23] Even though I typically refer to "issues," I actually consider a rule/counter-rule issue (e.g., negligence and contributory negligence) to be the equivalent of one analysis issue on an exam, not two.

Sample Exam Answer #1D

Negligence

Can Able recover from Lawnco in negligence because Lawnco failed to inspect the Model L-100 for wear while knowing that a worn safety feature can result in injury to the user?

Liability for negligence exists when the plaintiff proves that a duty was owed to him, that the defendant breached the duty, and that the defendant's act was the cause in fact and proximate cause of the plaintiff's injury.

Duty

A duty is owed to all foreseeable plaintiffs. Able was a foreseeable, plaintiff: Able was a user and Lawnco had actual knowledge that a worn out safety mechanism can result in injury to the user.

Breach

A breach of duty is found when the defendant's conduct was unreasonable, as was here when Lawnco failed to inspect some Model L-100s, while knowing that the safety mechanisms wear out and knowing that an improper safety can cause injury.

Cause in Fact: But For

Cause in fact is established when, but for defendant's conduct, plaintiff would not have suffered the injury. Here, if the safety mechanism had been working properly, Able would not have been injured.

Proximate Cause

Proximate cause exists when there is no external intervening and superseding force to cut off liability; no such force is found here.

Damages

The injury required is also stated.

Thus, Lawnco was negligent.

Contributory Negligence

Will Lawnco be able to avoid liability to Able on the ground that Able was contributorily negligent in failing to read the instructions and use the mower properly?

Contributory negligence is conduct on the part of the plaintiff, contributing as a legal cause—cause in fact and proximate cause—to the harm he has suffered, which falls below the standard to which he is required to conform for his own protection; under the common law, it is a bar to recovery.

Legal Causation: Cause in Fact

Cause in fact is established, again, using the but for test: Able's failure to read the instructions and operate the machinery in the prescribed manner was a legal cause of the injury: if

he had read the instructions and operated the mower in the prescribed manner, he would not have been injured.

Causation: Proximate Cause
There is no superseding event or policy consideration to insulate Able from his own carelessness.

Unreasonable Conduct
The warning signs ("ALWAYS READ OPERATING INSTRUCTIONS BEFORE USING ANY EQUIPMENT") and the booklet of instructions which he was given were for his own protection. His failure to take heed of the signs and read the booklet was conduct which fell below the standard that he should have conformed to for his own safety.

Therefore, Able was contributorily negligent and will be barred from recovering damages.

Sample Exam Answer #1D: Dissecting the Answer

Sample Answer #1D is virtually identical with Sample Answer #1A by way of substantive content. We can easily see that the major difference is the use of sub-headings. In effect, this is one big "rule mop-up" (elements clearly satisfied for simple analysis and complex analysis issues).[24] It seems that Sample Answer #1D is even better than Sample Answer #1A. If headings and sub-headings are good, how can Answer #1D be anything but great? The answer is simple: While I recommend this detail for bar exam takers, I do not recommend this generally for law school students. The bar exam is not as tough as law school exams and you will have the time to get into this detail on the bar exam; on law school exams, I am concerned that you will run out of time. In short, this kind of detail is needed for analysis issues, but for rule/counter-rule issues, you may not have the luxury of time. If you do have that time, that is great. Give the professor the detail that you want. On the other hand, bear in mind that Sample Exam Answer #1D is really just one issue: there is no analysis and to go into such detail for one issue may cause you to run out of time for other issues.

Thus, to repeat, if time is on your side, fine, go into the detail as per Sample Answer #1D. If time is not on your side, use Sample Answer #1A as your guide. It is a bit shorter and it will enable you to get the job done nicely.

The moral here, yet again, is that HIRRAC™ is just a tool. It is not a substitute for thinking or for using reasonable judgment.

HYPOTHETICAL #2: MAJORITY RULE/MINORITY RULE

Now let us go over another type of rule/counter-rule issue: the majority rule/minority rule issue. This hypo, Hypothetical #2, is a variation of the Hypothetical #1 and has been covered previously.[25] Again, for purposes of completion, we follow the hypo with a diagram and a good scratch outline.

---

[24] See Chapters 14 and 15.
[25] See Chapter 11, "Categorizing the Issues," Hypothetical #4.

Hypothetical #2

[Rule/Counter-Rule: Majority Rule/Minority Rule]

Lawnco is a business located in the State of Westmoreland. Lawnco's business is the renting of various kinds of gardening machines and tools. One of the machines that Lawnco rents is an electric lawn-mower, Model L-100. On all such models, there is a safety feature to prevent a certain type of injury to the user. From time to time, the safety feature on the Model L-100 will wear out because of use. Lawnco negligently fails to regularly inspect each Model L-100 to make sure that the safety feature is in good working order. A worn out safety mechanism can result in injury to the user.

Able comes onto Lawnco's premises to rent a Model L-100. Throughout Lawnco's store, there are numerous signs, in large red print, that state: "ALWAYS READ OPERATING INSTRUCTIONS BEFORE USING ANY EQUIPMENT." Able is quite literate and he saw the signs. In addition, all customers of Lawnco receive a booklet of operating instructions for the machine or tool that the customer rents. Able received such a booklet for the Model L-100, but failed to read the booklet before operating the mower. Able then proceeded to use the Model L-100 in a manner not prescribed and was injured.

If the mower had a properly functioning safety feature, Able would not have been injured. Able was not aware that the safety feature was worn out. Further, even without the safety feature, if Able had read the operating instructions and used the mower in the manner prescribed, he would not have been injured.

Lawnco was 70 % responsible for Able's injury.

The manufacturer is no longer in existence. You are to assume that the doctrine of strict liability does not apply on these facts in this jurisdiction. You are also to omit any discussion of the Uniform Commercial Code.

Can Able recover? Discuss.

**borbri** Diagram

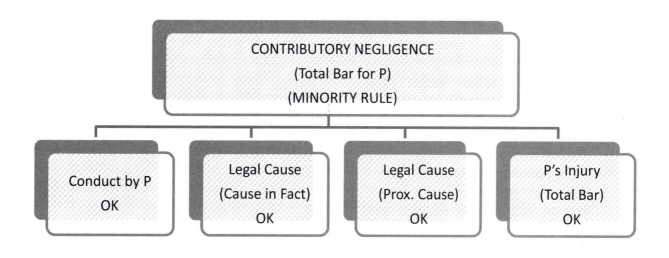

CONTRIBUTORY NEGLIGENCE
(Total Bar for P)
(MINORITY RULE)

Conduct by P
OK

Legal Cause
(Cause in Fact)
OK

Legal Cause
(Prox. Cause)
OK

P's Injury
(Total Bar)
OK

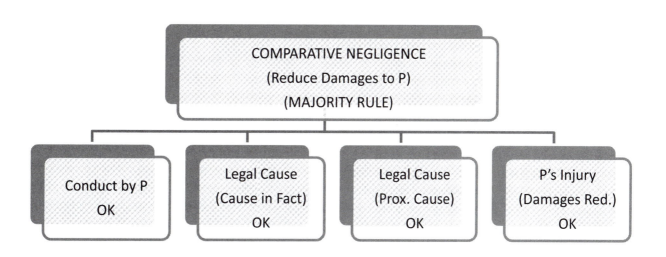

COMPARATIVE NEGLIGENCE
(Reduce Damages to P)
(MAJORITY RULE)

Conduct by P
OK

Legal Cause
(Cause in Fact)
OK

Legal Cause
(Prox. Cause)
OK

P's Injury
(Damages Red.)
OK

Sample Scratch Outline #2

L v. A: Contributory Negligence: Failure to read/Improper Use of equipment

L v. A: Comparative Negligence: Failure to read/Improper Use of equipment

....

We can answer this question in either of two different ways. The first way will be consistent with Sample Answer #1A. The second way will be consistent with Sample Answer #1B. Remember that either way is acceptable. Remember also that in both cases, all elements of the rule are clearly satisfied: the outcome is dependent solely on the rule of law that the jurisdiction in question would adopt. If contributory negligence is the rule that is adopted, Able loses; if comparative negligence is the rule that is adopted, Able wins (70 percent of his damages).

The important points that you should keep in mind when you study these sample answers are: (1) The format is in an HIRRAC™ format. (2) All elements of each rule are absolutely and clearly satisfied. (3) As such, there is no creativity or analysis involved. (4) Indeed, if you tried to do an "analysis," you would waste your time and become frustrated. (5) But you *will* have to do an application: apply the rule to the facts to establish that all elements are indeed satisfied.

Sample Exam Answer #2A: A Great Answer

<u>Contributory Negligence</u>
Will Lawnco be able to avoid liability to Able on the ground that Able was contributorily negligent in failing to read the instructions and improperly using the mower?

Contributory negligence is conduct on the part of the plaintiff, contributing as a legal cause—cause in fact and proximate cause—to the harm he has suffered, which falls below the standard to which he is required to conform for his own protection; under the common law, it is a bar to recovery.

Able's failure to read the instructions and operate the machinery in the prescribed manner was a legal cause of the injury: if he had read the instructions and operated the mower in the prescribed manner, he would not have been injured. The warning signs ("ALWAYS READ OPERATING INSTRUCTIONS BEFORE USING ANY EQUIPMENT") and the booklet of instructions which he was given were for his own protection. His failure to take heed of the signs and read the booklet was conduct which fell below the standard that he should have conformed to for his own safety.

Therefore, Able was contributorily negligent and, if this doctrine is recognized in this jurisdiction, he will be barred from recovering damages.

<u>Comparative Negligence</u>
Will Able be able to recover at least some of his damages from Lawnco, even if Able's injuries were partially caused by his negligence in failing to read the instructions and use the mower properly?

Where the plaintiff's negligence was a cause of his injury, his damages are reduced in proportion to his negligence but his action is not barred.

As discussed above in the discussion of contributory negligence, Able's failure to read the instructions when he saw the sign telling him to read the instructions is conduct which was a legal cause of his injury. Since Able was 30 percent responsible, his damages should be reduced by 30 percent.

Therefore, if the jurisdiction follows the rule comparative negligence, Able will recover 70 percent of his damages.

Sample Exam #2A: Dissecting the Answer

Notice how we tackle the contributory negligence issue: heading, issue, rule, and application. Notice, too, again, that there is no analysis. After we finish off the contributory negligence issue, we address the comparative negligence issue in similar fashion.

Some students may wonder: why do we not address negligence? The reason is this: the facts state that Lawnco was negligent: "Lawnco negligently fails to regularly inspect . . . ." This is a preclusion fact. There is, therefore, no reason to address this issue.

Some students, however, want to let the professor know that negligence is a "given." Consequently, some students will break out of the HIRRAC™ format and state as the very first sentence of their essay: "The facts state that Lawnco was negligent. No discussion of Lawnco's liability, therefore, is necessary." Immediately thereafter, these students go into their first HIRRAC™. If you want to do this, that is fine. If you are not certain what your professor wants, check with your professor.

Through the years, some students have asked me this question: "Should I not, in my application, state which rule (majority or minority) is the 'better rule'? We have discussed in class which rule is superior. Should I not discuss this in my answer? Furthermore, if I give the 'reasons' for which rule is better, is this not 'analysis'?"

Here is my response to this question: I do not think that most teachers want a discussion of which rule is better. If, however, your professor does want such a discussion, then by all means, put it in your application. In any event, this is not "analysis." Remember that analysis is your creative reasons—not your professor's—why the element exists/does not exist. In college, it was okay to "regurgitate" it back to the professor. That is not the standard in law school, however. Still, if your professor wants such a discussion, invariably, you will be "regurgitating" what the professor stated in class. As such, your discussion is not original thinking and, therefore, is not analysis (at least in the manner that I define it).

Sample Exam Answer #2B: Another Great Answer

Now let us look at Sample Answer #2B, an answer just a little more sophisticated than Sample Answer #2A. Which one do you use as a model? Whichever one you find easier to write.

Sample Exam Answer #2B

Contributory Negligence/Comparative Negligence

Will Lawnco be able to avoid liability to Able on the ground that Able was contributorily negligent in failing to read the instructions and improperly using the mower, or will Able be able to recover at least some of his damages from Lawnco, even if Able's injuries were partially caused by his negligence in failing to read the instructions and use the mower properly?

Contributory negligence is conduct on the part of the plaintiff, contributing as a legal cause—cause in fact and proximate cause—to the harm he has suffered, which falls below the standard to which he is required to conform for his own protection; under the common law, it is a bar to recovery.

Able's failure to read the instructions and operate the machinery in the prescribed manner was a legal cause of the injury: if he had read the instructions and operated the mower in the prescribed manner, he would not have been injured. The warning signs ("ALWAYS READ OPERATING INSTRUCTIONS BEFORE USING ANY EQUIPMENT") and the booklet of instructions which he was given were for his own protection. His failure to take heed of the signs and read the booklet was conduct which fell below the standard that he should have conformed to for his own safety. Therefore, Able was contributorily negligent and, if this doctrine is recognized in this jurisdiction, he will be barred from recovering damages.

However, as discussed above, although Able's failure to read the instructions when he saw the sign telling him to read the instructions is conduct which was a legal cause of his injury, under comparative negligence, since Able was 30 percent responsible, his damages should be reduced by 30 percent.

Therefore, if the jurisdiction follows the rule of comparative negligence, Able will recover 70 percent of his damages.

Sample Exam Answer #2B: Dissecting the Answer

You will note that Sample Exam Answer #2B is virtually identical to Sample Exam Answer #2A. Indeed, the issues, rules, and applications are the same. What we have done here is simply combine the two issues. Do you have to combine issues? As we have stated previously, the answer is, no. The moral: feel free to experiment with a style that works for you—so long as you stay within the basic HIRRAC™ structure. Remember to use HIRRAC™ as a tool, but never become a slave to it or let it override your good common sense. Remember also that while it is okay to combine rule/counter-rule issues, never combine analysis issues.

HYPOTHETICAL #3: RULE/COROLLARY TO THE RULE

Our last hypothetical, a landlord-tenant problem, deals with the final type of rule/counter-rule issue: the rule and the corollary to the rule. We have previously studied this hypothetical too.[26] As before, we follow the hypo with a diagram and a good scratch outline.

---

[26] See Chapter 11, "Categorizing the Issues," Hypothetical #5.

Hypothetical #3

[Rule/Counter-Rule: Rule/Corollary to the Rule]

Lenore owns the Whiteacre apartment complex. The complex is rented entirely by low income tenants. Through the years, Lenore has lost interest in the building. As a result, rats and roaches are common throughout. Hot water is seldom available. Toilets regularly overflow due to old plumbing, which must be replaced. Heat in the winter is seldom available.

The tenants have repeatedly informed Lenore of this situation, but she refuses to do anything. The tenants want to know what, if anything, they can do. Moving out, however, is not an option.

Discuss.

Diagram

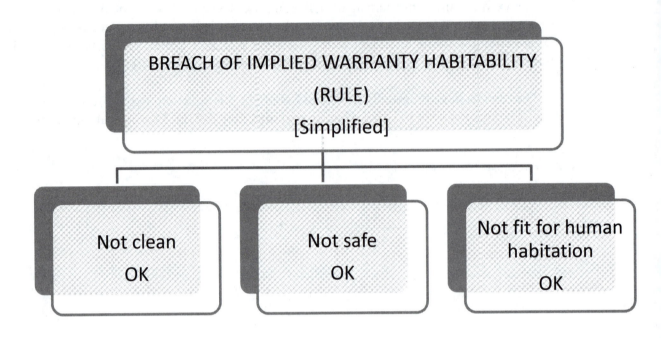

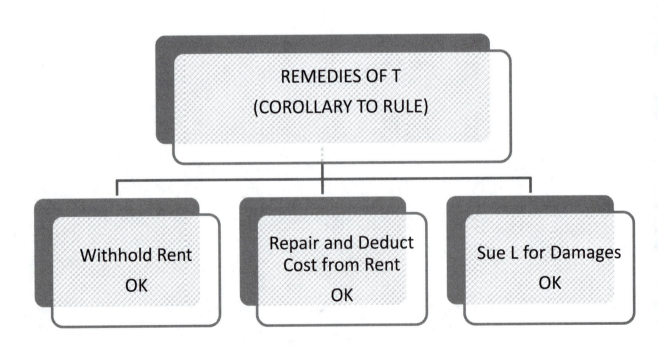

Sample Scratch Outline #3

Tenants v. Lenore: Breach Implied Warranty of Habitability:
                                   Vermin/Toilet Overflow/Old Plumbing/No Heat

Tenants v. Lenore: Remedy for Breach:
                                   Withhold Rent; Repair and Deduct; Damages

....

How do we answer this problem? It should not be a surprise to you that we answer it in the HIRRAC format. Let us look at some good samples.

Sample Exam Answer #3A: An Excellent Answer

This answer is quite good because it follows the HIRRAC™ structure for the cause of action (rule) and the remedies (corollary to the rule).

Sample Exam Answer #3A

Implied Warranty of Habitability

Can the tenants sue Lenore for breach of the implied warranty of habitability for an apartment building, which is vermin-infested, has old and improperly working plumbing and often no heat in the wintertime?

The implied warranty of habitability states that a landlord must deliver and maintain, throughout the lease, premises which are safe, clean, and fit for human habitation.

An apartment that has vermin infestation, along with overflowing sewage and lack of heat in the winter, is unclean and a threat to one's health and safety.

Therefore, the landlord breached the warranty.

Remedy: Rent Withholding[27]

When the landlord breaches the implied warranty of habitability, can the tenants avail themselves of rent withholding?

When the landlord breaches the implied warranty of habitability, tenants may typically withhold rent, equal to the damages suffered or the pro-rata diminution in value due to lack of heat, plumbing problems, and emotional distress (from vermin); jurisdictions often require that the withheld rent must be deposited into escrow.

Whatever the agreed rent is, the tenant may therefore withhold rent, either a percentage or the entire amount, depending upon the severity of the landlord's breach.

Rent withholding is therefore one remedy.

Remedy: Repair and Deduct

When the landlord breaches the implied warranty of habitability, can the tenants make the repairs themselves and deduct the cost from their rent?

In some jurisdictions, tenants may withhold rent and deduct the cost, not to exceed a stated amount, typically not more than one month's rent, and not to include the value of the tenants' own labor.

For some of the repairs, such as vermin eradication, the tenants may be able to repair and

---

[27] Note that between the heading of this issue and the conclusion of the preceding issue, I have triple-spaced. I do this because when I double-space between paragraphs, triple spacing between issues makes my essay easier to read and gives my answer a "nicer" look. You will also note, however, that when I do a "sub-HIRRAC™" for complex analysis issues, I do not triple space. There, I double-space to make it clear that the elements (e.g., duty, breach of duty, etc.) that I HIRRAC™ are all part of a greater problem (e.g., negligence).

deduct because the cost may be within the dollar parameters of the local statute. The tenants will probably not be able to repair and deduct for new plumbing since the cost will probably be too great.

Repair and deduct is, therefore, another remedy.

Remedy: Damages
When the landlord breaches the implied warranty of habitability, can the tenants sue for damages?

When the landlord breaches the implied warranty of habitability, some jurisdictions[28] also allow a suit for damages, including a suit for punitives when the landlord's behavior is outrageous.

As the building defects are very substantial and the landlord chooses to do nothing, the tenants may wish to continue to pay rent and sue for damages, including punitive damages.

A suit for damages is therefore appropriate.

---

[28] We have labeled this issue a "rule/corollary to the rule" type of rule/counter-rule issue. Indeed, it is. Still, do you also see how it is *also* a "majority rule/minority rule" type of rule/counter-rule issue? ("... some jurisdictions . . .") We bring this to your attention purposefully. On your exams, if you see an issue which overlaps with *several* types of categories, that is okay. The key to success is to know whether you must "analyze" or "apply." That one issue can be a "rule/corollary to the rule" as well as a "majority rule/minority rule" issue should in no way frustrate you.

Sample Exam Answer #3B: Yet Another Excellent Answer

Although Sample Exam Answer #3A is correct, we can make it a little more "lean." Let us look at Sample Exam Answer #3B.

Sample Exam Answer #3B

<u>Implied Warranty of Habitability</u>
Can the tenants sue Lenore for breach of the implied warranty of habitability for an apartment building which is vermin-infested, has old and improperly working plumbing, and often has no heat in the wintertime?

The implied warranty of habitability states that a landlord must deliver and maintain, throughout the lease, premises which are safe, clean, and fit for human habitation.

An apartment which has vermin infestation, along with overflowing sewage and lack of heat in the winter, is unclean and a threat to one's health and safety.

Therefore, the landlord breached the warranty.

<u>Remedies: Withhold Rent, Repair and Deduct, and Damages</u>
When there is a breach of the implied warranty of habitability, what remedies are available to the tenants?

When there is a breach of the implied warranty of habitability, the tenants can either withhold rent, repair and deduct, or sue the landlord for damages, depending upon the jurisdiction.[29]

If the tenants withhold rent, they will not have to pay any rent if there is a total breach; otherwise they will be allowed to withhold a pro-rata amount.

In some jurisdictions, tenants may withhold rent and deduct the cost, not to exceed a stated amount, typically not more than rent for one month, and not to include the tenants' own labor. For some of the repairs, such as vermin eradication, the tenants may be able to repair and deduct since the cost may be within the dollar parameters of the local statute. The tenants will probably not be able to repair and deduct for new plumbing since the cost will probably be too great.

In other jurisdictions, tenants can pay rent and sue for damages, including punitives. Since Lenore chose to do nothing, punitives may be appropriate.

The remedies are therefore: withhold; repair and deduct; or sue for damages.

---

[29] See footnote 26, supra. Note also that within this HIRRAC™ (remedies) we are dealing with three rules: withholding rent; repair and deduct; and damages. Does this mean we are dealing with HIRRRAC™? The point, as stated earlier, is to use HIRRAC™ as a tool, but never feel burdened by it. You use HIRRAC™. Do not let HIRRAC™ use you!

Sample Exam Answer #3B: Dissecting the Answer

This answer is as good as Sample Exam Answer #3A. The only difference is that here, all of the rules that relate to the corollary have been combined into one HIRRAC™. Again, use the format in #3A or #3B, whichever one suits your own writing needs better.

SUMMARY OF CHAPTER 16

To summarize this chapter: whenever you have a rule/counter-rule issue, you may HIRRAC™ the rule and then HIRRAC™ the counter-rule: use two separate "HIRRACs™." It may look "baby" but it really is okay and it will work. On the other hand, if you choose, combine the several issues into one HIRRAC™. This latter approach may be a little more "sophisticated." Both work just fine, however.

Most importantly, when you HIRRAC™ a rule/counter-rule issue, remember that the "A" stands for application, *not* analysis. If you try to do an analysis in a rule/counter-rule issue, you will get very frustrated: no analysis is possible with a rule/counter-rule issue.

CHAPTER 17
USING HIRRAC™ TO ANSWER A COMBINATION ISSUE

In this chapter, we discuss answering the last of the major issues: the combination issue.[1] You will recall that in a combination issue, one or more elements of the rule applicable to the issue is in dispute *and* one or more of the elements of that rule has more than one definition. In Hypothetical #1, we deal with a classical combination issue. The problem should be somewhat familiar to you, as we have visited this hypothetical earlier.[2] As usual, we follow up the hypothetical with a diagram and good scratch outline.

HYPOTHETICAL #1: ANALYSIS WITH RULE/COUNTER-RULE

Hypothetical #1 is the adverse possession problem involving Oscar, the owner, and Max, the manager.

---

[1] See Chapter 11, "Categorizing the Issues," for a discussion of the "combination issue."
[2] See Chapter 11, "Categorizing the Issues," Hypothetical #6.

Hypothetical #1

[Combination Issue: Analysis with Rule/Counter-Rule]

Oscar owns a 35-unit apartment building. There are a few cracks throughout the building, but nothing that affects a tenant's health and safety. Indeed, the building is quite sound. Oscar does not live on the premises.

In January 1988, Oscar hires Max Smith to manage the apartment house. Max does such a fine job in managing the apartment house that Oscar decides that he, Oscar, can finally take a well-deserved vacation. Oscar tells Max to continue to do the fine job that he, Max, is doing. Oscar then books a one-year cruise on the Queen Elizabeth II and sets sail on July 4, 1989.

In August 1989, Max sends out a letter to all tenants. The letter reads:

Dear Tenant:

Oscar is gone. I am in control here. You are to see me for all problems regarding your apartment. You will make your check payable to "Max Smith."

Sincerely,

Max Smith

Following receipt of the letter from Max, all of the tenants make their rent checks out to "Max Smith." Max deposits the checks into his personal checking account, which he just opened.

Several months later, a vacant apartment is repainted by Max and rented out on a month-to-month basis. All other tenants have leases for a term for years for one year.

Meanwhile, Oscar loves traveling so much that he decides to stay overseas for awhile after the cruise ends. In this regard, he telephones Max and lets Max know that he, Oscar, will be gone for a few more years. When Oscar asks how everything is going, Max replies, "The building is better now than when you were running it." The two then hang up. They have the same conversation twice for the duration that Oscar is overseas.

In 1999, Oscar decides that he is tired of traveling. He has also run up quite a few debts while overseas. Oscar comes back to the United States and prepares to sell the apartment house to pay off all of his debts.

The jurisdiction within which the apartment building lies provides in its Civil Code: "Any action to recover the possession of real property must be commenced within seven years from the time that an actual entry was made by the one in possession."

Discuss.

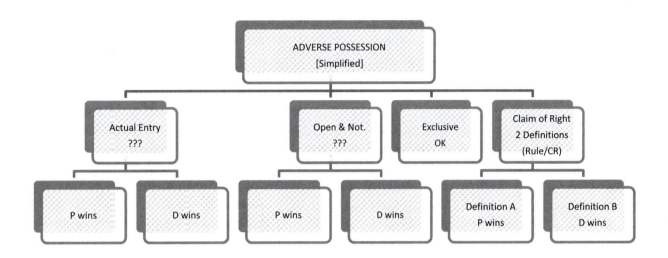

Sample Scratch Outline #1

Max v. Oscar: Adverse Possession

    Actual entry: Letter to tenants; new lease; checks deposited in Max's name; repainting

    Open and notorious: Letter to tenants; new lease; checks deposited in Max's name; repainting

    Hostile: Conversation with Oscar

    Claim of right: Good Faith Rule: Max a manager
    Claim of right: Bad Faith Rule: Max a manager

    Elements satisfied: Continuous and exclusive[3]

....

The problem that this adverse possession question presents is this: Some of the elements (actual entry, open and notorious, and hostile) are in dispute because they can go "either way." For example, based upon the definition of actual entry (a substantial physical occupation of the land), we can make a creative argument why Max did make an actual entry; we can also make a creative argument, based upon that same definition, why Max did not make an actual entry. The same point holds true for open and notorious and hostile. Consequently, these elements (actual entry, open and notorious, and hostile) must be "analyzed," element by element, in our traditional HIRRAC™ format.

However, when we get to "claim of right," we are no longer looking at "analysis." Claim of right can "go either way"—but not because of a creative argument. The reason that claim of right can go either way is this: We have several definitions of claim of right. Claim of right deals with the intent of the possessor. Some jurisdictions define claim of right one way, while other jurisdictions define claim of right another way.

One definition of claim of right is that the possessor must have made a good faith mistake: "I truly believed that the land was mine." If such a definition is used, Max must absolutely and clearly lose: As manager, he had to know that the apartment building was not his.

However, another definition of claim of right is that the possessor had taken possession of the land in bad faith: "I knew the land was not mine but I took it anyway." If such a definition is used for claim of right, Max must win. Again, as manager, he had to know that the apartment building was not his.

---

[3] You may recall from Chapter 14, "Using HIRRAC™ to Answer a Simple Analysis Issue," that some professors want a discussion of all elements, not just those that are in dispute. In such case, you can address those elements as part of the "rule mop-up." See Chapter 14 for a detailed discussion.

Sample scratch Outline #1 takes this split of authority into account.[4]

Sample Exam Answer #1A: An Excellent Answer

Now let us see how we may answer this problem,[5] using the HIRRAC™ format.

---

[4] In this combination issue, because several elements of the rule are in dispute, we have a complex analysis issue. Additionally, because claim of right also is in dispute (but *solely* because we can define it in one of two ways), we have a rule/counter-rule issue (more specifically, of a "majority rule/minority rule" type).

[5] Hypothetical #1 of this chapter contains three elements to analyze (actual entry, open and notorious, and hostility) and one rule/counter-rule issue (claim of right). This means that there are a total of four issues to discuss on the exam (I count "the rule" and "the counter-rule" as one issue). For a typical one-hour exam, I usually give a total of six or seven issues. Therefore, Hypothetical #1 is equal to about four-sevenths of a typical exam. Complete examinations are covered in Chapter 19, "Sample Exams."

Adverse Possession

Can Max prevent Oscar from selling the apartment building because Max in fact is the new owner under the doctrine of adverse possession?

To obtain title by adverse possession, there must be an actual entry that is open and notorious, hostile, exclusive, under claim of right, and continuous for the statutory period.

Actual Entry[6]

Did Max make an actual entry of Oscar's apartment house when he sent a letter to all the tenants stating that he was in control and all checks were to be made out to him, he entered into a new lease with a tenant and had the apartment painted, and deposited rent checks into his own account?

An actual entry is a substantial physical occupation of the land.

By repainting the apartment, entering into a month-to-month lease with a new tenant while others have leases for a term for years, and ordering the tenants to pay him personally, Max was occupying the land in a substantial manner because, although at first blush it seems that Max is not doing much, in fact no true owner could do more. Indeed, the month-to-month lease was a break with tradition and, in this regard, Max again was doing what any owner would do: convey the type of lease that he chooses to convey without being concerned about tradition or prior conduct.

On the other hand, although Max did all these things, that is what he was hired to do—be the agent for Oscar, especially while Oscar is gone. Under such circumstances, it would be reasonable for Max to exercise his independent judgment. Further, a variance of one lease for one apartment is not an act that is so unusual that it could be deemed to be outside the scope of the duties of Max. After all, managers are charged with getting new tenants. Finally, even the checking account in Max's name is consistent with his employment-related duties: with Oscar away, Max must reasonably be expected to pay for expenses of the apartment house and an account solely in his name would facilitate such payments.

Thus, Max did not make an actual entry.

Open and Notorious[7]

Assuming that Max did make an actual entry, was his occupation also open and notorious by his letter to the tenants, the execution of the new lease, the repainting, and the deposit of the checks into his own checking account?

---

[6] Note how I indent the element headings (actual entry, etc.) by one inch, while the "big" issue of adverse possession is indented .5 inch. This makes it clear to the professor that the elements are all part of the greater problem of adverse possession.

[7] Note how while I typically triple-space between issues, I double-space between elements. Again, this makes it clear that the elements are all part of the greater problem of the "big" issue (in this case, adverse possession).

An occupation is open and notorious if the true owner, upon visiting the premises, would have been made aware that another is occupying the premises.

* * *

Therefore, the occupation was not open and notorious.

<u>Hostile</u>

* * *

Max's occupation was therefore hostile.

<u>Claim of Right</u>[8]
Was Max's occupation of Oscar's building as a manager under claim of right?

In some jurisdictions, claim of right means that the possessor had a good faith, albeit mistaken, intent to claim the property as his own. In other jurisdictions, claim of right means that the possessor had a bad faith intent to claim the property as his own: he knew it was not his but he intended to claim it anyway.[9]

If the State of Westmoreland uses the good faith standard for the definition of claim of right, Max must lose: He was hired as a manager of the property and as such could not have had a good faith belief that the building was his. On the other hand, if the State of Westmoreland uses a bad faith standard for the definition of claim of right, Max must win, for the same reason: He knew the property was not his.

Consequently, Max may satisfy the requirement of claim of right.[10]

For the foregoing reasons, even if Max satisfied the claim of right requirement, Max did not acquire the property by adverse possession.[11]

---

[8] Could I have tackled this as two separate issues? Could I have done a HIRRAC™ for "Claim of Right: Good Faith" and a separate HIRRAC™ for "Claim of Right: Bad Faith"? Absolutely! Recall that we discussed that for rule/counter-rule issues, you may (but are not required to) combine the issues. Never, however, combine issues that are analysis issues.

[9] As stated earlier, there is yet another standard: the objective standard. To repeat what I stated earlier in this text, I have omitted this standard from this answer because my purpose here is to teach essay exam writing, not substantive law.

[10] If the professor grading this exam is one who wants a discussion of all elements, including those that are not in dispute, the student could begin at this point with his "rule mop-up," a discussion of those elements of the rule that are clearly satisfied. See footnote 3, supra. See also Chapter 14, "Using HIRRAC™ to Answer a Simple Analysis Issue."

[11] I previously concluded that Max did not make an actual entry; I also concluded that his entry was not open and notorious.

Sample Exam Answer 1A: Dissecting the Answer

Let us now examine Sample Exam Answer #1A. The elements that deal with actual entry, open and notorious, and hostility are identical to the hypothetical discussed in Chapter 15, "Answering a Complex Analysis Issue."[12] We, therefore, shall, devote our time here to discussing the claim of right issue, the rule/counter-rule aspect of this combination issue.

1. *Heading: "Claim of right:"* As we have discussed in previous chapters,[13] headings are more than useful. I consider them critical. Headings help the professor to know what the student is going to discuss (and you can never go wrong by making a professor's job easier). Headings also help the student: The student knows that his or her discussion has certain boundaries. In this case, the scope of the discussion is claim of right. Note that we do not list the parties because we have only one set of parties: Oscar and Max.

2. *Issue statement: "Was Max's occupation of Oscar's building as a manager under claim of right?"* Recall that when you are dealing with a rule/counter-rule issue (which we are dealing with in this combination issue) a good issue statement should include the parties, the legal issue and the key facts. In Sample Exam Answer #1A, we have the parties (Max and Oscar); the legal issue/element (claim of right); and the key facts (as manager).

3. *(Two) rules of law: "In some jurisdictions, claim of right means . . . good faith . . . . In other jurisdictions, claim of right means . . . bad faith. . . ."* Here are the two rules: (1) good faith and (2) bad faith. This aspect of the problem is the rule/counter-rule issue (majority rule/minority rule issue): some jurisdictions believe claim of right means one thing and other jurisdictions believe that claim of right means another thing. Thus, here are the two "Rs" of HIRRAC™.

4. *Application: "If the State of Westmoreland uses the good faith standard for the definition of claim of right, Max must lose: He was hired as a manager of the property and as such could not have had a good faith belief that the building was his. On the other hand, if the State of Westmoreland uses a bad faith standard for the definition of claim of right, Max must win, for the same reason: He knew the property was not his."*

Keep in mind that what we are doing here is applying each rule to the facts. We take the facts to show that if claim of right means good faith, Max absolutely and clearly could not have had good faith. Nevertheless, if claim of right means bad faith, Max absolutely and clearly had bad faith.[14] Notice that analysis is not a part of this HIRRAC™: the "A" here (as part of the "rule/counter-rule issue") stands for "application."

---

[12] See Sample Exam Answer #1A.

[13] See for example Chapter 15, "Using HIRRAC™ to Answer a Complex Analysis Issue," Sample Exam Answer #1A.

[14] Up until this point, we have always stated that in an application, all of the elements of the rule are absolutely and clearly satisfied. Certainly Max has absolutely and clearly satisfied all of the elements of adverse possession if the jurisdiction defines claim of right to require "bad faith." However, he has clearly not satisfied all of the elements of adverse possession if claim of right is defined as requiring good faith. Why, then, in such case, should we bother to discuss the other elements of adverse possession? We address this concern in Chapter 18, "Answering a 'Non-Issue' Issue."

4. *Conclusion: "Consequently, Max may satisfy the requirement of claim of right."* This is then followed by the overall conclusion for the adverse possession issue.

If this does not seem too hard for you, pat yourself on the back. The reason that it does not seem so hard is because you are now starting to feel very comfortable with law school essay exams and the HIRRAC™ method.

HYPOTHETICAL #2: ANALYSIS WITH RULE/COUNTER-RULE WITH ANALYSIS

Now let us look at one last combination issue, a torts problem that we discussed in Chapter 11, "Categorizing the Issues."[15] As usual, we have included a diagram and a good "scratch" outline of the issues.

This is as difficult a problem as you will ever get in law school. If you can master this, you can master anything. The key is to break down the rule into elements. On the exam, you might well want to diagram this out, as I have.

---

[15] Hypothetical #7.

Hypothetical #2

[Combination Issue: Analysis with Rule/Counter-Rule with Analysis]

The day after Christmas, a group of adults knocked on the door of Yule's home and asked for the discarded Christmas tree that Yule had just placed on his porch for the trash man. Yule reluctantly agreed, although he saw in the street the large pile of similar trees, which the group had collected. In addition, Yule had read warnings in the newspaper concerning the danger faced by young neighborhood groups in burning discarded Christmas trees in large piles. He warned them to "be careful." The pile of trees was then dragged by the group to a vacant lot in the neighborhood.

One member of the group, Bob, struck a match and applied it to a corner of the pile. Bob then snapped off a burning branch and lunged toward Tiny, Bob's friend. Tiny was frightened and he dashed into the adjacent street. Tiny was injured when hit by an oncoming car without any fault on the part of the driver.

Discuss the liability of Yule.

Diagram

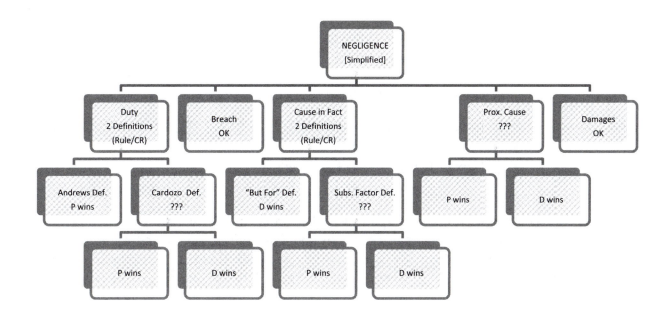

    As I stated at the beginning of this hypothetical, this is as tough as you can get. It is complicated. For such a problem (or any problem, if you are a visual learner), you may wish to diagram this out on scratch paper on your actual exam (and practice diagramming out problems in practice exams as you get ready to take your finals).

Sample Scratch Outline #2

Tiny v. Yule: Negligence

Duty: Cardozo Approach: Warnings given; Newspaper account; Reluctant agreement; Bob's lunging

Duty: Andrews Approach: Warnings given; Newspaper account; Reluctant agreement; Bob's lunging

Cause In Fact: Substantial Factor Test: Match applied to corner of pile[16]

Proximate Cause: Bob's lunging[17]

....

This is a very difficult hypothetical. The problem that we have in this negligence question is this: Duty can be defined in one of two ways: Cardozo's definition and Andrews' definition (and herein is the rule/counter-rule issue of this problem). However, if we use Cardozo's definition, it is disputable whether a duty exists (and herein is the analysis aspect within the rule/counter-rule issue).

Sample Exam Answer #2A: An Excellent Answer

Let us now examine how we answer Hypothetical #2.

---

[16] Recall from our discussion in Chapter 11, "Categorizing the Issues," that under the "but for" test, cause in fact is not satisfied: even without Yule's tree, the fire could have been set. Therefore, cause in fact, using the "but for" test, is not in dispute. (But see next footnote.) However, cause in fact, using the "substantial factor" test, is in dispute. Hence, it is included in the scratch outline. We discuss this aspect of the problem in greater length in Chapter 18, "Answering a 'Non-Issue' Issue."

[17] Of course, we could include in our scratch outline the elements that are clearly satisfied: cause in fact (the "but for" test) and damages: Most teachers certainly would want a discussion of both tests for cause in fact. Note, also, that proximate cause has two definitions: the Restatement test and the foreseeability test. In this sample answer, we have included only the Restatement test (a hindsight approach). Again, the purpose is not to teach substantive law, but essay writing. In this regard, I have indicated in the diagram that the schematic is "simplified."

Sample Exam Answer #2A

Negligence
Is Yule liable to Tiny in negligence?

To establish negligence, a plaintiff must prove duty, breach of duty, cause in fact, proximate cause, and damages.

Duty: Cardozo's Approach
Did Yule owe Tiny a duty of care, as defined by Cardozo, when he read warnings, told the group to "be careful" and gave the tree to the group reluctantly, and Bob subsequently lunged at Tiny?

Under Cardozo's approach, a duty is owed to those in the foreseeable zone of danger.

Because Yule read the warnings in the newspaper concerning the problem of people setting trees on fire, warned the group to "be careful," and only reluctantly gave the tree to the group, Yule must have foreseen a problem; otherwise, he would not have shown the concern that he exhibited. One does not give warnings unless one foresees danger.

In the alternative, because Bob purposefully lunged at Tiny, it is doubtful that this was a foreseeable risk because friends are generally not expected to create a risk to each other.

Therefore, under Cardozo's approach, Yule did not owe a duty to Tiny.

Duty: Andrews Approach
On the same facts, under the Andrews approach, did Yule owe Tiny a duty?

Under the Andrews approach, a duty is owed to the whole world, which duty is cut off only by the restrictive rules of proximate cause.

In order to determine whether Yule owed Tiny a duty, we must discuss whether any rules of proximate cause will cut off liability, which is discussed below.

* * *

Sample Exam Answer #2A: Dissecting the Answer

Let us now examine Sample Exam Answer #2A. It is a complex analysis issue because multiple elements of the rule are in dispute; a few of the elements (duty, cause in fact, and proximate cause) can go either way on the facts that are given. Additionally, it is also a rule/counter-rule issue (because duty can be defined in one of two ways: Cardozo defines duty in one way and Andrews defines it in another way).

1. *Heading: "Negligence."* This allows the professor to zero in on the problem with ease.

2. *Issue statement: "Is Yule liable to Tiny in negligence?"* This is the broad issue.

3. *Rule of law: "To establish negligence, a plaintiff must prove duty, breach of duty, cause in fact, proximate cause and damages."* The issue is negligence—and so is the rule of law. Of course, this is the "first R" of our HIRRAC™ formulation.

Because this combination issue is partly a complex analysis issue, we are going to isolate those elements of the rule that are in dispute. We shall indent the material that follows so you may see clearly that the overall problem that we are still dealing with is negligence. (Note that we also indented the sub-headings in Sample Exam Answer #2A. Note, too, that while we indent the sub-headings, we do not indent the text that follows.)

(i) *Heading: "Duty: Cardozo's Approach."* Again, a heading is a good idea for purposes of focus.

(ii) *Issue statement: "Did Yule owe Tiny a duty of care, as defined by Cardozo . . ."* The issue statement has the parties (Tiny v. Yule), the element in dispute (duty), and the key facts that are triggering the element (read warnings, etc.)

(iii) *Rule of law: "Under Cardozo's approach, a duty is owed to those in the foreseeable zone of danger."* As always, because the issue (element) is duty, the rule of law must define duty. This, of course, is the "second R" of our HIRRAC™ formulation.

(iv) *Analysis: "Because Yule read the warnings in the newspaper . . . Yule must have foreseen a problem; otherwise he would not have shown the concern that he exhibited. One does not give warnings unless one foresees danger."* This is the analysis for why a duty was owed. In short, one does not give warnings unless one can foresee a danger.

Notice that the foundation for the analysis is the key facts. Notice, too, that we have a good analysis because the student takes the key facts that are given and builds on to those facts a creative argument to prove that a duty exists.

You may also recall that there is a test to determine if you have indeed done an analysis: ask the question, "Why?"[18] If we ask that question here, it is not an intelligent question because the response to the question would be, "I told you why; didn't you pay attention?" Indeed, Sample

---

[18] See Chapter 14, "Using HIRRAC™ to Answer a Simple Analysis Issue."

Answer 2A completely answers our inquiry as to why Yule owed Tiny a duty to not give the group the tree.

In the next paragraph, we take the key facts that are given, prefaced by words of transition, build on to those facts a different argument to prove that a duty did not exist. *"In the alternative, because Bob purposefully lunged at Tiny, it is doubtful that this was a foreseeable risk because friends are generally not expected to create a risk to each other."* Note the use of the word, "because." As we have discussed earlier, if you force yourself to use the word, "because," you will assure yourself that you will follow up with *reasons*—which is the heart of analysis.

Now that we have completed our analysis for duty, we move on to our conclusion.

(v) *Conclusion: "Therefore, under Cardozo's approach, Yule did not owe a duty to Tiny."* This ends our discussion of Cardozo's approach to duty. Remember, however, that we do not want to ever "conclude ourselves out of points." Even though we have concluded that no duty was owed, we will still proceed to discuss the Andrews approach to duty and the other elements that are in dispute.[19]

Now let us study several other sample answers. These samples will illustrate points previously covered in other hypos and in other chapters. However, because the points made are so important, it is worth our time to visit them again.

Sample Exam Answer #2B: Conclusory and No Analysis

As you will see from this sample answer, there is no analysis. Again, you learn how to do analysis by seeing what does not qualify as analysis.

---

[19] For those elements of the rule that are not in dispute, we will cover them in the so-called "rule mop-up." See Chapter 14, "Using HIRRAC to Answer a Simple Analysis Issue."

<u>Negligence</u>
To establish negligence, a plaintiff must prove duty, breach of duty, cause in fact, proximate cause and damages.

<u>Duty: Cardozo's Approach</u>
Did Yule owe Tiny a duty of care, as defined by Cardozo, when he read warnings, told the group to be "be careful" and gave the tree to the group reluctantly, and Bob subsequently lunged at Tiny?

Under Cardozo's approach, a duty is owed to those in the foreseeable zone of danger.

Because Yule read the warnings in the newspaper concerning the problem of people setting piles of trees on fire, warned the group to "be careful" and only reluctantly gave the tree to the group, a duty was owed.

In the alternative, because Bob purposefully lunged at Tiny, this was not a foreseeable risk.

* * *

Sample Exam Answer #2B: Dissecting the Answer

Take a close look at Sample Exam Answer #2B. The heading and issue of negligence is perfect, as is the heading (that is, sub-heading), issue, and rule of duty. In fact, it is identical to Sample Exam Answer #2A. The difference between #2A and #2B is that there is no analysis in Sample Exam Answer #2B.

In Sample Exam Answer #2B, our fictitious student has stated the facts ("Because Yule read the warnings in the newspaper concerning the problem of people setting piles of trees on fire, warned the . . . and only reluctantly gave the tree to the group") and added on a conclusion ("a duty was owed"). There is no creative argument. There are no reasons given as to *why* a duty was owed. In summary, this paragraph does not demonstrate good analysis. The professor will say it is "conclusory" and give it little (if any) credit.

One last point: Yes, the student used the word "because," but still failed to do an analysis. The point here is that HIRRAC™, as I have often stated, is merely an organizational tool and not a substitute for thinking. This sample answer proves that point.

The same criticism that we just made applies with respect to the "analysis" as to why a duty was not owed: there is no analysis. We have a mere conclusion.

We now move on to a new sample answer.

Sample Exam Answer #2C: No Analysis (to an Extreme)

Sample Exam Answer #2C has the same problems that #2B has, but even more so. Sample Exam Answer #2C is truly a restatement of the facts with a conclusion tacked on.

Sample Exam Answer #2C

<u>Negligence</u>

To establish negligence, a plaintiff must prove duty, breach of duty, cause in fact, proximate cause and damages.

<u>Duty: Cardozo's Approach</u>

Did Yule owe Tiny a duty of care, as defined by Cardozo, when he read warnings, told the group to "be careful" and gave the tree to the group reluctantly, and Bob subsequently lunged at Tiny?

Under Cardozo's approach, a duty is owed to those in the foreseeable zone of danger.

The facts state that Yule read the warnings in the newspaper concerning the problem of people setting piles of trees on fire, warned the group to "be careful," and only reluctantly gave the tree to the group. Therefore, Yule owed a duty to Tiny.

* * *

Sample Exam Answer #2C: Dissecting the Answer

There is clearly no analysis. We have a restatement of facts and conclusion. Remember to *always* state your reasons—your creative reasons when you do an analysis.

SUMMARY OF CHAPTER 17

Now let us briefly summarize this chapter. When you have a complex analysis issue, some of the elements will be in dispute because, based upon the sole definition of each of those elements, the outcome can "go either way" on the facts given. The plaintiff may win, but so may the defendant.

Additionally, another element(s) will be in dispute because of the definition that we give it: Some jurisdictions will define the element one way but other jurisdictions will define the element in another way. Moreover, once you determine what the definition is (as we did with "duty," in Sample Exam Answer #2A), the outcome may not be certain because based upon that definition (for example, Cardozo's approach to duty), the outcome can "go either way" on the facts given.

In all cases, you will HIRRAC™ the answer. You will state the general issue (negligence); state the rule of law (duty, breach, cause in fact, proximate cause, and damages). You then begin isolating the elements in dispute (duty). How do you do this? Essentially, you do a HIRRAC™ for each element (or, as some students call it, a "sub-HIRRAC™"): provide a sub-heading (Duty: Cardozo's View); give a complete issue statement ("Did Yule owe Tiny a duty of care when . . ."); state the rule of duty; analyze whether a duty existed/did not exist; conclude.

We are now ready to discuss what is for some students a very troubling matter: When do you discuss something when it is not an issue?

barbri

CHAPTER 18
ANSWERING A "NON-ISSUE" ISSUE

When you have a simple analysis issue, one element of the rule of law is in dispute; all of the other elements are absolutely and clearly satisfied.[1] With a complex analysis issue, several elements of the rule are in dispute.[2] When you address a rule/counter-rule issue, all of the elements of the rule are absolutely and clearly satisfied.[3] There is, therefore, a common thread running through every analysis issue and every rule/counter-rule issue: Every element of every rule is either absolutely and clearly satisfied (rule/counter-rule) or arguably satisfied (analysis).

UNDERSTANDING THE "NON-ISSUE" ISSUE

However, when we come to the "non-issue" issue, something unusual is going to happen: we are going to have to address an element(s) of the rule which is absolutely and clearly *not* satisfied—and which will never be satisfied. Not now. Not in a thousand years.

HYPOTHETICAL #1

Let us illustrate this point with Hypothetical #1, a variation of the burglary issue that we previously discussed.[4] Read Hypothetical #1 carefully and see how it differs from the hypo that we previously discussed. We provide a diagram Hypothetical #1 after the hypothetical.

---

[1] See Chapter 11, "Categorizing the Issues."
[2] *Ibid.*
[3] *Ibid.*
[4] See Chapter 14, "Using HIRRAC™ to Answer a Simple Analysis Issue," Hypothetical #1.

Hypothetical #1

In June 2010, Charles graduated from college with a B.S. degree in accounting. Prior to beginning work in September for an accounting firm, Charles decided to travel across the United States in his 2005 Dodge minivan, seeing small towns and just enjoying himself. Not being financially well off, however, Charles felt he could economize by sleeping in the back of his station wagon. In this way, he would not have to pay for a motel room nightly.

While traveling through State X, Charles pulled over from the public highway to catch a few hours of sleep. It was a cool day so Charles rolled up all the windows of his car. For safety reasons, he also locked all of the doors of his car. By 10:30 AM, with the sun shining brightly, Charles fell asleep.

An hour later, Dan walked by. Dan saw Charles' wallet lying next to Charles. Being low on funds, Dan decided that it would be easy to take Charles' wallet. Dan then broke the glass nearest Charles with the intent of snatching Charles' wallet; Dan put his hand into the car and succeeded in taking the wallet. Charles' person, however, was not harmed in any way.

Assuming that State X's Penal Code codifies the common law, what crimes, if any, has Dan committed? Discuss.

Hypothetical #1 Explained

How does this hypo differ from the one that we covered previously? Look carefully. In the present hypo: (1) "It was a cool *day*"; (2) the time was "10:30 *AM*"; and (3) the "*sun* [was] shining brightly."

There should be no doubt in your mind: Dan broke and entered during *daytime* hours—not during the nighttime hours. As such, and as a matter of law, Dan cannot be guilty of common law burglary. Because Dan cannot be guilty of common law burglary, you may reasonably be thinking to yourself, "Why then should I even discuss common law burglary?"

Indeed, on a practical level, you should not discuss common law burglary. For example, if you were the district attorney, would you file charges against Dan for common law burglary? Of course not: One element (nighttime) is absolutely and clearly not satisfied—and it will never be satisfied. Further, for Dan to be guilty of common law burglary, the state must prove *all* elements of the crime beyond a reasonable doubt. Dan did not commit common law burglary. It is that simple.

However, a number of your professors may be interested in testing your theoretical understanding of the law of common law burglary. As such, you would want to let them know that burglary does not exist because one element (nighttime) is not satisfied.

How would you let them know that you know that common law burglary on these facts cannot exist? You do so by using the HIRRAC™ method, of course.

Sample Exam Answer #1: An Excellent Answer[5]

---

[5] Of course, an excellent answer could have been written by changing the order of the answer: The first element that we addressed could have been "nighttime" and the last could have been "dwelling house." Remember: These are all minor differences. The point to always keep in mind is that all good answers will address (1) why the car was/was not a dwelling house; (2) why the nighttime element was not satisfied; (3) why the other elements were satisfied. HIRRAC™ will assist you in addressing these points.

Sample Exam Answer #1

<u>Burglary</u>
Can the State convict Dan of burglary on the ground that the car was a dwelling house, since Charles was sleeping in it while on his trip?

A burglary is the breaking and entering of the dwelling house of another in the nighttime with the intent to commit a felony therein.

<u>Dwelling house</u>
A dwelling house is a place of human habitation.

Although Dan broke into Charles' car while Charles was sleeping in it, the car would not qualify as a dwelling house because a car is typically not thought of as being something used for habitation; it is used for travel. Moreover, even though Charles was sleeping in the car at the time, this should not make a car a dwelling, since every time a person would take a nap in his car, that would transform the car into a dwelling, not the intent of the common law, which was to protect a person in his home. Finally, sleeping in a car even for a few months should not change the characterization of the car, because it was still used by Charles for travel around the country; it was not used exclusively as a place to sleep, wash, and entertain, as homes are typically used.

On the other hand, although the car was used for travel, it was also used as a place for sleeping, a characteristic of a place for human habitation. Indeed, when Dan broke into the car, it was stationary with Charles sleeping in it. As such, the car took on more of the characteristics of a home than a car. Additionally, even though the car went from being a car to a dwelling for the two months that Charles was on the road and then back again to a car, this is no different than a structure that is used as a store, then transformed into a residential apartment for two months, and then back to a store again upon the tenant vacating the premises; the focus should be on the time that humans use it for habitation-like purposes.

Therefore, the car was a dwelling house

<u>Breaking</u>
A breaking is the creation of a breach, which Dan accomplished when he "broke the glass" window of the car.

<u>Entry</u>
An entry exists if any part of the defendant intrudes; this existed when Dan put his hand through the window.

<u>Nighttime</u>
It was not nighttime, the period between sunset and sunrise, since it took place at 10:30 AM and the sun was shining.

<u>Intent to commit felony</u>

The intent to commit a felony element is met since Dan intended to take the wallet before he broke the window and, under common law, all larceny was a felony.

Therefore, because the nighttime element was not satisfied, Dan did not commit a burglary.

Sample Exam Answer #1: Dissecting the Answer

Do you now see what a "non-issue" issue is? All of the elements are either absolutely satisfied (breaking; entering; and intent to commit a felony), or are arguably satisfied (dwelling house)—with the exception of one element: "nighttime." This one element cannot be satisfied on the facts given.

Be aware of this type of "issue." It can appear on any one of your exams. Now, you know how to address it if it does.

KNOWING WHEN TO RAISE A "NON-ISSUE" ISSUE

Now that you know how to handle a non-issue issue, *when* do you raise a non-issue issue? Here is a good guideline (if not a bright line test). Assuming your professor tests on these issues (I do not), ask yourself this question: Would a good lawyer even think of this issue? If the answer is yes, raise it. If the answer is no, do not raise it. Thus, in Hypothetical #1, a good lawyer would at least think about common law burglary, and then dismiss it. Hence, you could raise this on the exam, as we did in Sample Answer #1. On the other hand, no good lawyer would think about raising fraud or the Rule Against Perpetuities in Hypothetical #1. Hence, you would not raise these issues.

Now let us move on to sample exams.

CHAPTER 19
SAMPLE EXAMS

In this chapter, we have provided you with two complete examinations. The first is an actual torts question from the California Bar Exam. The second is an exam that I recently gave to my own property students. Each examination in this chapter is one hour in duration. You will find it most beneficial to take these exams under timed conditions and study the sample answers afterward. You should note that most issues on the California Bar Exam are not analysis issues; most are application issues (that is, some type of rule/counter-rule). Most issues for my own exams are analysis issues.

Each answer is in the HIRRAC™ format. We have heavily annotated the answers by extensive use of footnotes. Indeed, virtually every sentence is footnoted. We think that you will find this to be very helpful in understanding what goes into a good answer.

It is, however, important that you keep in mind that the sample answers are just that: samples. Although they are good answers, they have been purposefully designed not to be "perfect" answers. In this respect, you will have a standard that you can readily achieve.

You should also be aware that because these answers are samples, there is much room for disagreement: You may very well tackle the issues in a different order, for example. You will certainly think of different creative arguments for the analysis. You may even think of issues that we did not discuss. Your conclusion may be different. Remember: It is possible for ten students to answer the question differently—and each of the ten students can get an "A" for the final grade.

Nonetheless, all good answers will have issue statements, rules, and analyses. Let us now examine the questions and answers.

SAMPLE EXAM #1: TORTS

Abel and Baker were working on a scaffold lawfully erected over a public sidewalk. Abel, contrary to an express rule of his employer, was not wearing a hard hat.

While trying to park her automobile near one of the supports of the scaffold, Diana maneuvered it into such a position that she knew there was a risk of knocking the scaffold down if she backed without someone to guide her. She appealed for help to Sam, a stranger who was passing by. Sam just laughed. Angered, Diana proceeded to back her auto without assistance and knocked a support out from under the scaffold, causing Abel and Baker to fall.

Abel severely fractured his skull and was taken unconscious to a hospital. If he had been wearing his hard hat, he would have suffered only a slight concussion with minimal disability.

Baker sustained a fracture of a vertebra, but he was able to walk and felt only sight pain. The fracture could have been easily diagnosed by X-ray and a medical doctor of average competence could have successfully treated it by immobilization. Instead of visiting a physician, Baker worked the rest of the day. While driving his car home later that day, Baker stopped at an intersection and his car was struck from the rear by a car driven by Ed. The collision caused only slight damage to Baker's car, but it was sufficiently severe to aggravate the fracture in Baker's back, resulting in paralysis.

Diana and Sam settled Baker's claims against them and received general releases from him. Abel sued Diana and Sam. Baker sued Ed. Assume that Diana, Sam and Ed raise all appropriate defenses.

1.   What rights, if any, does Abel have against Diana? Sam? Discuss.

2.   What rights, if any, does Baker have against Ed? Discuss.

SAMPLE EXAM ANSWER #1

1. Abel v. Diana[6]

<u>Battery</u>[7]

Did Diana have the requisite intent to commit a battery against Abel when she backed her car unassisted and knew of the risk of knocking the scaffold down?[8]

A battery is the intentional and unpermitted offensive or harmful touching of the person of another.[9] Intent exists if the defendant was substantially certain of the result.[10]

When Diana backed her car unassisted and knew of the risk of knocking the scaffold down, she crossed the line from negligence (foreseeability) to intent (substantially certain): she actually knew what the consequence of her act would be—that she would knock the scaffold down.[11]

However, although Diana may have been substantially certain that the scaffold would fall down, it is not a foregone conclusion that follows that she was substantially certain that she would cause men to fall along with the scaffold. Although workers are often on a scaffold, workers do go to lunch and take breaks.[12]

Therefore, Diana did not have the requisite intent.[13]

---

[6] Always identify and number the interrogatories for your professor. Make his or her job easy. Further, where there are several interrogatories, it is a very good idea first to address interrogatory #1 and then address interrogatory #2. That makes sense, does it not? Unfortunately, for whatever reason, not all students tackle the interrogatories in the order presented. Remember: you want to stand out because you write a good exam. You do not want to stand out because you were the only one in the class to discuss "Baker v. Ed" before "Abel v. Diana."

[7] Headings are a critical part of the HIRRAC™ formula. With a heading, which is the legal issue, the professor knows exactly what the student is going to discuss. We underline our headings for emphasis and clarity.

[8] This is a simple analysis issue: all elements are satisfied except one—intent. The issue statement includes (1) the parties (2) the legal issue (3) the element in dispute and (4) the key facts. Parenthetically, you also could have addressed this as a "non-issue" issue. See chapter 18. In any event, the point is that a good lawyer would address this issue in some manner. Remember, do not obsess over whether this issue is a certain type of rule/counter-rule issue or a combination issue. The key is always to ask yourself, *Are all elements of the rule absolutely and clearly satisfied?* If yes, you have only to do an application; you do not have analysis. If the answer is no, if an element(s) can go either way based on the facts, if it is in a gray zone, you have an analysis. In any event, your format is HIRRAC™.

[9] The issue is battery; the rule of law is therefore battery.

[10] We have isolated the disputable element ("intent") by defining it.

[11] Here is our analysis for why intent exists. We take the key facts that we are given and build onto those facts a creative argument to prove that Diana had the requisite intent. We believe that she really did not have the requisite intent. Consequently, this is our "weaker" argument and we begin with our weaker argument so that we may conclude on our "strong" side. Of course, you could take a contrary view on this. That is never a problem for an analysis issue.

[12] This paragraph is our "other side" of the analysis. Here, we establish by creative argument that Diana was not substantially certain of the results. Can you think of other or even better arguments? Of course, you could. Note, too, that we preface our analysis with a transitional word, "However." This lets the professor know that we are switching sides.

[13] We conclude that Diana did not have the requisite intent.

Assuming Diana did have the requisite intent, she touched Abel, and the touching was harmful, evidenced by his injuries. Moreover, the touching was not permitted.[14]

Negligence[15]

Can Abel prevail against Diana in negligence because she backed the car unassisted, knowing of the risk of knocking the scaffold down?[16]

To state a claim in negligence, the plaintiff must establish duty, breach of duty, cause in fact, proximate cause, and damages.[17]

Duty: Cardozo

Did Diana owe a duty of care to Abel?[18] Under Cardozo's view a duty is owed to those in the foreseeable zone of danger.[19] Because Diana knew of the danger of knocking the scaffold down—and since workers are often on scaffolds—it was foreseeable that someone like Abel would be injured.[20]

---

[14] This paragraph is our "rule mop-up." In the "rule mop-up," we summarily dispose of those elements which are absolutely and clearly satisfied. Notice that while generally you are *never* to assume, it is proper to assume when you need to so that you do not "conclude yourself" out of points. We further develop when to make assumptions in Chapter 20. You also will note that the "rule mop-up" is done in very summary fashion. The reason for the summary treatment is this: We are in the first issue of the exam and we want to make certain that we have plenty of time to finish. You will also note that we have concluded that intent does not exist (barring battery as a matter of law). Nevertheless, we still include the "rule mop-up." The lesson here (and I state this again) is, never "conclude yourself out of points." Of course, if your professor does not want a "rule mop-up," you would totally omit this paragraph.

[15] We now move on to the next issue. Note that we triple-space between issues (but double-space between elements). The negligence issue will be part of a rule/counter-rule issue: The rule (or cause of action) is negligence and the exception to the rule (or the affirmative defense) is contributory negligence and (the exception to the exception is) comparative negligence. Notice again the use of underlined headings and sub-headings to make it easy for the professor to read. We should also note here that we are going to go into this negligence issue in some depth. Consequently, you may well criticize our handling of this negligence issue on the ground that it is too long: we could have "shortened" it up. For example, we could have omitted all of the "sub-issue" statements. All this is true. Remember: Ten people can answer an exam in ten different ways—and each of them can receive an "A" for a final grade. Remember too: This answer is a *sample answer*. It is not a model and it is not perfect. The answer is not intended to be inserted between Numbers and Deuteronomy.

[16] This paragraph is the issue statement. Because the issue is a "rule/counter-rule" issue, the issue statement will contain three things: (1) the parties; (2) the legal issue; and (3) the key facts that are triggering the issue. The reason that we have a rule/counter-rule issue involved is because every element of negligence is absolutely and clearly satisfied. If you think that not every element is clearly satisfied, that is okay, too: it is quite possible in any given fact pattern for one person to think that the issue is a rule/counter-rule issue and another to think that it is an analysis issue. For example, in this issue, you may have wanted to handle Abel's lack of a hard hat as a proximate cause issue and not as a contributory negligence issue. The moral is this: So long as you understand what you are doing—and explain it to the professor in a lawyer-like manner—you will be fine.

[17] This paragraph is our rule of negligence.

[18] We now break out each element with the idea of establishing that each element is absolutely and clearly satisfied.

[19] This is one rule of law: Cardozo's view.

[20] Here we have our *application* (not analysis): we let the professor know that on these facts, a duty existed. Remember that when we do an "application" as part of a rule/counter-rule issue, we do not have any creative argument. Creative arguments are used when we have to perform an "analysis." Note, too, that for rule/counter-rule issues, you often may typically put the issue, rule, application, and conclusion all in one paragraph (unlike analysis issues). That is because application issues are much shorter than analysis issues (and one neat paragraph is more pleasing to the eye than four short choppy paragraphs). Of course, if you feel more comfortable putting the issue, rule,

Duty: Andrews

Under Andrews' view, a duty is owed to everyone.[21] Using this broad view of duty, Diana clearly owed a duty to Abel.[22]

Breach

Did Diana breach her duty when she proceeded, knowing of the danger?[23] A breach of duty exists when the defendant acts unreasonably.[24] It was unreasonable for Diana to proceed knowing of the risk: that the scaffold could come down.[25] Considering the gravity of proceeding as she did, a reasonable person would have waited until some passerby would have rendered assistance.

Cause in fact: But for and Substantial Factor

Was Diana's knocking down the scaffolding the cause in fact of Abel's injury?[26] Cause in fact exists if "but for" the defendant's act, the injury would not have happened; another test is whether the defendant's conduct was the cause in fact of the plaintiff's injury.[27] But for Diana knocking down the scaffold, Abel would not have been injured; if it were the sine qua non of the accident, Diana's conduct was necessarily also a substantial factor.[28]

Proximate Cause

Was Diana's knocking down the scaffolding the proximate cause of Abel's injury?[29] Under the rules of proximate cause, if there is a superseding event, liability will be cut off.[30] There is no superseding event here.[31]

Damages

Abel suffered injuries: He has damages.[32]
Diana was therefore negligent.[33]

---

application, and conclusion in separate paragraphs, that is fine, too. Again, for analysis issues, you must use a separate paragraph for each part of the HIRRAC™ formula.

[21] This sentence is the rule according to Andrews' view.

[22] We have here a short application to let the professor know that a duty clearly exists using Andrews' definition.

[23] We now go to the next element: breach of duty.

[24] We define the term.

[25] In this sentence and the one that follows, we apply the rule to the facts: we tell the professor that on these facts Diana clearly breached her duty.

[26] The next element: cause in fact.

[27] I give the two different definitions here for cause in fact. Could I have broken them down into two separate rules? The answer is, yes. However, for rule/counter-rule issues (application), you can combine if you wish. I do so here because I am starting to get nervous for time.

[28] We apply the rule to the facts: Diana's backing her car in the manner that she did was the cause in fact of Abel's injury: But for (*sine qua non*) her action, the scaffold would not have fallen down. Necessarily, it also was a substantial factor.

[29] The next element is proximate cause.

[30] We give the rule of proximate cause.

[31] A brief application: there is, in effect, no reason to cut off Diana's liability. Of course, it might be that Abel's failure to go to the doctor is a superseding event. Nonetheless, I chose to cover that aspect of the problem within the context of contributory negligence. Remember, this is law school and there may be several good answers to a problem. Yet again, we see the theme of "ambiguity with precision."

[32] Damages are covered summarily.

[33] Here is the overall conclusion.

<u>Contributory Negligence</u>[34]

Can Diana avoid liability because Abel was contributorily negligent when he failed to wear his hard hat, in violation of company rules?[35]

Contributory negligence is conduct on the part of the plaintiff, contributing as a legal cause, cause in fact and proximate cause, to the harm he has suffered, which falls below the standard to which he is required to conform for his own protection; under the common law, it is a bar to recovery.[36]

By failing to comply with company rules, which mandated that he wear his hard hat, Abel contributed to the harm that he suffered: if he had worn it, he would have suffered a slight concussion. He was required to wear the hat for his own protection: to prevent injury to himself.[37]

Therefore, under the common law, Abel will be denied recovery.[38]

<u>Comparative Negligence</u>[39]

Can Abel still recover from Diana, notwithstanding his own negligence in failing to wear a hard hat, under the doctrine of comparative negligence?[40]

Modernly, in a pure comparative negligence jurisdiction, where the plaintiff's negligence was a cause of his injury, his damages are reduced in proportion to his negligence but his action is not barred.[41] However, in some comparative negligence jurisdictions, the plaintiff has his entire claim barred if his negligence is greater than the defendant's.

In a pure comparative negligence jurisdiction, Abel will recover from Diana. He will,

---

[34] This is the affirmative defense, the "counter-rule," with an underlined heading for emphasis.

[35] This is the issue statement, which contains: (1) the parties; (2) the legal issue; and (3) the key facts.

[36] The heading and issue statement deals with contributory negligence. The rule of law must therefore define contributory negligence. You will note that this time, I do not break out the elements as I did for negligence. Time is a factor and one has to use a rule of common sense. Remember to use HIRRAC™ but not be a slave to it. The key is always to proceed in a logical progression. HIRRAC™ helps you do that. Never, however, be a slave to HIRRAC™.

[37] This paragraph is our application: We let the professor know that on the facts given, Abel was contributorily negligent. Note that there is no creativity (analysis) here.

[38] This is the conclusion for this issue.

[39] Here is another "counter-rule": comparative negligence. This is the exception to the exception (contributory negligence).

[40] This is the issue statement with the parties, the legal issue, and the key facts.

[41] There are two rules of comparative negligence: a so-called "pure" comparative negligence and a so-called "50 percent" comparative negligence. This sentence deals with the pure comparative negligence rule. The next sentence deals with the 50 percent comparative negligence rule. Notice the twist in this issue: the "counter-rule" is comparative negligence—but there are two rules for comparative negligence: a majority rule and a minority rule. Thus, we have a rule/exception to the rule/exception to the rule issue (negligence/contributory negligence/comparative negligence) and, with respect to one of the exceptions to the rule (comparative negligence) we have a majority rule (pure comparative negligence) and a minority rule (50 percent comparative negligence). Confusing? Not really. Just remember to keep in mind the one critical question: *Are all elements of the rule absolutely and clearly satisfied?* If the answer is yes, you have a rule/counter-rule issue (and no analysis). If the answer is no, you have an analysis issue (requiring creativity or reasons).

however, have his damages reduced pro rata.[42] Nevertheless, in some comparative negligence jurisdictions, if Abel's negligence is deemed to be greater than Diana's, Abel will be denied recovery.[43] In this respect, it is similar to contributory negligence.[44]

Abel v. Sam

Negligence[45]

Is Sam, the passerby, liable to Abel in negligence when he failed to assist Diana backing in her car?[46]

Negligence is defined as duty, breach of duty, cause in fact, proximate cause, and damages.[47] Barring a special relationship or a statute, a person has no duty to act.[48]

Because Sam is a passerby, a stranger and not in any special relationship, he is under no duty to act.[49]

Therefore, Sam is not liable to Abel in negligence.[50]

2. Baker v. Ed[51]

Negligence[52]

Is Ed liable to Baker for negligence when Ed crashed into Baker's car, aggravating a pre-existing injury?[53]

Negligence requires duty, breach, cause in fact, proximate cause, and damages.[54]

Ed owed a duty to Baker to drive safely. Ed breached that duty by striking Baker's stopped car. Ed's striking Baker was also the cause in fact of Baker's injury. Baker's preexisting weakness, caused by Diana, is not a superseding event to prevent a finding of proximate cause: Under the "eggshell skull" theory, a defendant must take the plaintiff as he finds him. Finally, Baker suffered

---

[42] This sentence is our application for the pure comparative negligence rule.

[43] This sentence is our application for the "50 percent" comparative negligence rule.

[44] This sentence serves as our conclusion.

[45] This is a classical "non-issue" issue, which we discussed in the last chapter.

[46] This is our issue statement.

[47] The issue is negligence; the rule therefore defines negligence.

[48] We isolate the element in dispute. This "non-issue" issue exists because duty cannot be established on these facts. Not now. Not ever.

[49] We let the professor know that a duty cannot be found on these facts.

[50] This is the conclusion.

[51] We have finished dealing with the first interrogatory. We now proceed to the second.

[52] We have yet another negligence issue to deal with. But this time it will be part of a combination issue. The rule is negligence and the counter-rule will be contributory negligence. However, there will be one element of contributory negligence that will be in dispute, as you shall see.

[53] This is our issue statement: parties, legal issue, and key facts.

[54] We have restated the rule in shorthand fashion. Many professors will have no objection if you simply state: "See definition above." I do not like it, personally. When I teach essay writing for the California Bar Exam, I tell my students to never write, "See above." My feeling is that rewriting one sentence ("Negligence requires: duty, breach, cause in fact, proximate cause and damages") is not going to waste too much time and it helps keep the flow.

injuries from the crash with Ed.[55]

Therefore, Ed was negligent.[56]

<u>Contributory Negligence</u>[57]
Was Baker's failure to obtain medical assistance conduct which qualifies as contributory negligence, because if he did receive such assistance, he would have been immobilized and would not have travelled home from work and been struck by Ed's car?[58]

Contributory negligence is conduct on the part of the plaintiff, contributing as a legal cause, cause in fact and proximate cause, to the harm he has suffered, which falls below the standard to which he is required to conform for his own protection; under the common law, it is a bar to recovery.[59] Conduct falls below the standard when it is unreasonable.[60]

A person who falls from a scaffold should reasonably be expected to get medical diagnosis and treatment because severe injuries can exist without immediate symptoms. In this regard, Baker's failure to obtain medical assistance was negligent conduct[61]

However,[62] if one does not feel hurt, it is not unreasonable to continue with one's daily routine because if one does not feel great pain, one typically does not go to a doctor. To go to a doctor for a checkup whenever something happens—which does not immediately result in pain—could become expensive and be looked at as unusual if not over-reactive behavior.[63]

Therefore, Baker was not contributorily negligent.[64]

<u>Comparative Negligence</u>
Even if Ed was deemed to be negligent, in a pure comparative negligence jurisdiction, he would merely have his damages reduced.[65]

---

[55] In this paragraph, we have an abbreviated application for all of the elements of the rule. Remember: you must always be aware of the time factor.

[56] Here is our conclusion.

[57] Here is the next heading.

[58] Here is the issue statement. Because we are dealing with a simple analysis issue, the issue statement should include four points: (1) the parties; (2) the legal issue; (3) the element in dispute; and (4) the key facts that are triggering that element.

[59] The rule is contributory negligence because the issue is contributory negligence.

[60] We now isolate the element of the rule of law that is in dispute by defining that element.

[61] This paragraph (what we believe to be the "weaker" side) contains our analysis—our reasons—of why Baker's failure to go to a doctor was unreasonable conduct.

[62] I use a word of transition to let the professor know that I am switching sides.

[63] This paragraph is the analysis for the "other side," what we perceive to be the stronger side. Remember: there is no problem if you felt that the stronger side was that Baker acted unreasonably.

[64] This is our conclusion. You will note that we do not have a rule mop-up. The reason that we do not is because (1) the other elements of contributory negligence are not, in all probability, going to be worth much point wise, and (2) we want to make certain that we have the time to get to the comparative negligence issue. Remember to use your time smartly.

[65] We cover this issue in a very cursory manner: It is identical to the comparative negligence issue previously covered.

SAMPLE EXAM #2: PROPERTY

Opel owns 100 acres that she subdivides into 100 one-acre lots. Thereafter, Opel constructs a single-family house on each lot. To ensure the development will be a tranquil and clutter-free place for homeowners, Opel inserts a provision in some of the deeds that states, "Except for community-installed traffic signs, no signs of any kind are allowed." Opel sells off all of the lots. Zev is one of the later purchasers and acquires lot 91. The restriction was in the deeds to the first five lots sold but is not in Zev's deed. Zev, a political activist, puts an 8 ½ inch by 11 inch sign in his front window. The sign states, "End World Hunger." Several neighbors complain about Zev's sign to the AAA Homeowners' Association ("AAA"), the local homeowners' association. Each of the 100 homeowners in question belongs to AAA. AAA contacts Zev and demands that he take down the sign. Zev refuses. Thereafter, AAA files suit against Zev, seeking an injunction to force Zev to take down his sign.

AAA owns no land.

Will AAA prevail in its suit against Zev? Discuss. Omit from your discussion any reference to nuisance, the First Amendment, due process, or equal protection.

SAMPLE EXAM ANSWER #2

<u>Implied Reciprocal Negative Easement</u>[1]

Can AAA prevail against Zev and prevent him from putting up his "End World Hunger" sign when some people in the development had a restriction in their deeds against all signs and Zev, a later purchaser, did not?[2]

An implied reciprocal negative easement arises when a common grantor conveys a parcel with restrictions and, by so conveying, the remaining lots retained by the common grantor are similarly and reciprocally restricted.[3] An implied reciprocal negative easement, where recognized,[4] may be either a new type of negative easement, or merely a theory to sustain several elements of a running covenant (discussed below).[5]

When Opel conveyed the first five lots with the express restriction,[6] then all of the remaining lots became bound too because[7] it would make no sense for Opel to have only the first five lots bound in this community but not the others. Moreover,[8] while the ancient common law recognized only four negative easements (light, air, water flow from an artificial stream, and support), that is not a good reason for not recognizing a new one. Law evolves and we should be prepared to recognize new negative easements as needs develop. Evolution, after all, is an integral part of our common law heritage. Further,[9] because easements "run," the restriction runs to all subsequent purchasers taking from Opel, such as Zev, so long as Zev had notice (see below).

Nonetheless,[10] to impute this restriction to Zev is to essentially vitiate the Statute of Frauds,[11] something that has taken centuries to develop and should not be taken lightly. In this regard,[12] if Opel had wanted Zev to be bound, she should have simply put it in the deed. Further,[13] if this implied reciprocal negative easement is a new type of negative easement, that is something that should not be adopted in a cavalier manner. The courts of England were hesitant about creating new types of negative easements and, considering that our legal system is based on the

---

[1] Here is the first legal issue and heading that I will write on.

[2] Here is the issue that I discuss. This is a simple analysis issue: only one element will be in dispute.

[3] The issue is implied reciprocal negative easements, and so my rule is an implied reciprocal negative easement. This is the "R1" of my HIRRAC™ formulation.

[4] I let the professor know that not all jurisdictions recognize this doctrine.

[5] This is the "R2" of my HIRRAC™ formulation. In all frankness, you could have answered this question quite readily without putting in this sentence. I have stated this many times in this text, and I state it again here because it is so important: The point is that HIRRAC™ is merely an organizational tool and you should not be bound to it like a servant. Let it work for you. You should not work for it.

[6] These are the key facts. What follows is my creative argument.

[7] Here is that important word "because." If you insert this word, you will virtually assure yourself that you will follow with creative argument—your reasons (aka analysis).

[8] I make one more argument, based on policy considerations.

[9] I tie up one last point: that easements run. Could I have put this into a separate HIRRAC™? I suppose that I could have. But the point was so simple that I decided to put it in the last sentence of this paragraph of analysis. Remember, yet again, that HIRRAC™ is merely a tool. Never become a slave to it.

[10] I switch sides here.

[11] Here is an argument in opposition to the theory of implied reciprocal negative easements.

[12] I further develop my policy argument.

[13] I make yet another policy argument.

330

English common law, we should be wary about creating new interests that were foreign to our common law ancestors.

Thus, the implied reciprocal negative easement theory should not be recognized as binding on Zev.[14]

Burden of the Covenant in Equity[15]

As an alternative theory, does the burden of the covenant run with the land in equity (AAA seeks an injunction, traditionally, an equitable remedy), to bind Zev?[16]

For the burden of the covenant to run with the land in equity, the original parties must be bound (Statute of Frauds), they must have intended that the successor to the original promisor be bound, the promise must touch and concern the burdened land, and the successor (Zev) must have had notice.[17]

Statute of Frauds[18]

Were Opel and "Mr. 1" (the purchaser of the first lot, whoever that was) bound, when there was a restriction in Mr. 1's deed but no express restriction in the lots retained by Opel?[19]

For the original parties (Opel and Mr. 1) to be bound,[20] there must be compliance with the Statute of Frauds because an equitable servitude is an interest in land.[21] Further, the other lots must also be bound.[22] The implied reciprocal negative easement, where recognized, satisfies the requirement of binding both the original parties and the successors.[23]

Here, there was compliance with the Statute of Frauds because Opel executed—presumably she executed, that is, signed—and delivered the deed to Mr. 1.[24] While the facts do not state whether Mr. 1 signed the deed too, that is irrelevant because in American law, accepting is the equivalent of signing, and it is tradition in Anglo-American jurisprudence that only the grantor need sign the deed. Further, to the extent that Opel herself needs also to be bound (along with her remaining lots 2-100), these lots were bound by way of the implied reciprocal negative easement

---

[14] I conclude.

[15] Note how I triple-space between issues.

[16] This is going to be a complex analysis issue: multiple elements of the rule will be in dispute.

[17] Here is the "R1" of my HIRRAC™ formulation.

[18] Notice how I indent this "sub-heading" to make it clear to the professor (or bar grader) that this element is part and parcel of the greater problem of the burden running in equity. I also double-space (not triple-space) within elements.

[19] Here is my issue statement.

[20] This sentence is the "R2"of my HIRRAC™ formulation. Note that the *original* parties must be bound, that is, Opel and Mr. 1. If they are not bound, Zev cannot be bound.

[21] While some jurisdictions hold that a real covenant is not an interest in land (hence, there is no need to comply with the Statute of Frauds), all jurisdictions agree that an equitable servitude is an interest in land.

[22] Is this "R3"? Perhaps it is! Perhaps we have HIRRRAC™. So what! Remember to use HIRRAC™ (or HIRRRAC™) as a tool; never be afraid of it or enslaved by it.

[23] Is this "R4"? Is this HIRRRRAC™? See preceding note.

[24] If the original parties are not bound none are bound and that is the end of it. I think that the facts clearly imply that Opel signed the deed (and on the actual exam, none of my students indicated or even hinted at anything else). This answer, therefore, will not take issue with this point.

theory that was discussed above: that each lot was similarly and reciprocally bound after Opel conveyed to Mr. 1.

On the other hand,[25] if the jurisdiction in question takes the Statute of Frauds more seriously and does not recognize the implied reciprocal negative easement, then lots following lot #5 (those that did not have the express restriction), could not be bound. In this regard, there is good reason to hold Opel to a higher standard:[26] the Statute of Frauds was developed to preclude a "he says, she says" endless debate on who thought what and when. As a matter of policy, to force people to comply with the formalities long established, we should not give an "easy pass" to someone like Opel. Harshness here will ensure less litigation in the future. In such case, if the implied reciprocal negative easement theory is not recognized, Zev was not bound.

Thus, the Statute of Frauds or the form of the covenant would not have been satisfied.[27]

Intent

Assuming that the original parties were bound,[28] did the original parties (Opel and Mr. 1), intend successors to be bound by the promise in Mr. 1's deed and the lots remaining in Opel?

For the parties to have intended successors to the promisor to be bound, no magic words (such as "heirs and assigns") are necessary; rather, we look to the totality of the circumstances.[29]

Although no magic words are necessary,[30] they certainly are probative, and we do not have words such as "heirs and assigns" to indicate that the successors to lots 2-100 (including Zev's) were bound. Further,[31] because Opel is a developer, she should be held to a higher standard: If all are to be bound, she should either put it in everyone's deed or use words that will make it clear that all are to be bound. Finally,[32] where the wording is not clear, as here, the balance should be struck in favor of free alienability and lesser restrictions, especially when the restrictions deal with political speech ("End World Hunger").

On the other hand,[33] it would make no sense to prevent signs in some lots and not on others. If the intent by the original parties (Opel and Mr. 1) is to have a clutter-free community, then all of the community was intended (implicitly) to be bound. Further, it is only reasonable to believe that if Mr. 1 were himself bound, he would want everyone else to be bound along with him: that it would be unreasonable to believe he would accept a deed to be bound but that most of the other people in the community would not be so bound. Additionally,[34] the implied reciprocal

---

[25] I switch sides here.

[26] What follows is a policy argument opposing the implied reciprocal negative easement theory.

[27] Here is my conclusion. Of course, if the original parties (Opel and Mr. 1) are not bound, then Zev cannot be bound. I continue, however, because you never conclude yourself out of points.

[28] Although I have concluded that the form of the covenant did not bind Zev, I do not want to conclude myself out of points. Hence, I go on to discuss the issue of intent.

[29] Here is my rule of law, the "R2" of my HIRRAC™ formulation.

[30] Here begins the first of several arguments to establish why the original parties intended Zev to be bound.

[31] I make another argument here, based on policy considerations.

[32] I make one last argument, also based on policy.

[33] I switch sides. The argument that follows is based on logic.

[34] I make one final argument, based on the implied reciprocal negative easement theory.

negative easement is available to establish not just the form of the contract to bind those not the original parties, but also to establish the intent: that the original parties intended via the implied reciprocal negative easement to bind all in the subdivision. Indeed, it would not make sense to say that the implied reciprocal negative easement theory bound successors (form of the covenant) but that the original parties did not intend these successors to be bound.

Therefore, Opel and Mr. 1 intended successors like Zev to be bound.

Touch and Concern: Common Law View
Does the covenant not to have any signs in the community touch and concern the land, as the common law understood the term?

A promise touches and concerns the land when it relates to the land.[35] A promise relates to the land on the burden side of the covenant when it either reduces the landowner's rights to the land or reduces the value of the land.[36]

Because the covenant prevents Zev from putting up a sign, the covenant necessarily restricts his rights with respect to the land because[37] but for the covenant, Zev would be allowed to do this without suffering any penalty whatsoever.

On the other hand,[38] the covenant does not deal with the land itself;[39] rather, it deals with actions of Zev personally on the land. Speech, as such, does not "touch" in a layperson's sense of touching, as a building does on the land. In this regard, the covenant in question appears more like a personal covenant. Moreover,[40] the promise does not reduce Zev's property value: Because of the covenant, uniformity will reign and not be subject to odd people engaging in odd behavior that only drives down property values. For example,[41] in the absence of a covenant regarding the color of a house, someone might paint their house yellow with orange polka dots. While such a covenant restricts rights, it also actually increases the value of other homeowners' property in the subdivision.

Therefore, the promise does not touch and concern.

Touch and Concern: Restatement View
Does the covenant in question touch and concern under the Restatement's view?

Under the Restatement, the touch and concern requirement is abolished. Under the Restatement, a covenant will be upheld unless it is unconscionable, or if the covenant violates public policy.

---

[35] Here is my rule of law, the "R2" of my HIRRAC™ formulation.

[36] Here is my rule of law, the "R3" of my HIRRAC™ or HIRRRAC™ formulation (see above for further elucidation).

[37] Here again is that important word, "because." For further elucidation, see above.

[38] I switch sides. The argument that follows is essentially the same as in a prior year's exam.

[39] Here I argue that because the covenant does not literally "touch," as with a promise to maintain a wall, it is more consistent with a personal covenant.

[40] Here I make another argument, based on an alternative definition of touch and concern.

[41] I argue here by analogy.

The covenant here is unconscionable and violates public policy because[42] it stifles free speech and the marketplace of ideas. Society should want ideas furthered and a covenant that restricts such a flow is not in the interests of society.

Nonetheless, while such an argument could be made for government controlled property, that argument loses much of its steam in a privately controlled environment. While Zev's sign is small and "politically correct" if everyone in the community put up such a sign—and perhaps signs that are not so "correct,"—the neighborhood would soon turn into a cluttered kaleidoscope of correct and "incorrect" signs, drawings, and even pictures. The subdivision, but for the covenant, could turn into a fools' lair.

Thus, the covenant is not unconscionable.

Notice: Common Grantor[43]
Did Zev have notice of the restriction because there is a common grantor?

Notice may be actual, record, or inquiry. In some jurisdictions, a deed out from a common grantor imparts record notice: notice from the public records; in other jurisdictions, it does not impart notice.

Because Opel conveyed all the deeds in question, in those jurisdictions that recognize such notice, Zev would have notice to find the five deeds that had the express restriction. It might be difficult to research, but it is not impossible.

Notice: Inquiry Notice
Was Zev put on inquiry when no one else had signs on their property?

Inquiry notice arises when one is apprised of facts that would lead a reasonable person to investigate further; the investigation can include an interrogation of those in possession of the property.[44]

Had Zev knocked on his neighbors' doors and inquired about whether it is permissible to hang a sign in his window, he would have found out about the restriction at a certain point.[45]

However,[46] it is improbable that Zev would have even known to ask whether he could put up a sign, "End World Hunger."[47] You don't know what you don't know, and to put this burden on Zev means that every act he engages in with respect to his property (paint color; type of flower

---

[42] Notice the important word, "because." Use this word and you will almost certainly force yourself to do an analysis (give your reasons).

[43] This issue is a straight rule/counter-rule (majority rule/minority rule). An analysis here is not possible. It is straight application.

[44] Here is my rule of law. Note that I could have broken this down into two rules, so that I have an "R2" and an "R3." Yet, again, I did this purposefully to show you that HIRRAC™ is just a tool; it is not holy writ.

[45] Here is my analysis.

[46] I now switch sides.

[47] Here and in the next sentence, I make a logical argument why Zev did not have notice.

planted; number of guests he invites; etc.), he would first have to ask to learn if it is permissible. That is too much for anyone to ask. Moreover,[48] even if Zev had the foresight to ask his neighbor, his neighbor would have responded, "In my deed I can't do that." From that, Zev would have to make the jump that because his neighbor is restricted, Zev, too, is restricted. Thus, in effect, Zev would have to have notice of an implied reciprocal negative easement, a legal theory not recognized in all jurisdictions and certainly not well understood by lawyers, judges, and scholars (not clear if an implied reciprocal negative easement is a new negative easement or a theory to sustain the form and intent elements of a running covenant). This is simply too much of a burden to put on any layperson.

Thus, Zev did not have notice and the burden of the covenant does not run in equity.

Benefit of the Covenant: Vertical Privity
Assuming the burden does run to Zev, is AAA in vertical privity—that is, does it have standing to sue—when it owns no property in the subdivision?[49]

Vertical privity typically is not required for the benefit of the covenant to run (AAA is not an original promisee), but standing is nonetheless an issue.[50]

Although AAA does not own any property and, therefore, from a traditional perspective is not in vertical privity and, thus, has no standing to sue Zev,[51] it is a question of expediency to allow the homeowner's association to enforce covenants. If it were found that AAA does not have standing (is not in vertical privity), then other homeowners would have to bring suit. It is time-effective to allow AAA to bring suit and consistent with the expanding and evolving idea of the common law: that law evolves to keep up with changes in society. Subdivisions did not exist at the time of *Tulk v. Moxhay*, but they do now.[52]

Hence, AAA is in vertical privity.

---

[48] I make one more argument.

[49] Never conclude yourself out of points. Hence, I preface the issue statement with, "Assuming the burden runs to Zev . . . ."

[50] What is this, no "R2" for HIRRAC™? I make the point, yet again: use HIRRAC™ but do not be a slave to it.

[51] Here is my analysis for why AAA is not in vertical privity. Should I next proceed to put the other side in a separate paragraph? Generally, I should, but because the argument against privity is so short, I decided to put all of this in one paragraph. Generally, however, you should put your analysis for each side in two separate paragraphs.

[52] Note the policy arguments I use.

barbri

CHAPTER 20
MAKING ASSUMPTIONS

A common concern for law school students is, when does one make an assumption? Very often, students will make unwarranted assumptions. When this happens, the professor will write on the essay, "Don't assume anything." Yet there are times when you will have to make an assumption to address the issue. Thus, *when* is it permissible for you to make an assumption? When is it not permissible?

WHEN YOU MUST ASSUME

There are two times when it is not only appropriate to assume, but essential to assume. We touched on both of these scenarios previously. We now go into them in greater depth.

Assume So that You Do Not Conclude Yourself Out of Points

You always assume when you do not want to conclude yourself out of points. Consider this example, one that we previously have covered in these materials.

If you have a complex analysis issue (multiple elements of a rule in dispute) that deals with negligence and you resolve the first issue in favor of the defendant, that is, that the defendant did not owe the plaintiff a duty of due care, then that is the end of the game for the plaintiff. If defendant does not owe the plaintiff a duty, then negligence cannot lie as a matter of law. Yet, as we have also discussed, it would be foolish for you not to continue discussing the other issues. You want to get all possible points on the essay. Thus, you would write, "Assuming, however, that defendant did owe plaintiff a duty to be careful, did the defendant breach that duty when he . . . ."

This, therefore, is the first scenario where you will assume. Again, you assume when it is necessary so that you do not otherwise conclude yourself out of points.

There is one other scenario where you must assume.

Assume When the Facts Force You to Assume

The other time you must assume is when the facts force you to make an assumption. How can that be? Consider this hypothetical.

Suppose we have the following fact pattern: Larry (L) leases an apartment to Tom (T). The lease is for three years. Soon after moving in, T finds that there are many problems with the apartment and, we will stipulate, that because of these problems, L has breached the covenant of quiet enjoyment.[1] T finally moves out after four months. L sues T for the balance due on the lease. The question is whether T can avail himself of the remedy of constructive eviction and avoid liability under the lease and L's claim for rent due.[2]

---

[1] The covenant of quiet enjoyment is implied in every lease and states that a landlord cannot substantially interfere with the tenant's peaceful enjoyment of the premises.

[2] The remedy of constructive evictions states that if the landlord breaches the covenant of quiet enjoyment

Does a tenant move out in a timely manner when he takes four months to move out? The answer is: *It depends*. Without any other facts to go on, if it is easy to get another apartment, four months may well be unreasonable. On the other hand, if it is difficult for T to get another apartment (because of a tight market), then four months time to get a new apartment might be very reasonable.

Notice what has happened: the tenant moved out in four months' time. Those are the facts given. Is four months a reasonable period? It depends: If we *assume* that it is easy to get another place, four months is too long a period. However, if we *assume* that it is difficult to get another apartment, then four months may be a very quick period of time.

Thus, when we assume: (1) there is an underlying factual basis for our assumption (here, it was a given that tenant moved out in four months); and (2) we must assume both ways. First, we must make the assumption favorable for the plaintiff. Then, alternatively, we must make the assumption favorable to the defendant. Why is this so?

Suppose that we had stated in our answer, "Because T took four months to move out, this was too long a period of time. Therefore, he was not constructively evicted." Would this be correct? No. We have assumed that four months is too long a period. On what basis can we make such an assumption? What would be the consequences if the vacancy rate in the city were less than one-tenth of one percent? Would four months be too long under those circumstances? Of course, it would not.

On the other hand, let us suppose that we wrote, "Because T took four months to move out, this was a very reasonable period of time." Would this be correct? Again, the answer would have to be, no. We have now assumed that four months is a short and reasonable time to move out. On what basis can we make this assumption? What would be the consequence if the vacancy rate in the city were thirty-three percent? Would four months be reasonable under those circumstances? Of course, it would not.

Consequently, when there are *facts in the problem* that will allow you to make a reasonable assumption, you must assume in favor of the plaintiff *and* the defendant. You can never assume facts in favor of one side only.

HYPOTHETICAL #1

Hypothetical #1, a contracts problem, raises this issue.

---

and the tenant moves out in a timely manner, the tenant is relieved of further liability under the lease. Timeliness is dependent upon the totality of the circumstances.

Hypothetical #1

[Making Assumptions]

[Simple Analysis Issue]

Alice was in the women's department in Marcy's Department Store. Alice saw a rack of coats with the following sign on the rack: "SALE: TAKE 50 % OFF THE PRICE TAG." Alice took one coat off the rack and took it to the cashier to purchase. The price tag was $800. Alice took out $400 plus applicable sales tax and tendered it to the cashier. The store manager saw the transaction. The manager approached Alice and told her that the coat that she selected was not on sale and that it was put on the sale rack by mistake. Alice did not know that the coat was not on sale at the time she took it off the rack and presented it to the cashier for purchase.

Can Marcy's avoid the sale?

Hypothetical #1: Forcing You to Assume

Appreciate the problem that we are dealing with. Marcy's will want to avoid the contract with Alice. Can it avoid the contract? It can, but only on the grounds of unilateral mistake. The rule is that the offeror (Marcy's) can avoid the contract only if the offeree (Alice) knew or should have known of the mistake. There are no facts to indicate that Alice knew. Are there any facts to indicate that Alice *should have known*? No. However, *if we assume* that there was something unusual about the coat that she wanted (by way of price or quality), then she should have known that something was wrong. But, *on the other hand, if we assume* that there was nothing unusual about the coat, then there was no reason for her to believe that there was a problem. Do you get the idea?

Let us see how we would address this issue in a HIRRAC™ format.

Sample Exam Answer #1A : A Very Good Answer

<u>Unilateral Mistake</u>

Can Marcy's avoid the contract with Alice on the theory of unilateral mistake, because Alice should have known that Marcy's placed the coat on the rack by mistake?

In a unilateral mistake, the offeror can avoid the contract if the offeree knew or should have known of the offeror's mistake. Whether an offeree should have known of the offeror's mistake is dependent on the totality of the circumstances.

Because the coat was mistakenly hanging on the sales rack and assuming that the coat Alice selected was of the same or similar quality and in the same price range as the other coats, then Alice would have no way of knowing that the coat in question was not on sale. With nothing unusual to observe, Alice cannot have the burden of asking a store salesperson if everything is correctly marked; she would have a right in such case to rely on the store's price tag marking system.

However, assuming that the coat in question was much higher in price and/or of much finer or different quality than the other coats, then Alice should have suspected that something was wrong. For example, if all of the other coats had a price tag of $75, Alice should have suspected that something was wrong.

In such latter case, Marcy's could avoid the contract.

Sample Exam Answer #1A: Dissecting the Answer

Sample Answer #1A is a good answer. We are forced from the facts to discuss mistake (the facts tell us that Marcy's made a mistake). The only difficult problem is addressing the assumption. How do we do it? We address the assumption in our analysis—and we approach it from two sides: favorable to Alice and favorable to Marcy's.

Sample Exam Answer #1B: A Poor Answer

Now we will contrast Sample Exam Answer #1A with Sample Exam Answer #1B. Do you see a difference in the analysis? Sample Answer #1B assumes that there were facts sufficient to put Alice on notice.

Sample Exam Answer #1B

<u>Unilateral Mistake</u>

Can Marcy's avoid the contract with Alice on the theory of unilateral mistake, since Alice should have known that Marcy's placed the coat on the rack by mistake?

In a unilateral mistake, the offeror can avoid the contract if the offeree knew or should have known of the offeror's mistake. Whether an offeree should have known of the offeror's mistake is dependent on the totality of the circumstances.

The coat in question must have been much higher in price for it not to be on sale. Therefore, Alice should have known of the store's mistake.

Sample Exam Answer #1B: Dissecting the Answer

This answer simply assumes facts that are not appropriate. There is no basis to make this one-sided assumption. Thus, before you make any assumption, remember to be certain that there are facts to support the assumption. Remember also that when you assume, make the assumption favorable for the plaintiff *and* the defendant.

We are now ready to wind down. We now move to the last chapter of this material.

CHAPTER 21
FINAL THOUGHTS AND MAXIMS FOR SUCCESS

We have covered a tremendous amount of material in these pages. At this point, for reinforcement purposes, it will be good to review the highlights. I call this segment my "Maxims for Success."

MAXIM #1

All law is made up of rules. Never lose sight of this. Keep this in mind when you are preparing for class and studying for your final exams—especially for your final exams. Remember that although your professor may spend the entire class time discussing "policy," it is improbable that the entire exam will be policy. Rather, you will have to know rules of law. So make sure that you know all of the rules for which you are responsible.

MAXIM #2

All rules are made up of elements. It is not enough for you to know the rules. You must also know the definitions of the elements of the rules. Why is this? Because the chances are very good that you will not just be tested on "battery." Rather, you will be tested on an element of battery: "person." You cannot discuss whether a "plate," for example, is a "person" for the law of battery unless you know what a "person" is.

MAXIM #3

A case may require a court to determine which rule to use. Because all law is made up of rules, sometimes a court must determine which rule of law should be used to resolve a dispute between the parties. For example, the court may have to decide whether it should adopt the rule of contributory negligence or comparative negligence.

MAXIM #4

The court may know which rule to use, but must define an element of the rule. Sometimes the problem does not revolve around the rule. Rather it revolves around the definition of an element. For example, for purposes of the law of battery, how does one define the term, "person"? Keep in mind that this is virtually all that appellate courts do: articulate which rule should be used (Maxim #3) or the definition of an element of a rule (Maxim #4). If you keep these maxims in mind, you will make your preparation time for class discussion very productive and efficient.

MAXIM #5

A case may require a court to determine which rule to use, and define an element of that rule. This does not happen too often, but it does happen. In any event, do you see how it is just a variation (combination) of maxims #3 and #4? Further, is this not consistent with the first two maxims (all law is made up of rules and all rules are made up of elements)? It certainly is.

MAXIM #6

A course outline must include rules and elements of rules (and their definitions), at least to the extent that your professor holds you responsible. There is nothing wrong with using a good commercial outline to get an overview of the subject to fill in a missing gap of knowledge that you have. Nevertheless, you will learn best by active learning: creating your own work of art. Remember that you are going to have to memorize many (very many) rules of law and definitions of elements of rules. You can memorize these rules and elements by rote (which is very inefficient) or you can memorize them by *doing*. If you memorize by doing—by creating your own course outline—you will have no problem in assimilating the massive amounts of material that you will encounter. Nevertheless, do not get carried away: synthesize only that material for which you are responsible. The corollary to this is to forget about case names; you typically do not need to know case names. You need to know rules and elements. You need to know case names, but in only two circumstances. The first is when your professor tells you that he or she wants you to know case names. The second is where the case stands for an entire doctrine, not just a rule of law. An example of a case standing for an entire doctrine and not just a rule of law is *Erie*.

MAXIM #7

Do plenty of practice exams. You will learn best by doing. This means that the more practice exams that you do, the more you will learn. Consequently, if you do *dozens* of practice exams for each course, you will do well. Why is this true? Because proximate cause is proximate cause: the professor can change the names and the places, but once you understand what proximate cause is, it does not matter if a surgeon commits malpractice or a plumber installs a pipe negligently. So, do much practice, practice, and more practice!

MAXIM #8

Keep your exam (scratch) outlines short so that you do not write your exams twice. When a student tells me that he or she has a problem in finishing exams, often the problem is the result of having too much detail in the scratch outline. Remember to avoid stating rules of law and analyses. If your outlines include rules and analyses, you will never be able to finish.

MAXIM #9

On the exam, pay close attention to key facts because key facts trigger the issues. When you read your cases, you are sensitive to those facts that are the key facts. Key facts, you will recall, are those facts, which, if changed or eliminated, would change the outcome of the case. Key facts trigger the legal dispute between the parties. On the exam, you will also have to deal with key facts: They trigger the issues that you will discuss. In this regard, pay careful attention to adjectives, adverbs, and action verbs.

MAXIM #10

Once you see an issue, ask yourself, "Are all of the elements of the rule absolutely and clearly satisfied?" If the answer is yes, you have a rule/counter rule (application) issue. Ask yourself this question will mean the difference between an "A" and a "B" for a final grade. Why is this true? If all of the elements of the rule are clearly satisfied, you will "apply" the rule to the facts because you have nothing to "analyze."

MAXIM #11

If not all of the elements are clearly satisfied, you have an analysis issue. This is when you will have to engage in "analysis"—when an element(s) of the rule is not clearly satisfied on the facts given. Analysis is tough because you will have to do "creative thinking."

MAXIM #12

Remember the "formula" for analysis: *FACTS GIVEN + CREATIVE ARGUMENT = PROVES ELEMENT IN DISPUTE and FACTS GIVEN + CREATIVE ARGUMENT = DISPROVES THE ELEMENT.* We take the facts that we are given (the key facts) and build onto those key facts a creative argument to prove that the element that is in dispute does exist. Then, we take the facts that we are given (the same or different key facts) and build onto those facts a different creative argument to prove that the element in dispute does not exist. The point to remember is that analysis is your *reasons* for *why* the element exists *and* does not exist. Remember that ten people can come up with ten different reasons—and they can each get an "A" on the final exam.

MAXIM #13

Never merely repeat facts in analysis. The purpose of the key facts in your analysis is to provide a foundation for your creative arguments. Nevertheless, you should never have a sentence of *pure* facts in your "analysis." If you do, you are merely repeating the facts and stating a conclusion. You will get little credit for that. Work in the word, "because," and that will help you follow up with your reasons, that is, your analysis.

MAXIM #14

Be prepared for a combination issue. You may not just get "analysis" issues and "rule/counter-rule" issues. You may also get so-called "combination" issues: a rule/counter-rule issue *and* one or more elements of the rule or counter-rule are in dispute from a factual perspective.

MAXIM #15

Always HIRRAC™ your answers. Irrespective of the type of issue that you have, you must HIRRAC™ your answers. For an analysis issue, HIRRAC™ stands for: Issue, Rule, Rule, Analysis, and Conclusion. For a rule/counter-rule issue, HIRRAC™ stands for: Issue, Rule, Rule, Application, and Conclusion. HIRRAC™ is not a substitute for thinking, however. It is a good organizational tool. If you have a professor who says, "I don't want to see HIRRAC™," then you must ask the professor what he or she wants. It is inconceivable that the professor does not want the problem identified, the rule of law stated, and an analysis or application performed. Still, when in doubt, ask your professor.

MAXIM #16

Do not make assumptions unless (1) you are assuming so that you do not "conclude yourself out of points," or (2) you have facts to support the assumption—and then make sure that you make the assumption favorable for both the plaintiff and defendant. These are the only two times when you make an assumption. In the second scenario, when you do make an assumption (it will be part of your analysis), make sure that you make it favorable for each side.

MAXIM #17

Keep a proper perspective! Law school is tough, but you do not have to make it tougher than it is. Remember to keep a proper perspective: Eat well. Get exercise. Put down the books one day a week and enjoy yourself. Go to a movie; read a newspaper; listen to the birds chirp. Do it with your spouse or mate. After all, when you come right down to it, law school is not the most important thing in life. Having your health and someone to care about you is. So be good to your mates. Do not ignore them.

I wish you health, happiness, prosperity, and much success in law school—and in the practice of law.